P9-DHA-199

Edward Said

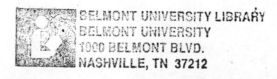

Edward Said

A Critical Introduction

Valerie Kennedy

Polity Press

The right of Valerie Kennedy to be identified as author of this work has been asserted in accordance with the Copyright, Designs and Patents Act 1988.

First published in 2000 by Polity Press in association with Blackwell Publishers Ltd

Editorial office:
Polity Press
65 Bridge Street
Cambridge CB2 1UR, UK

Marketing and production:
Blackwell Publishers Ltd
108 Cowley Road
Oxford OX4 1JF, UK

Published in the USA by
Blackwell Publishers Inc.
Commerce Place
350 Main Street
Malden, MA 02148, USA

ISBN 0-7456-2018-3
ISBN 0-7456-2019-1 (pbk)

A catalogue record for this book is available from the British Library and has been applied for from the Library of Congress.

Typeset in 10.5 on 12 pt Palatino
by Best-set Typesetter Ltd., Hong Kong
Printed in Great Britain by MPG Books Limited, Bodmin, Cornwall

This book is printed on acid-free paper.

Key Contemporary Thinkers

Published

Jeremy Ahearne, *Michel de Certeau: Interpretation and its Other*

Peter Burke, *The French Historical Revolution: The Annales School 1929–1989*

Michael Caesar, *Umberto Eco: Philosophy, Semiotics and the Work of Fiction*

Colin Davis, *Levinas: An Introduction*

Simon Evnine, *Donald Davidson*

Edward Fullbrook and Kate Fullbrook, *Simone de Beauvoir: A Critical Introduction*

Andrew Gamble, *Hayek: The Iron Cage of Liberty*

Philip Hansen, *Hannah Arendt: Politics, History and Citizenship*

Sean Homer, *Fredric Jameson: Marxism, Hermeneutics, Postmodernism*

Christopher Hookway, *Quine: Language, Experience and Reality*

Christina Howells, *Derrida: Deconstruction from Phenomenology to Ethics*

Simon Jarvis, *Adorno: A Critical Introduction*

Douglas Kellner, *Jean Baudrillard: From Marxism to Post-Modernism and Beyond*

Valerie Kennedy, *Edward Said*

Chandran Kukathas and Philip Pettit, *Rawls: A Theory of Justice and its Critics*

James McGilvray, *Chomsky: Language, Mind, and Politics*

Lois McNay, *Foucault: A Critical Introduction*

Philip Manning, *Erving Goffman and Modern Sociology*

Michael Moriarty, *Roland Barthes*

William Outhwaite, *Habermas: A Critical Introduction*

John Preston, *Feyerabend: Philosophy, Science and Society*

Susan Sellers, *Hélène Cixous: Authorship, Autobiography and Love*

David Silverman, *Harvey Sacks: Social Science and Conversation Analysis*

Dennis Smith, *Zygmunt Bauman: Prophet of Postmodernity*

Geoffrey Stokes, *Popper: Philosophy, Politics and Scientific Method*

Georgia Warnke, *Gadamer: Hermeneutics, Tradition and Reason*

James Williams, *Lyotard: Towards a Postmodern Philosophy*

Jonathan Wolff, *Robert Nozick: Property, Justice and the Minimal State*

Forthcoming

Maria Baghramian, *Hilary Putnam*

Sara Beardsworth, *Kristeva*

Mark Cain, *Fodor: Language, Mind and Philosophy*
James Carey, *Innis and McLuhan*
Rosemary Cowan, Cornell West: *The Politics of Redemption*
George Crowder, Isaiah Berlin: *Liberty, Pluralism and Liberalism*
Thomas D'Andrea, *Alasdair MacIntyre*
Eric Dunning, *Norbert Elias*
Jocelyn Dunphy, *Paul Ricoeur*
Matthew Elton, *Daniel Dennett*
Nigel Gibson, *Frantz Fanon*
Graeme Gilloch, *Walter Benjamin*
Karen Green, *Dummett: Philosophy of Language*
Espen Hammer, *Stanley Cavell*
Keith Hart, *C.L.R. James*
Fred Inglis, *Clifford Geertz: Culture, Custom and Ethics*
Sarah Kay, *Žižek: A Critical Introduction*
Paul Kelly, *Ronald Dworkin*
Carl Levy, *Antonio Gramsci*
Moya Lloyd, *Judith Butler*
Dermot Moran, *Edmund Husserl*
Harold Noonan, *Frege*
Steve Redhead, *Paul Virilio: Theorist for an Accelerated Culture*
Chris Rojek, *Stuart Hall and Cultural Studies*
Wes Sharrock and Rupert Read, *Kuhn*
Nick Smith, *Charles Taylor*
Nicholas Walker, *Heidegger*

Contents

Acknowledgements

Many thanks to Susanne Kappeler for initiating this project. I would also like to thank Lester Barber, Stephen Buick, Thomas F. Daughton, Jamil Khadir, Anthony Lake, Hasna Lebbady and Sita Schutt for reading and discussing part or all of various versions of this text, and for their support and encouragement. Thanks to Mohammed Dahbi and Michael Toler for copies of articles and to Francesca Cauchi for reading the proofs and help with the index. I would also like to thank Bilkent University, Ankara, Turkey, for some financial support for this project.

I would like to express my most grateful thanks to Edward W. Said for his gracious permission to reproduce material from the following works:

Culture and Imperialism (World English language rights, excluding the USA).

'Opponents, audiences, constituencies, and community'; 'Interview', in *Diacritics*, 1976; 'Shattered myths', 'From silence to sound and back again', 'Figures, configurations, transfigurations'; 'Interview' in *boundary 2*, 1993; 'Homage to a belly-dancer'; 'Interview' in *Edward Said: A Critical Reader*, ed. Michael Sprinker; 'Interview' in *A Critical Sense*, ed. Peter Osborne; 'The Arab Right Wing'; 'The Arab-American war', 'Identity, negation, and violence'; 'The Other Arab Muslims'; 'Orientalism reconsidered'; 'The politics of knowledge'.

I would also like to thank the following for their kind permission to reproduce material from the following works:

Random House UK and Chatto and Windus for *Culture and Imperialism* by Edward Said; Faber and Faber Ltd. for 'Tradition and

the Individual Talent', in *The Sacred Wood* (new edition, 1997) by
T. S. Eliot; Harcourt Inc. for 'Tradition and the Individual Talent' in
Selected Essays by T. S. Eliot.

I would also like to thank Random House USA for permission to
reproduce material as follows:

From *Orientalism* by Edward W. Said. Copyright © 1978 by
Edward W. Said. Reprinted by permission of Pantheon Books, a
Division of Random House Inc.; From *Culture and Imperialism* by
Edward W. Said. Copyright © 1993 by Edward W. Said. Reprinted
by permission of Alfred A. Knopf Inc.

Abbreviations

Works by Said

Books

ALS   *After the Last Sky* (1986)
B   *Beginnings* (1975)
BV   *Blaming the Victims* (1988)
CI   *Culture and Imperialism* (1993)
CIs   *Covering Islam* (1981)
JC   *Joseph Conrad and the Fiction of Autobiography* (1966)
ME   *Musical Elaborations* (1991)
O   *Orientalism* (1978)
PandS   *The Pen and the Sword* (1994)
PD   *Peace and Its Discontents* (1995)
PolD   *The Politics of Dispossession* (1995)
QP   *The Question of Palestine* (1979)
RI   *Representations of the Intellectual* (1994)
WTC   *The World, the Text, and the Critic* (1983)

Interviews

D   *Diacritics* interview (1976)
I   Interview with Jennifer Wicke and Michael Sprinker (1992)

Articles

F   'Figures, configurations, transfigurations' (1990)
FW   Foreword to *Little Mountain* by Elias Khoury (1989)

Int   Introduction to *Days of Dust* by Halim Barakat (1983)
OR   'Orientalism reconsidered' (1985)
O   'Opponents, audiences, constituencies, and community' (1982)
RC   'Representing the colonized' (1989)
SM   'Shattered myths' (1975)

Works by other authors

Homi Bhabha

LC   *The Location of Culture* (1994)
Free 'Freedom's basis in the indeterminate' (1995)

Benyamin Netanyahu

APN   *A Place Among the Nations: Israel and the World* (1993)

Gayatri Spivak

CSS   'Can the subaltern speak?' (1993)
HTR   'How to read a "culturally different" book' (1994)
IM   *Imaginary Maps: Three Stories by Mahasweta Devi* (1995)
IOW   *In Other Worlds: Essays in Cultural Politics* (1987)
OTM   *Outside in the Teaching Machine* (1993)
PCC   *The Post-Colonial Critic: Interviews, Strategies, Dialogue* (1990)
RS   'The Rani of Sirmur' (1984)
TWT   'Three women's texts and a critique of imperialism' (1985)

Introduction

Edward Said: a significant figure

As a literary and cultural critic and social commentator, Edward
Said is a highly significant and at times controversial figure in contemporary intellectual life. His *œuvre* is impressive in terms of both
scope and importance, and he has exercised a significant influence
in the field of cultural and postcolonial studies. His writings on Orientalism and related phenomena have provided the inspiration for
a large number of new studies, including many which extend his
work in unexpected ways or in ways which implicitly or explicitly
challenge his own ideas. A writer of avowedly conservative literary
and cultural biases, Said has increasingly come to analyse the
complex and vital relationship between literature, politics and
culture. This analysis has taken three main forms in his work. First,
two of his most important books, *Orientalism* and *Culture and Imperialism*, consider the relationship between the West and the East in
the colonial and postcolonial contexts. Second, Said has been
directly concerned both with Palestine and the situation of Palestinians in the Middle East, and with larger issues related to the
Arabo-Islamic world and its relationship with and representation in
and by the West. Third, he has devoted considerable time and
energy to defining the role and responsibilities of the intellectual in
the contemporary world.[1]

The first main area of his work deals with the political implications of Western colonialism and imperialism and the West's domination and representation of the East or, more generally, the

non-European world. *Orientalism*, first published in 1978, examines the development of Western conceptions and representations of the Orient from the middle of the eighteenth century to the present. Orientalism is seen as a set of academic disciplines concerned with studying the Orient, but also as a style of thought based on an existential difference between the Orient and the Occident. Both these are related to the development of the institutional and administrative procedures of Western imperialism. The book offers a variety of perspectives on the proliferating discourses of Orientalism in such disparate areas as literature, linguistic and other types of scholarship, travel writing, anthropology and colonial administration. The varying definitions and views of Orientalism are not always completely consistent, but the book's central argument about the interdependence of the political and the cultural dimensions of Orientalism and their effects on literary works provided a dramatically new insight in mainstream literary criticism. It has since proved to be one of the key sources, if not *the* key source, of inspiration for much later work by others in the fields of literary, critical and cultural theory, especially in postcolonial studies. *Culture and Imperialism* continues and extends the work begun in *Orientalism* by documenting the imperial complicities of some major works of the Western literary (and in one case, musical) canon. The book's final chapter looks at the geopolitics of the postcolonial world and pays particular and critical attention to America's role in it.

The second main focus of Said's work is the analysis of the situation in Palestine, Israel and the Middle East more generally. His main concern has always been the condition of the Palestinian people, but he has also constantly written about larger political and cultural issues related to the Arabo-Islamic world and its relationship with the West, including the ways in which it is constructed and represented by the West. Said sees his work in this area as being intimately connected to his work on Orientalism. *Orientalism* was quickly followed by *The Question of Palestine* (1979) and *Covering Islam* (1981). The Introduction to *Covering Islam* argues that the three books deal with the relation between 'Islam, the Arabs, and the Orient', on the one hand, and 'the West, France, Britain, and in particular the United States', on the other.[2] He has also said, in the Afterword to the 1995 edition of *Orientalism*, that his position on the Palestinian issue has not changed in its essentials since the original publication of *The Question of Palestine*.[3] The many essays that he has written since then bear out this statement. Two main concerns emerge. The first is the documentation of Palestinian existence in the nineteenth and twentieth centuries, with emphasis on the need for a Palestinian narrative to counter the pro-Israeli narrative of events in the Middle East. This is accompanied by the analysis of the distortions, prejudices and racism that all too often characterize the representation of Islam and Arabs, especially Palestinian Arabs, by the Western media and academia. Secondly, Said has consistently provided a critique of US government policy in the Middle East, and of the Israeli and Arab governments and their actions, including those of the recently established Palestinian Authority.

Said's third central topic is the function of criticism in the contemporary world, especially the role and responsibilities of the intellectual. Two key texts here are *The World, the Text, and the Critic* (1983) and *Representations of the Intellectual* (1994). In the first, Said puts forward his own theoretical position, provides a commentary on aspects of contemporary critical theory which is often scathing, and offers some perceptive and idiosyncratic accounts of certain individual writers. He proposes a model of secular criticism, criticizes much contemporary theory because of its detachment from the problems and constraints of the real world and explains why Foucault rather than Derrida provides part of the inspiration for his own approach. Said's later writings show his increasing impatience with Foucault's work, which he comes to see as more and more detached from real-life political and social issues, and thus as ineffectual, since it fails to challenge the *status quo* or bring about change. For Said, the key words for the intellectual are scepticism, memory and, above all, 'the critical sense'.[4] In *Representations of the Intellectual* he develops his argument that the intellectual should not be seduced by power or official approval, but should remain unco-opted if not uncommitted, ready to challenge orthodoxies and received ideas and to change the world.

The interrelation of these three major areas in Said's work is one reason for Said's special position in contemporary Western intellectual life. Others are the wide scope and the rich variety of his analyses of literary works and political and cultural phenomena, and the courage he has shown in expressing his political convictions. He is in many ways the restless embodiment of his own ideal of the unco-opted critical intellectual who refuses to accept orthodoxy of any kind. The reasons for this can be found in the way in which Said has assumed the contradictions and conflicts subsequent to the accident of his birth and the events of his life. Said has made the facts of his birth and his experiences a central strand in his work, uniting the personal and the public dimensions of his life in writing which is compelling and often provocative.[5]

A man of more than one world[6]

Said was born in November 1935 in Talbiya, West Jerusalem, in what was then British Mandate Palestine.[7] His father's family, from Jerusalem, was middle-class, conventional, formal and Anglican. His mother's, from Safad and later Nazareth, was also middle-class but less conventional and more artistically inclined. The family lived mostly in Cairo, but spent long periods in Palestine in 1942 and 1947, and spent their summers in the Lebanese village of Dhour el Shweir for twenty-seven years, beginning in 1943. As a Christian, but a Protestant rather than a member of the Orthodox Church, Said grew up as part of a minority inside a minority. As he says to Imre Salusinszky, 'Although Palestinians, we were Anglicans: so we were a minority within the Christian minority in an Islamic majority setting.'[8] He was baptized in the Anglican cathedral of St George, and in 1947 spent some months at St George's school, where his father had also studied.[9] In Cairo, he attended Gezira primary school, the Cairo School for American Children and finally Victoria College. The family left Jerusalem for good in December 1947, before the Palestinian–Israeli war of 1947 and the expulsion and dispossession of many Palestinians in the *annakba*, or catastrophe, and returned to Cairo. At the British-run Victoria College, Said was often punished as a troublemaker, partly for speaking Arabic rather than English. Finally he left and was sent to the USA by his father, where he completed his secondary education at Mount Hermon, a boarding school in Massachusetts, before going on to study at Princeton and Harvard. He took up a teaching position at Columbia, where he became University Professor of English and Comparative Literature.[10]

From the 1970s onwards, Said has sought to turn his initial sense of alienation in the USA and his growing awareness of a divided allegiance as both a Palestinian Arab and an American citizen into something positive by bringing together the two sides of his experience. As he said in an interview, until about 1967 his career was almost purely that of the literary academic. After that date his two lives as American academic and concerned Middle Easterner began to come together in his work. This was due to the Six Day War of 1967 and subsequent events in the Middle East, and to Said's growing awareness of the interrelation of politics and literature and of his own responsibilities.[11] From the late 1960s to the mid-1970s Said moved from being a traditional humanist academic to become one of the most significant Anglophone cultural and political commentators of the later twentieth century.

He has striven for a vision of transnational human interaction avoiding both sectarianism and politics based on divisive notions of ethnic or religious identity. He has written about some aspects of his early life in Palestine and Egypt, his initial feeling of alienation when he arrived in the USA, and the implications of being a man of two worlds, notably in the 1998 essay 'Between worlds' and in his 1999 memoir *Out of Place*. He has also discussed both the current situation and the complex mixture of feelings occasioned by his journeys back to Palestine-Israel in 1992, 1996 and 1998 in a series of articles originally published in the *London Review of Books*. The more general issue of exile and dispossession is approached in several other essays: Said has come to see his own position as a relatively privileged exile as one variant of the situation of displacement which he sees as a typical feature of the late twentieth century.

Said has returned to Palestine-Israel only a few times since he and his family left in 1947. On the first of these occasions, in 1992, he was accompanied by his second wife, Miriam, his son, Wadie, and his daughter, Naila, aged 20 and 18 respectively. On his second journey, in 1996, he travelled alone, but he spent some time with his son who was then working as a translator for the Jerusalem Media and Communication Centre in the Occupied Territories. In 1998 he returned to make a film for a British television channel about the Palestinians. As might be expected, the feelings aroused by these journeys are strong and conflicting. There is the shock of recognition on seeing the Said family home in West Jerusalem again, and then anger and sadness at the discovery that the house is now inhabited by a 'right-wing fundamentalist Christian and militantly pro-Zionist group'.[12] Generally, Said has a sense of a history finished, places lost, a country where, with the exception of Arab Nazareth, he can no longer feel at home. Moreover, when he visits Gaza, both in 1992 and 1996, he finds conditions worse than those he saw in the South African townships in 1991. Finally, while feeling a sense of solidarity with Palestinians in Israel and the Occupied Territories, Said recognizes that it would be very hard for him to live there, since his own state of exile is relatively liberated and privileged by comparison.[13] The 1996 visit reveals a similar mixture of emotions, with the added detail that by then all of Said's books have been removed from bookshops in Gaza and on the West Bank on the orders of Yasser Arafat.[14] The film shown on British television in May 1998 on the anniversary of the establishment of the state of Israel covers similar ground. In addition, Said narrates his visit to Hebron and bears witness to the continuing confiscation and destruction of Palestinian land and property by Israeli soldiers acting on the orders of the state, and the continuing encroachments of Israeli settlers on land under the jurisdiction of the Palestinian Authority. He notes with some bitterness that the Palestinian Authority seems to be doing nothing to stop this process.

Said's accounts of these journeys are complemented by several pieces in which he explores the condition of exile more generally as a late twentieth-century phenomenon, notably 'Reflections on exile' and 'The mind of winter: reflections on life in exile', both published in 1984. These argue that it is part of the contemporary intellectual's role to speak for the displaced and dispossessed, and to use the freedom of exile for positive ends. Indeed, Said uses the image of exile or migrancy elsewhere in his work to characterize the role of the intellectual in the late twentieth century. He argues that the intellectual should be a marginal or migrant figure who helps to produce new types of knowledge as well as to criticize abuses of power and the obfuscations and distortions of official discourse.[15]

Above all, Said's work shows a consistent independence of thought, which is his most outstanding characteristic. He has tried to embrace the contradictions and divisions of his position in order to use them for positive ends. Yet if his chosen position as a man between two cultures, worlds and languages has enabled him to make connections which few, if any, had made before, then it also has certain negative consequences. First, despite his desire to allow the marginalized to speak, he is consistently blind to gender, and women are certainly under-represented in his work. Second, there is a potential clash between the detachment of the scholarly humanist and the commitment of the polemicist who argues for Palestinian rights.

Said's blindness to gender characterizes almost all of his work. It is rare for him to analyse a work by a woman, although there are exceptions to this,[16] and he has shown himself to be aware of his deficiencies in this respect. As he has said to Peter Osborne, there are no 'heroines' in *Orientalism*,[17] and *After the Last Sky* also comments on its own failure to pay attention to Palestinian women.[18] Said's neglect of gender is ironic for two reasons. First, his demystification of the construction of the Oriental as Other in *Orientalism* parallels feminism's focus on the woman as Other; second, one of the types of scholarly work inspired by *Orientalism* is the study of women's role in Orientalism as travellers, writers and artists. Said's neglect of gender may be at least partially explained by certain features of his context and upbringing. Neither the Palestinian society nor the class into which he was born, nor the elite British and American educational institutions which he attended as a student and at which he later taught, encouraged any awareness of gender as an important theoretical factor or fact of real life. Indeed, Said has spent most of his life as a student and teacher in typical patriarchal institutions, all-male worlds where women's role and presence were negligible, at least until the recent past.

There is also a potential contradiction between the humanist scholar and the Palestinian polemicist. However, Said does not accept the values of the comfortable world of the Western academic elite uncritically. On the contrary, despite the distance between both his current situation and his class origins, on the one hand, and the poverty and dispossession of the majority of Palestinians on the other, he has tried to forge an oppositional form of Western humanism which defends the rights of the underprivileged. A look at his early works will show both his initial conservatism and the gradual shift from purely literary to more worldly and political analyses.

Early criticism: from *Joseph Conrad* to *The World, the Text, and the Critic*

In *Joseph Conrad and the Fiction of Autobiography*, the focus is on Conrad the great writer and the short stories as significant works of literature. The book avoids those features of Conrad's writing on which Said focuses in *Orientalism* and *Culture and Imperialism*, that is, the themes of colonial domination and exploitation. Said uses the historical context of Conrad's work primarily as a means of elucidating the letters and short stories as dramatizations of Conrad's individual psychodrama, although sometimes he does suggest that changes in Conrad are caused by the changes in the external political environment (*JC*, pp. 73, 75). Although Said refers to Conrad's awareness of himself as someone who was 'the product of cross-bred nationalities' (p. 69), he does not note that, as a Pole, Conrad has suffered Russian colonization, and came to identify himself, at least partially, with the worldview of another imperial power, Britain. The complexities of this potentially contradictory situation are not even signalled, much less analysed, and neither is the potential parallel between Said's own experiences and those of Conrad, although a much later autobiographical piece explores this point.[19]

Said's next book was *Beginnings: Intention and Method* (1975), which established his reputation as one of America's foremost contemporary literary critics. As Said himself says in a later interview with Imre Salusinszky, it is somewhat 'ventriloquistic', the work of a writer seeking his own voice through the works and voices of others.[20] While it shows his continued interest in Conrad, it works on a much broader historical and theoretical basis, relating literature to philosophy, psychology, and critical and cultural theory. Said discusses the development of the European novel from the eighteenth to the twentieth century and sees it in terms of 'beginnings', 'authority' and 'molestation'. The novel is seen as having a 'quasi-paternal role' until the advent of modernism when this role is exchanged for 'an almost total supplementarity' (*B*, p. 151). The problem of locating a beginning point in critical theory is approached from the point of view of certain types of French critical thought such as structuralism, poststructuralism (Foucault) and deconstruction (Derrida). Derrida's ideas are not examined at any length, although he is important in exposing the problems of structuralism (pp. 339–43). The book relates literature to other types of narrative, but to those of philosophy (Vico, Marx, Kierkegaard, Nietzsche), psychology (Freud) and critical and cultural theory (Foucault, Derrida, Lévi-Strauss), rather than those of history, politics or economics. The theory of narrative authority and molestation pays no attention to the specific historical or political contexts of texts. For example, *Nostromo* is read through its author's psychobiography, and the colonial and postcolonial contexts of both author and text are ignored (pp. 100–37).

Nonetheless, *Beginnings* is important since it indicates three of Said's later major concerns. These are, first, his growing consciousness about what is involved in the activities of creative writing and criticism, and of the implications of his own position in relation to the European critical tradition and to the American academy. The second is his exploration of secular beginnings rather than divine origins. Thirdly, Said's desire to consider literature in connection with other forms of human activity, that is, as worldly, emerges alongside his awareness of the conservatism of his own 'cultural biases' (*B*, pp. xiii–xiv).

After *Beginnings*, 'Shattered myths' (1975) and the 1976 *Diacritics* interview indicate the way in which Said's work underwent a fundamental change of direction in the mid-1970s.[21] In 'Shattered myths' many of the key themes and ideas of *Orientalism* are already present. For example, Said pinpoints what he calls the 'key reduction' of Orientalism, the hierarchical opposition between Westerners and Easterners, describing it in terms which appear almost unchanged in *Orientalism* (SM, pp. 413–14, *O*, p. 49). He also focuses on a number of over-generalizing and demeaning stereotypes of Arabs (pp. 417, 421–2) and on Renan's anti-Semitic linguistic studies (pp. 431–3) as he does in the later work. Said identifies Orientalism's institutional basis, underscores its 'political, social, and even economic significance' (pp. 425–6) and indirectly evokes the issue of representation (pp. 440–1) which is to be so important and so problematic in *Orientalism* (*O*, p. 273). What is lacking, interestingly, is any reference to Foucault's ideas of the archive or a discourse or systems of disciplinary control.

The *Diacritics* interview, conversely, is directly concerned with literary theory, Foucault's ideas of discourse and the question of intellectual responsibility. It opens with a discussion of Said's view of the reception of what both he and his interviewer call the 'critical avant-garde' in American universities. Said recognizes the value of the work done by critics such as Harold Bloom as innovative and exciting, but regrets 'its comparative neglect of historical, you might say *archival* concern' (D, pp. 30–1, emphasis in the original, and see p. 33). In a parallel fashion, Said finds the 'New New critics', especially the deconstructionists at Yale, 'quietistic' in that 'They seem uninterested in political questions.' He declares that he shares a number of their interests, but also notes that he feels 'separated from [them] on a great many other grounds', notably in relation to politics (p. 35).

Evoking his two lives as teacher and politically involved individual, he explains that the links between the two are beginning to emerge in his work. He states: 'I guess that what moves me mostly is anger at injustice, an intolerance of oppression, and some fairly unoriginal ideas about freedom and knowledge' (p. 36). The phrase looks forward to many of his later pronouncements on intellectual responsibility. The rest of the interview is taken up with the project of the book on Orientalism, including some illuminating references to Foucault's ideas. Foucault functions as an enabling figure who connects the realm of theory with the realm of worldly concerns of power, domination and representation. Said praises Foucault's attack on the figure of the author as originating figure (p. 40), but he describes Foucault's diagnosis of the systematic and constraining nature of discourse as even more important (pp. 36, 41). Defining Orientalism as a 'myth-system', Said describes himself as 'an Oriental writing back at the Orientalists . . . I am also writing *to* them, as it were, by dismantling the structure of their discipline' (p. 47, emphasis in the original). Here Said describes himself as outside the field of discourse of Orientalism, writing from the Archimedean point outside the system that he is so sceptical about elsewhere.

By 1976 Said can be seen to be in the process of formulating his central ideas about critical responsibility. These are his scepticism about 'technical criticism', and his desire to link literature, history and politics by using theory to analyse the structures of social and political power and domination. These concerns lead him to formulate his key concepts of worldliness and secular criticism in *The World, the Text, and the Critic*.

For Said, to say that texts are worldly means that 'they are . . . a part of the social world, human life, and of course the historical moments in which they are located and interpreted' (*WTC* p. 4).[22] If texts are worldly, then criticism must also deal with the world. One of the recurrent complaints about theory in Said's writing in the 1970s and 1980s is that 'American or even European literary theory now explicitly accepts the principle of noninterference.' Conversely, he believes that 'criticism and the critical consciousness' should take account of 'The realities of power and authority' as well as those of resistance (*WTC*, pp. 3, 5). In 'Reflections on American "left" literary criticism', first published in 1979, Said laments the lack of 'real opposition' in academic work, finding it 'for the most part stunningly silent' about the relationships between intellectuals, culture and the power and authority of the state. However, he quotes Foucault, Ohmann, Poulantzas and unnamed 'Feminist critics' as partial exceptions to this rule (*WTC* pp. 160, 169–70).

Said finds both formalism and structuralism wanting: formalism since it treats literary texts in abstraction from their social and political contexts, and structuralism for not being able to deal adequately with texts, their authors or intentions.[23] Said's unease with the structuralist project is primarily that it denies the specificity of the literary text and obliterates historical change and domination with its over-emphasis on system and method (*B*, pp. 319, 335, 337, 338). He exempts both Derrida and Foucault from these criticisms, and finds Foucault more congenial and suggestive for his own work than Derrida. As he says in the 1983 essay, 'Criticism between culture and system' (first published as 'The problem of textuality' in 1978), 'Derrida's criticism moves us *into* the text, Foucault's *in* and *out*' (*WTC*, p. 183, emphasis in the original). The essay documents Said's reservations about Derrida's reading of texts.[24] Derrida's work is seen as excessively abstract, over-reliant on the philosophical systems which it deconstructs, and tending to assume that concepts such as *différance* can remain both permanently undecidable and practical at the same time (pp. 209–10). Most importantly, for Said, Derrida does not provide enough 'specification' about the institutional basis and the power relations that underlie the Western metaphysical tradition. His work also ignores oppression and cannot criticize its own ethnocentrism (pp. 209, 212). However, although Foucault does include power relations in his work, his approach is also found wanting by Said. He has a passive and sterile view of how power works, he pays no attention to such notions as class struggle, state power, economic domination and so on, and there is no equivalent of Gramsci's idea of hegemony in his work. Finally, Foucault is unable to account for historical change and does not include Europe's domination of the non-European world in his analysis (pp. 221–3).

After the mid-1970s, there is in Said's work a sense of an ever-growing impatience with writers who do not actively seek to promote change or, at least, a new awareness of the situation, whether within the academy or outside it. For him, it is one of the functions of the intellectual in the wider world to work towards this change in reality and awareness. In terms of his own *œuvre*, *Orientalism* may be said to have achieved precisely this.

Overview

This study will begin by discussing *Orientalism* as a groundbreaking book, and the only one, as Said says in his Afterword to the 1995 edition, that he wrote as one continuous project.[25] Chapter 1 will present *Orientalism*'s scope and arguments. It will then analyse three central problematic aspects of the book: the issue of definition, the use of Foucault, Gramsci and the tradition of literary humanism and the conflicts in methodology and values which Said's eclectic approach entails, and the book's almost total neglect of gender as a theoretical category. Finally, 'Orientalism reconsidered' and Said's 'Afterword' to the 1995 edition of the book will be discussed in relation to questions of positionality and to Said's plea for alternative forms of knowledge and secularity.

Secularity is also a key term for Said in his writings on Palestine and the Middle East, to be examined in chapter 2. Said offers several versions of the Palestinian narrative, and he challenges what Foucault calls the 'regime of truth',[26] that is, the assumptions underlying discussions of Israeli and Palestinian history. He also provides a critique of all of the major players in the area, as well as of Zionism, the policies of the US and Israeli governments and the role of the American media. Much of his writing on these issues is characterized by his equivocal position both inside and outside the Middle East situation and by his vacillations on the issues of objectivity and representation.

The third chapter will argue that *Culture and Imperialism* continues both the work begun in *Orientalism* in connecting literature and politics, and the attempt to analyse some aspects of American domination and neo-imperialism in the contemporary world that characterizes Said's writings on Palestine. The organization, scope and main arguments of the book will be presented, the methodological framework – especially the use of T. S. Eliot, Fanon, Raymond Williams and Foucault – analysed, and the three elements of Said's search for a third way examined and evaluated. These are: first, the radical elements in his work; second, his contrasting conservative preferences and priorities; and finally, his call for alternative modes of reading and interpretation and for secular opposition to official conformism, religious fundamentalism and coercive systems of thought of every kind.

The final chapter of the book will focus on what might be called Said's legacy to the fields of postcolonial studies, whose development owes a great deal to Said's ideas especially in relation to postcolonial theory and colonial discourse analysis. However, there are important differences in approach between Said and postcolonial theorists such as Homi Bhabha and Gayatri Spivak, notably regarding such matters as history, theory and positionality. Said's work has been the inspiration for a more historicized and politicized approach to the literature of empire and imperial travel writing. It has also provided the impetus for the expansion of the field he began to open up with *Orientalism*, notably in the study of the genre of travel writing, especially travel writing by women.

Finally, since the issue of positionality is one of the themes of this study of Said, it is necessary to situate my own perspective. Said's journey from the colonized periphery to the metropolitan neo-colonial centre was dictated by historical, political, and family necessities. My journey has been different. Born a British citizen, I have moved from near the centre to the periphery. Since 1976 I have been living and teaching in Kenya, Morocco and Turkey. The two journeys are in many ways incomparable. Still, tinged with post-colonial complicity as my journey inevitably is, it has also allowed me to arrive at perspectives on political and cultural issues that I could never have had if I had stayed in Europe. Without Said's work, neither contemporary literary studies nor postcolonial theory would be quite the same: one major reason for this is *Orientalism*.

1

Orientalism

Orientalism is theoretically inconsistent, and I designed it that way.[1]

Introduction

It is almost impossible to overestimate the significance of *Orientalism* for the study of literature in English in the Anglo-American academic context. First published in 1978, it introduced a global perspective of political and economic realities to which literary studies had hitherto remained closed.[2] Said brought politics into literary studies by insisting that scholarly Orientalism needs to be seen in the context of Western perceptions of the Orient dating back to Classical times. He argued that these perceptions need to be seen in relation to the Western domination of the Orient through colonialism and imperialism as well as neo-colonialism.[3] A corollary of this argument is that Western academic institutions are compromised by their relation to power, especially in departments such as Area Studies.[4]

In the late 1970s, these were radical ideas. In both Britain and the USA the dominant pedagogical mode was still generally that of the New Criticism. Additionally, in the former, the moral perspective of F. R. Leavis was a powerful influence. In both places there were cautious attempts to introduce elements of structuralist, Marxist or feminist theory by various marginal groups or individuals. While the 'crisis in English studies' was beginning to make itself felt (at least in Britain), the institutional solutions to it were unthought of or in their very early stages. These solutions later took the shape of the inclusion, some would say the dominance, of theory in the field, and the establishment of Women's, Cultural and Ethnic Studies courses, programmes and departments. In the late 1970s, the study of English or Comparative Literature consisted of courses on genre and period, on the technical and thematic characteristics of acknowledged canonical, great (usually male) writers such as Dickens, James or Shakespeare, with perhaps the occasional foray into structuralism, stylistics or linguistics. The linking of literary studies with the study of history or of politics was the domain only of the Marxists, and they were not generally central or influential in literature departments either in Britain or the USA in the period.[5]

Of course there were exceptions. By the late 1970s, on the fringes of university institutions in Britain and even more in the USA, both the feminist and the Civil Rights movements were beginning to make themselves felt as forces for change. But this process had not yet taken on its later amplitude and significance. On the theoretical front, the Anglo-American academic context was involved in its confrontation with structuralism and, later, post-structuralism through the works of writers like Barthes, Genette, Todorov and the *Tel quel* group, Foucault, Derrida and so on, many of which had been written in the 1950s and 1960s. In the late 1970s some of the key feminist texts of the late 1960s were beginning to have an impact, and some other key feminist studies of literature appeared. In short, the world of literary studies was a world which was only just beginning to be opened up to the influences of the outside world in the form of political, economic, and sexual realities which had hitherto generally been regarded as marginal to serious literary study.

It was into this closed world that *Orientalism* came in 1978. If the book is compared to the other critical productions of the time, the difference will be seen clearly. Kermode's *The Sense of an Ending* (1966), Fredric Jameson's *The Prison-House of Language* (1972), David Lodge's *The Modes of Modern Writing* (1977) or his *Working with Structuralism* (1981) did open up new philosophical or formalist perspectives, but they offered nothing comparable to *Orientalism*'s insistence on the inextricable connections between literature, history and politics. As Said has noted in the 'Afterword' to the 1995 edition of the book, he had trouble initially in interesting a publisher in the work.[6] However, *Orientalism* went on to become an epoch-making book, inaugurating not only changes in the study of

English and Comparative Literature in the form of new politicized and historicized readings of individual texts, but also opening up the fields of postcolonial studies.

The scope and arguments of *Orientalism*

Orientalism is composed of an Introduction and three long chapters. Many of Said's most important ideas appear in the Introduction, where his starting point is that 'the Orient is not an inert fact of nature', but that it is, like the Occident, 'man-made' (*O*, pp. 4, 5). This initial, apparently simple, but far-reaching statement opens up questions about the construction of the Orient and of Oriental people by Western scholars, travellers and imperialists. It also raises issues connected with representation, especially with the relation between representation, knowledge and power, which are both productive and problematic. These questions provide a wealth of insights into the relationship between the West and the Orient. They also contribute to a series of complex and at times contradictory or problematic arguments about various aspects of that relationship. Definitions of Orientalism as a field proliferate, and Said has a tendency to talk as if the discourse of Orientalism were always and everywhere the same. The book's all-male framework of reference, its concomitant neglect of the factors of class and gender and the problematic yoking together of Foucault, Gramsci and humanism all emerge first here.

Chapter 1, 'The Scope of Orientalism', offers an overview of the field. Beginning with a discussion of Orientalist discourse in the late nineteenth and twentieth centuries, it argues that this discourse is based on a transcendental dichotomy between the West and the Orient. The first is seen as 'rational, peaceful, liberal, logical, capable of holding real values, [and] without natural suspicion', and the latter as 'none of these things' (p. 49). The chapter introduces the key term 'imaginative geography', and offers a glance back at Western representations of the Orient, Islam, Muslims and Arabs before the mid-eighteenth century in order to suggest how the tradition, discourses and institutions of Orientalism came into being. It also opens the analysis of some aspects of the relation between the West and the East in the nineteenth and twentieth centuries. Napoleon's invasion of Egypt, along with the twenty-volume *Description de l'Egypte* published between 1809 and 1828, as well as the building of the Suez Canal (1854–69) are taken as key points, since they symbolize the material and textual European domination of the Orient characteristic of colonialism and imperialism.

At this point Said approaches the development of Orientalism by suggesting that it embodies a *'textual* attitude' (p. 92, emphasis in the original). This means that the discourse of Orientalism relies on images of the East and its inhabitants that are not derived from empirical evidence or experience but from other books. Said argues that this view of the Orient both pre-dates and survives the imperialist expansion of the nineteenth and twentieth centuries. He locates it in medieval texts, for example, and in the crude popular stereotyping of Arabs in the contemporary American media. He sees the situation in the middle of the twentieth century, when the formerly colonized countries had gained their independence, as a moment of crisis for the field. The Orient has now become the Third World, 'challenging and politically armed' to confront the West.[7] However, in Said's view, Orientalists have not risen to this new challenge, and he takes their failure to do so as a sign of the bankruptcy of the field in its contemporary form (p. 104).

Chapters 2 and 3 adopt a mainly chronological perspective. Chapter 2, entitled 'Orientalist Structures and Restructures', discusses what Said has defined as 'modern Orientalism' from the last third of the eighteenth century to around 1870, which he sees as part of the legacy of the Enlightenment (p. 118). However, in addition to the mainly chronological presentation of the systematic domination of the Orient by the West in the form of evolving imperialist and colonialist structures, Said offers 'the description of a set of devices common to the work of important poets, artists, and scholars' (p. 25). In the discussion of nineteenth-century Orientalism Said examines the works and careers of Silvestre de Sacy and Ernest Renan. Sacy is seen as the inaugurator of the tradition, while Renan provides both continuity and solidification of 'the official discourse of Orientalism' and of 'its intellectual and worldly institutions' (p. 130).

In his description of this discourse and its institutions, Said stresses the emergence of what he sees as the principle of binary opposition and comparison whereby Europe always emerges as superior to the Orient. A tripartite typology of Orientalist works is also introduced. Said identifies three different types of writer: the scientific writer, the creator of a personal aesthetic and the writer who combines the two. Edward William Lane's *The Manners and Customs of the Modern Egyptians* (1836) is taken as a prime example of the first category, Burton's *Pilgrimage to al-Madinah and Meccah* as typical of the second and Nerval's *Voyage en Orient* as representative of the third. Said discusses Lane's work at length since he sees Lane as typifying 'the increased specialization and institutionalization of knowledge about the Orient represented by the various Oriental societies' (p. 164). He concludes that scholarly Orientalism developed as an institution at the same time as colonialist and imperialist structures were established.

Although Said does not explicitly define imperialism and colonialism in *Orientalism*, it is clear that he uses the first to mean the domination of a distant territory by a Western metropolitan centre, which implies varying degrees of economic, political and military control, as well as cultural dominance. The latter is embodied in the discourses of the various domains associated with imperialism: trade, travel and exploration, science, and humanitarian and missionary activities. To some extent these domains might seem to be peripheral to imperialism, yet they are essential to it, since they provide much of the imperial rhetoric and representation necessary for the domination of one culture by another. Colonialism is seen as the establishment of settlements in a distant territory, usually but not always as a result of imperialist expansion, and as a process whereby settlers from the imperial power come to play a dominant and privileged role in the economic life of the territory.

The word 'imperialism' was not used in the sense defined above until the 1870s, notably after the beginning of 'classical imperialism', that is, the period of European expansionism involved in the scramble for Africa from 1880 onwards.[8] However, the use of imperialist rhetoric and representations that implied the superiority of Western culture and the inferiority and barbarity of other cultures had existed from the fifteenth century onwards. While colonialism usually follows imperialism, the activities of traders, missionaries, travellers and explorers paved the way for it. One of the things Said does in *Orientalism* is to provide some examples of the interrelations of imperialism, colonialism, and the discourses of domains associated with them.

Regarding the development of Orientalism as an institution, Said also explores the relation of the three types of Orientalist writing already identified to the idea of pilgrimage. Lane again represents the scientific or impersonal writer, Chateaubriand exemplifies the creator of the personal aesthetic, and Richard Burton, T. E. Lawrence and Charles Doughty the intermediate type. Said distinguishes between two different national versions of the pilgrimage. First there is the British version, where the realities of imperial possession limited imaginative possibilities to some extent. This is opposed to the French version where the lack of a real French imperial presence both provoked a sense of loss and allowed greater scope for the projection of this sense of loss and for other fantasies (pp. 168–70). However, as Moore-Gilbert has noted, French colonization of Algeria was well under way by the middle of the nineteenth century, which meant that France did have a real material involvement in the Orient.[9] Said goes on to contrast Lane and Chateaubriand as the prototypes of British and French Orientalist writers, and continues by discussing the writing of Lamartine, Nerval and Flaubert as writers belonging to the French version of the pilgrimage model. Nerval and Flaubert he sees as being particularly important, because the Orient is central to their work, 'both were geniuses', and both had 'a sympathetic, if perverse, vision of the Orient' (p. 180).

Said sees institutionalized Orientalism as the legacy of the nineteenth century to the twentieth, and the third chapter, 'Orientalism Now', examines this inheritance in the period after 1870. Before dealing with Anglo-French Orientalism and American neo-colonialism in the twentieth century in the third and fourth sections of the chapter, however, Said restates the characteristics of Orientalist dogma and makes an important distinction between latent and manifest Orientalism (see pp. 23–4 below). A sweeping indictment of the racism of nineteenth-century Orientalism follows, along with a rare recognition of its patriarchal nature. Said also notes the connections between Orientalism and theories of racial inequality and hierarchy (pp. 203–7). Kipling's idea of the 'White Man' and his civilizing role in the imperial world is analysed, and Said then moves on to examine some typical examples of Orientalist discourse. He sums up by saying that the major change in Orientalism after 1870 was one 'from an academic to an *instrumental* attitude' (p. 246, emphasis in the original).

This instrumental attitude is seen to have taken different forms in British and French Orientalism in the twentieth century, more specifically prior to and after World War I. Sir Hamilton Gibb and Louis Massignon are discussed as representatives of British and French Orientalism respectively. Said speaks explicitly of 'Islamic Orientalism' and comes to the conclusion that, from the post-World War I period until the present, it is characterized by 'its retrogressive position . . . its general methodological and ideological backwardness, and its comparative insularity' (p. 261). Said finally brings Massignon and Gibb together as the last two major representatives of what he calls 'the essentially *ecumenical* authority of European Orientalism' who took it 'as far as it could go'. 'After them', he says, 'the new reality – the new specialized style – was, broadly speaking, Anglo-American, and more narrowly speaking, it was American Social Scientese' (p. 284). The presentation of contemporary Orientalism focuses on the way in which Islam and Arabs are represented in the American media and elsewhere, and on the USA's cultural and political dominance of Arab countries. Although he ends with an appeal for alternative approaches to other cultures, Said also reasserts that his main purpose has been to dissect the already existing field rather than to provide such an alternative himself.

Said's approach in *Orientalism* is radical in several ways, and it was even more radical in 1978 than it is today. He foregrounds the Western textual construction of the Orient and argues that this textual production is an example of the Western 'will to power' over others, and that it is therefore intimately related to the material realities of political and economic domination which constitute colonialism, imperialism and neo-colonialism. However, Said also espouses a form of Western humanism that takes white, European, middle-class male experience as a key point of reference, although he is also concerned to contest this. He focuses on the West and the Western and gives scant acknowledgement of the work of non-Western postcolonial writers, at least until 'Orientalism reconsidered' (1985).[10] Moreover, he has little to say about class and gender as factors influencing the discourses and structures of Orientalism. Other problems arise from Said's attempts to reconcile Foucault, Gramsci and certain features of Western humanism. Foucault's ideas on discourse and power are evoked in conjunction with Gramsci's argument that culture is an important factor in establishing hegemony, that is the dominance of one people or group over another. But these perspectives occur alongside appeals to notions such as 'human reality' or 'human experience', which emerge from the philosophical tradition which both Foucault and Gramsci challenge.

I shall first comment on the problems arising from the multiple definitions of Orientalism as a field which the book offers. The methodological contradictions implied by Said's use of Foucault and Gramsci as well as humanism will then be examined. A critique of *Orientalism* in terms of gender will follow, and the conclusion will discuss some of Said's comments on the book in 'Orientalism recon-

sidered' and elsewhere which throw light both on *Orientalism* and
on the links between it and his other works.

The question of definition

Defining Orientalism proves to be a complex and contradictory
business. Some of the variations in perspective and emphasis in
Said's definitions can be seen as productive, and they can be
explained by the fact that he describes Orientalism as a discourse
in Foucault's meaning of the term. However, there is a vacillation
in the book between historical and ahistorical perspectives which is
disabling.[11]

The erratic appeal to historical contexts is clear in Said's initial
tripartite definition of Orientalism. First, it is an academic tradition
of study, teaching and writing about the Orient. Second, it is 'a style
of thought based upon an ontological and epistemological distinction made between "the Orient" and (most of the time) "the
Occident"'. Third, it is 'the corporate institution for dealing with
the Orient', or 'a Western style for dominating, restructuring, and
having authority over the Orient'. The first two meanings are not
historically located, but the third is situated as beginning in the
eighteenth century. It becomes clear immediately after this that Said
describes Orientalism as both an institution and a style since he is
defining it as a discourse in Foucauldian terms. Foucault defines a
discourse, or a set of 'discursive practices', as 'the delimitation of a
field of objects, the definition of a legitimate perspective for the
agent of knowledge, and the fixing of norms for the elaboration
of concepts and theories'.[12] That is, each discourse sets out the
parameters of a field of study or a type of intellectual activity, and
establishes a set of rules both for individuals participating in the
field or the activity and for the theoretical models that they create.
Further, a discourse may involve several different disciplines and
can be embodied 'in technical processes, in institutions, in patterns
for general behaviour', and in methods of communication and
teaching. It can also effect changes in mentalities and attitudes, since
it is related to power structures in society at large.[13] Said uses this
definition and argues that Foucault's concept of discourse can
help to explain 'the enormously systematic discipline by which
European culture was able to manage – and even produce – the
Orient politically, sociologically, militarily, ideologically, scientific-

ally, and imaginatively during the post-Enlightenment period' (*O*, pp. 2–3).

Said's second set of definitions of Orientalism seems to relate to the second of the three meanings given above, that is, to Orientalism as an ontological and epistemological distinction. Said argues that 'as much as the West itself, the Orient is an idea that has a history and a tradition of thought, imagery, and vocabulary that have given it reality and presence in and for the West.' However, he qualifies this statement in three ways: first, the Orient was not only or *'essentially* an idea' since it was and is also a reality; second, the Orient's status as an idea is intertwined with the domination of non-European countries by European ones; third, Orientalism 'is not an airy European fantasy about the Orient, but a created body of theory and practice in which, for many generations, there has been a considerable material investment'. The consequences of these qualifications, especially of the last two, are that the book is not primarily concerned with the correspondence between Orientalism's representations of the Orient and the real societies and cultures that were represented. Rather it deals with 'the internal consistency of Orientalism and its ideas about the Orient (the East as career) despite or beyond any correspondence, or lack thereof, with a "real" Orient' (p. 5). This passage introduces the problematic issue of the relationship between representation and truth, and although Said sidesteps the issue at this point, it will return to haunt his text on many later occasions.

At the beginning of the third section of chapter 1, Said offers another, this time a double, definition of Orientalism. It is 'the discipline by which the Orient was (and is) approached systematically, as a topic of learning, discovery, and practice', but also 'that collection of dreams, images, and vocabularies available to anyone who has tried to talk about what lies east of the dividing line' (p. 73). Although this double definition is not historically located, the historical perspective soon re-emerges as Said describes how the relation between Europe and the Orient was the product of the European expansion which came with imperialism and colonialism. The conflict between the two views of Orientalism here is compounded by the implication that the 'imperial institution' simply replaced the 'scholarly discourse' (p. 95), which is not at all what the rest of the book suggests. Moreover, Said is elsewhere at pains to point out that there was not only *one* scholarly discourse or imperial institution, but rather many interlocking discourses and institutions, which is what the Foucauldian perspective implies.

Lists of characteristics of Orientalist thought follow these two definitions. First come the four elements of eighteenth-century thought which laid the basis for modern Orientalism: '[European] expansion, historical confrontation, sympathy, [with the non-European and] classification' (p. 120). Then there is a classification of nineteenth-century Orientalist writers into three types, the scientific-impersonal, the scientific-personal and the personal mentioned above. In chapter 3, Said gives a list of four typical elements of Orientalist discourse in the twentieth century. These are: the use of generalizations, the 'binomial opposition of "ours" and "theirs"', the use of generalizing narrative descriptions and, finally, the 'synchronic essentialism' embodied in the use of transcendent, often derogatory categories such as 'Semitic' (pp. 227–40). Said argues that the opposition between 'our' world and 'theirs' always implies that 'our' world is superior to 'theirs' and that 'their' world depends on 'ours'.

The delineation of these different sets of categories is followed by the distinction between latent and manifest Orientalism at the beginning of the final chapter. This distinction cuts across Said's model of interlocking discourses and institutions, to some extent. While it may appear to be related to the earlier opposition between the systematic and the more imaginative approaches to the Orient, it does not cover the same ground. Latent Orientalism is 'an almost unconscious (and certainly an untouchable) positivity' while manifest Orientalism refers to 'the various stated views about Oriental society, languages, literatures, history, sociology, and so forth'. The term 'latent Orientalism' is not explicitly defined, but it seems to mean something like a collective and unconscious shared set of images and attitudes that does not change through time. Said uses this distinction to try to reconcile the historical and non-historical definitions of Orientalism which have characterized the book thus far, arguing that while manifest Orientalism changes from writer to writer and period to period, latent Orientalism does not (p. 206). As Peter Childs and Patrick Williams argue, latent Orientalism 'has strong affinities with certain concepts of ideology, particularly the "negative" version of ideology as false consciousness'.[14] This is true, although Said avoids using the word 'ideology', here as elsewhere. Somewhat confusingly, however, no sooner has Said made the distinction between latent and manifest Orientalism than he collapses it again, arguing that the two converged in the course of the nineteenth century (pp. 222–3).

The opposition between 'classical' studies of Orientalism and the descriptions of 'travellers, pilgrims, statesmen and the like' suggests that the split is now between the latent Orientalism of philologists and classical scholars, as opposed to the manifest Orientalism of writers, explorers and government administrators (pp. 222–3). This is somewhat different from what was suggested in the initial distinction, since this seemed to rely on an opposition between an unconscious or 'almost unconscious' set of predisposi-tions and a conscious set of theorizations, almost like the distinc-tion between deep structure and surface structure in language or between *langue* and *parole*.[15] The issue is not simplified by Said's recapitulation of the 'principal dogmas of Orientalism . . . today'. He summarizes them as follows. The West and the East are separ-ated by 'absolute and systematic difference', (ancient) abstrac-tions are always preferable to (contemporary) realities, the Orient is usually seen ahistorically as a uniform entity incapable of self-definition and, finally, the Orient is to be either feared or controlled (pp. 300–1).

There are several common points in these definitions. They are all marked by the vacillation between historical and ahistorical per-spectives, and between a homogenizing tendency and the recogni-tion that Orientalism is a varied and changing phenomenon. There is hesitation as to whether the Orient can be truly represented by Western writers or not, and contradictory positions are taken on the question of the relationship between scholarly and aesthetic Orient-alism and imperial institutions and colonial practices. That is, the book seems to suggest at times that scholarly Orientalism paved the way for imperialism and was then superseded by it, but at other moments imperialism is seen as coming to determine the develop-ment of scholarly Orientalism as a field. Many of these contradic-tions can be related to Said's use of the conflicting methodologies of Foucault, Gramsci and humanism.

Contradictory methods and values: Foucault, Gramsci and humanism

Said uses a Foucauldian strategy and mode of analysis of power and representation in *Orientalism*. However, he seems at times to hesitate between Foucault's ideas about the microstructures of power permeating the whole of political and civil society and a Gramscian conception of power as the domination of one state or group by another and the repression that this domination necessarily involves. Moreover, there is a significant difference between Foucault's and Gramsci's emphasis on the importance of the historical process, whatever the differences in the way they approach it, and the values of the Western humanist tradition to which Said appeals at various points in the book.

Said's use of Foucault: a problematic model

Foucault is perhaps the most important single theoretical source for Said. His work is unimaginable without Foucault's concepts of discourse and of discursive formations, his discussions of the relationships between power and knowledge, and his view that representations are always influenced by the systems of power in which they are located. Works such as Foucault's *Discipline and Punish*, *The Archaeology of Knowledge* and *The Order of Things* are key texts, and in a series of articles from 1972 to 1986 Said has engaged with Foucault's work in depth.[16] His evaluation of Foucault's work changes with time, notably in relation to Foucault's dismissal of the individual subject, work or author as useful or necessary analytic concepts.[17] Said is also increasingly sceptical about Foucault's conception of power because he comes to see it as leading to political inaction. Thus the relationship between Said's ideas and Foucault's in relation to such key concepts as discourse, power, representation, knowledge and objectivity is complex, shifting and at times contradictory. Three fundamental reasons for this are: first, the basic tension between them as regards the relationship between theory or analysis and action; second, their differing positions on whether or not such a thing as true representation is possible; and third, their different conceptualizations of power.

For Said, as for Gramsci, another key thinker and formative influence, theory and practice must go hand in hand; for Foucault, analysis rarely leads to action. Foucault's writings reject the possibility of any direct transition from his method of analysis to action. They expose the dangers and modes of operation of totalitarianism and of oppressive systems of thought and institutions, but they do not contribute to the destruction of totalitarianism or injustice in practice. This conflicts in the most fundamental way with the point of view expressed in many of Said's writings. Whether the domain is that of literary criticism, cultural theory or political commentary, Said sees the intellectual as someone who should bring about change and have an effect in the world of the academy or outside, or both. The dichotomy between theory and practice in Foucault is linked to the idea that representation is inevitably coloured by power, and that there can be no such thing as a 'true' representation.[18] In Said's writings, the movement from theory to practice and the appeal to a form of true representation is to be found in his work on Palestine and the Middle East, as well as in his discussions of the oppositional intellectual's role and responsibilities (see chapter 2). In *Orientalism* and *Culture and Imperialism*, Foucault's concept of representation is essential.

The third area where Said and Foucault diverge is in their conceptualizations of power. Foucault argues frequently that power comes 'from everywhere'.[19] That is, he reconceptualizes power in terms of what he calls a 'capillary' model of operation and propagation, rejecting the 'repressive hypothesis' which argues that power is imposed from above. This model, with its analysis of the microsystems of power operating through various discourses in the entire social and institutional body, is essential for Said. His dissection of the role of geographical and linguistic societies, scholarly institutions, disciplines such as anthropology and ethnography, and the contemporary media in both creating their subject and diffusing a body of authoritative knowledge, relies on Foucault's ideas of discourse, discipline and the connections between power and knowledge. Yet, at the same time, Foucault's 'capillary' model of power and his insistence that power is everywhere denies the possibility of identifying some of the specific sources of the type of power coming 'from above'. In *Orientalism* and in many of Said's writings on Palestine and the Middle East and on the issue of intellectual responsibility, there is a definite locus of power: the West, the European colonial powers, Israel or the USA. In Said's discussions of colonialism and neo-colonialism, power cannot be said in any meaningful way to come 'from everywhere', although it is embodied in a variety of discourses and institutions. As early as 1974 in 'An ethics of language', Said seems to doubt whether Foucault's notion of archaeology can help non-Western cultures resist domination, although in that article he finally reasserts Foucault's relevance to both radicalism in the West and nationalism in the Third World.[20] In 1978, at the time of writing *Orientalism*, Said seems relatively untroubled by Foucault's lack of attention to resistance; by 1993, when *Culture and Imperialism* was published, this has become more of a problem. Perhaps the most dramatic indication of the change in Said's view of Foucault is his comment in a 1997 article to the effect that Foucault's work is characterized by 'political hopelessness', and that it is nothing more than 'an intensely private, deeply eccentric, and insular version of history'.[21]

Said's choice of Foucault as one of his chief theoretical sources is thus ironic in several ways. The two share, in differing degrees, the emphasis on European or Western experience, an aspect of Foucault's work that Said criticizes in *Culture and Imperialism*, especially in relation to Foucault's neglect of imperialism in his analyses of power. In *Orientalism* Said sets out to reconnect European scholarship and literature on the Orient with the political contexts of imperialism, colonialism and neo-colonialism. Yet he chooses as one of his major theoretical sources a thinker who fails to connect the European and the non-European worlds, and who also refers to a model of power which obscures the role of a central locus of power in producing oppression. Moreover, Foucault's ideas often seem to deny the possibility of resistance; Said's adoption of a Foucauldian framework of ideas in *Orientalism* may be one reason why the book neglects resistance, while *Culture and Imperialism*, in moving away from Foucault, includes resistance as a key element in its analyses.

Foucault *in* Orientalism

In describing the '*textual* attitude' of the Orientalist tradition, Said uses Foucault's idea of a discourse to explain what he means: 'such texts can *create* not only knowledge but also the very reality they appear to describe. In time such knowledge and reality produce a tradition, or what Michel Foucault calls a discourse, whose material presence or weight, not the originality of a given author, is really responsible for the texts produced out of it' (p. 94, emphasis in the original). As Rashmi Bhatnagar says, 'Foucault's original contribution to the materialist conception of discourse' allows Said 'to improvise a convincing argument about the growth of institutional sites which accommodated the Orientalists, systematized their endeavour', and so on.[22] However, *Orientalism* as a whole shows that there are two major inconsistencies in Said's use of Foucault's concept of discourse. There is, first, the relationship between truth and representation, and in particular the question of whether there can be such a thing as true representation or whether any representation is, of necessity, to some extent a misrepresentation. Second, Said's conception of the relationships between discourse, knowledge and power differs from Foucault's, and the opposition between pure and interested knowledge is problematic for Said in a way that it is not for the French philosopher.

Concerning the relationship between truth and representation, Said takes at least two contradictory positions. First, there is a series of passages where he denies the relevance of the issue of any correspondence between Orientalist discourse and the reality it purports to describe. That is, the texts themselves, but not their individual authors, are seen to create rather than to reflect or refract reality. For example, in the Introduction, Said acknowledges the existence of the 'brute reality' of Oriental nations and cultures, but then notes that *Orientalism* will not discuss this reality. This is because the book is concerned with Orientalism's 'internal consistency' and not its 'correspondence, or lack thereof, with a "real" Orient'. He sees Orientalism as 'more particularly valuable as a sign of European-Atlantic power over the Orient than it is as a veridic discourse' about it. He develops the argument that the European presence in the Orient led to the creation of an invented 'Orient' as an object of study and readerly consumption. His analysis of Orientalist texts is thus concerned with them '*as representations*, not as "natural" depictions of the Orient', which means that he is concerned above all with textual and historical features and '*not* the correctness of the representation nor its fidelity to some great original' (pp. 5–6, 21, emphasis in the original).

So far, the perspective is consistently Foucauldian. However, other passages discuss Orientalist texts in ways that suggest that they do distort or misrepresent Oriental realities. For example, discussing d'Herbelot's narrative of the life of Mohammed in his *Bibliothèque orientale*, Said argues that 'the Orient is thus *Orientalized*.' This means that the Orient is identified 'as the province of the Orientalist', and it 'also forces the uninitiated Western reader to accept Orientalist codifications (like d'Herbelot's alphabetized *Bibliothèque*) as the *true* Orient.' He continues: 'Truth, in short, becomes a function of learned judgment, not of the material itself, which in time seems to owe even its existence to the Orientalist' (p. 67, emphasis in the original). Here, Said's emphasis on the way in which this invented Orient usurps the truth-claims of the real implies the idea of the misrepresentation or distortion of the original Orient. Later passages imply even more strongly that the Orient created by Orientalism misrepresents the reality. For example, having quoted Nietzsche's dictum that 'truths are illusions about which one has forgotten that this is what they are', Said says that 'Orientalism was such a system of truths, truths in Nietzsche's sense of the word.' Once again the idea of the 'real Orient' is present, if only by default. Confusingly, however, Said also talks about the 'objective discoveries' of Orientalism. By this he seems to mean the linguistic and historical systems and facts codified or reconstructed by Western scholars, although he once again qualifies the adjective 'objective' by claiming that, since these codifications or reconstructions are embodied in language, they cannot therefore be objective (pp. 203, 204). A little later, Said describes an important element in nineteenth-century Orientalism as being its development into a dogma. This meant that if a writer called something 'Oriental' the term was taken as objective description, but that the word was actually distorted by the set of power structures and ideological values in which Orientalism was implicated (p. 205). At this point Said's position on objectivity seems close to Fanon's view that 'For the native, objectivity is always directed against him.'[23]

Said's discussions of truth, discourse and representation are similarly vacillating. In the Introduction, he argues that what a culture circulates is 'not "truth" but representations' (O, p. 21). The discussion of these issues culminates in a long passage in the third section of the final chapter where Said seems to vacillate between the idea that true representation is theoretically possible and the opposite position that all representation is necessarily misrepresentation. He argues that all representations are necessarily unreliable because they are 'embedded first in the language and then in the culture, institutions, and political ambience of the representer'. Moreover, 'Representations are formations, or as Roland Barthes has said of all the operations of language, they are deformations.' If one follows this line of argument then there can be no such thing as a true representation, because all representations depend on language and on social power structures and institutions. However, elsewhere Said argues, rather differently, that his point is not about the 'misrepresentation of some Oriental essence', but that Orientalism as a system or discourse has an ideological purpose defined by its historical context (pp. 272–3). Another problem is that both the discourse of Orientalism *and* Said's analysis of it fail to do justice to the multiplicity and variousness of Oriental realities that is, they both homogenize their object of study (see pp. 30–1 and 35–41 below). Said's failure to acknowledge the heterogeneity of Orientalism may be one reason why his analysis of it becomes embroiled in contradictory definitions and redefinitions. Said finally states that the distinction between representation and misrepresentation 'is at best a matter of degree' (p. 272), which does not resolve the issue.

Said claims to be adopting a Foucauldian genealogical perspective, and he appeals to Foucault's notion of a discourse and the relationship between knowledge and power that it implies. However, if Said is later to accuse Foucault of neglecting the operation of European power in the non-European colonial context, of being in imagination *'with* rather than *against'* power (emphasis in the original),[24] and of neglecting the possibilities of resistance, then in *Orientalism* Said does something rather similar. For while the book undoubtedly focuses on the power of European Orientalist discourse to construct and represent the non-European Other, it ironically parallels that power itself in routinely identifying the colonizer and/or the Orientalist as all-powerful and the colonized as powerless. This identification locates all initiative as well as all control of the production of knowledge and of representation in the colonizing power and correspondingly negates to a very large extent the possibility of resistance or independent action on the part of the colonized.[25]

Moreover, the exclusive identification of power with the European colonizing countries and their institutions must be considered in relation to Said's recurrent presentation of Orientalism as a unified and dominant force that generally overrides any local or individual differences between its practitioners. Although Foucault's model of discourse would normally entail a variety of institutional and discursive practices, Said often speaks as if Orientalism were always and everywhere the same. This seems to suggest that differences between individual authors are ultimately less important than the perspectives they share which construct the Orient and its inhabitants as inherently different and inferior, although Said does insist on the importance of individual variation.

This vision of Orientalism as a homogeneous or monolithic entity has frequently been criticized,[26] although Peter Childs and Patrick Williams have argued that what Said is talking about is 'internal consistency', which should not be equated with 'absolute homogeneity' or 'monolithic uniformity'.[27] Robert Young provides a most illuminating comment on this aspect of Said's work. Young argues that Orientalism 'operates as a form of dislocation for the West', explaining that if the West's construction of the Orient 'does not really represent the East', then it 'signifies the West's own dislocation from itself, something inside that is presented, narrativized, as being outside'. That is, the Orient as constructed by the West can be interpreted as a projection of repressed desires and fears. That is why, as Young says, 'certain racial and gender theories were pro-

jected onto Orientalist stereotypes.' Young argues that Said recognizes the contradictory consequences of this type of projection only
intermittently, since he shares the assumptions of the European
humanist cultural heritage. This means that the contradictions
involved in that heritage re-emerge in the 'theoretical contradictions and conflicts' in Said's text.[28] As Ahmad says, 'humanism-as-
ideality is invoked precisely at the time when humanism-as-history
has been rejected so unequivocally' in *Orientalism*.[29]

To complement his analysis of the power structures and relations of Orientalism, Said turns to Gramsci's conceptualizations
of political and cultural hegemony, and of power as repression.
As Said says, Foucault's work contains nothing comparable to
Gramsci's notion of hegemony, that is, the domination of one state
by another,[30] which Said finds indispensable in analysing the relationship between Europe and the non-European Other. Finally,
Gramsci, like Raymond Williams, sees power as 'not invincible, not
impervious to dismantling, not unidirectional', which means that
there is at least the possibility of theorizing resistance.[31]

Gramsci in Orientalism

Said uses Gramsci in *Orientalism* in two ways. First, he links
Gramsci's distinction between political and civil society and his
view of culture operating within civil society to support political
domination with Foucault's idea of a discourse in order to try
to explain the 'durability and the strength' of Orientalism. Second,
he appeals to Gramsci's idea of providing a self-descriptive 'inventory' of the traces left by history on the individual when he
describes the *'personal dimension'* of his purposes in writing the book
(pp. 7, 25).

In the first case, Said's appeal to Gramsci can be seen as relatively
uncontentious: he uses the concept of hegemony (the domination
of one state by another) to supply what he sees as a lack in
Foucault's ideas. More specifically, he takes Orientalism as an example of how cultural hegemony works in civil society to reinforce
the ruling ideology of political society not by domination but by
consent. He also uses Gramsci's observation about the interdependence of political and civil society as the basis for his central argument that 'all academic knowledge about India and Egypt' in the
nineteenth century was affected by 'the gross political fact' that
these countries were British colonies (*O*, p. 11). What Gramsci's

ideas bring back into play are concepts such as 'ruling classes' and 'dominant interests' which are eliminated in Foucault's model of power as 'everywhere'. As Dennis Porter has observed, there is also a potential contradiction between discourse theory and the Gramscian notion of the domination of one state by another, because Gramsci's ideas foreground the notion of historical process, whereas discourse theory does not.[32] That is, Foucault's discourse theory often fails to historicize the relations between discourse and power, whereas Gramsci's analysis focuses on historical process and relates power to ideas such as the ruling classes and the dominant interests.

Said also uses the concept of cultural hegemony, or dominant cultural patterns and models, to justify linking the study of culture to a political phenomenon such as imperialism. Denying that to insist on the influence of imperialism on literary works demeans both culture and the works themselves, Said refers to Foucault, Gramsci and Raymond Williams. He argues that as an example of a dominant cultural form, Orientalism is 'a dynamic exchange between individual authors and the large political concerns shaped by the three great empires – British, French, and American' where the writing was produced. That is, the 'internal constraints' of Orientalism as a system were *'productive*, not unilaterally inhibiting' on individual writers (*O*, p. 14, emphasis in the original).

The second, perhaps more interesting use of Gramsci in *Orientalism* occurs when Said is discussing his personal position. He refers to Gramsci's injunction to the writer and critic to 'know thyself'. He quotes from *The Prison Notebooks* where as he notes, 'The starting-point of critical elaboration is the consciousness of what one really is, and is "knowing thyself" as a product of the historical process to date, which has deposited in you an infinity of traces, without leaving an inventory.' Noting that the English translation is incomplete, Said adds his own version of the final words of the sentence: 'therefore it is imperative at the outset to compile such an inventory.' Said responds to Gramsci's injunction by talking briefly about his 'Oriental' origins, his childhood, his Western education and his awareness of being a non-Westerner. He sees his study of Orientalism as being 'an attempt to inventory the traces upon me, the Oriental subject, of the culture whose domination has been so powerful a factor in the life of all Orientals'. He emphasizes his attempt to 'maintain a critical consciousness' as well as to use 'those instruments of historical, humanistic, and cultural research of which my education has made me the fortunate beneficiary'. He ends by asserting that he has never 'lost hold of the cultural reality of, the personal involvement in having been constituted as, "an Oriental"' (pp. 25–6).

The passage reveals several of the main reasons for the contradictions of *Orientalism*. First, in evoking the tools of 'historical, *humanistic*, and cultural research' (my emphasis), Said is appealing, ironically, to the tools of the tradition which gave birth both to imperialism and Orientalism. Second, by appealing to personal experience as the validation for his analysis of the general phenomenon of Orientalism, he falls into the kind of 'possessive exclusionism' that he rejects in *Orientalism* and in 'Orientalism reconsidered' (*O*, p. 322; OR, p. 229). In both he explicitly rejects the idea that 'only Muslims can write about Muslims, and so forth.' Third, in appealing to his individual 'critical consciousness' – a term which is central to his self-definition as an intellectual – he seems to imply that it is possible to stand outside the historical process. This is problematic because he also, contradictorily, characterizes himself as somebody who is a part of that process.[33] Finally, the passage shows once again Said's tendency to homogenize what is heterogeneous. Although he makes an indirect reference to his privileged status as an 'Oriental' in his allusion to being a 'fortunate beneficiary' of a certain type of Western education, he then nevertheless implies that his own experience is typical of that of all 'Orientals'. This is a clearly untenable position and one that he eschews elsewhere.

Foucault, Gramsci and humanism in Orientalism

One of the most problematic features of *Orientalism* is Said's attempt to link Foucault's ideas about discourse and Gramsci's concepts of cultural hegemony and the connections between political and civil society with his own oppositional version of humanism.[34] Said's relation to Western humanism is complex. Western humanism can be defined as the set of values and ideas associated with post-Enlightenment ideas of history as 'secular and progressive human self-development'.[35] As such, it involves an emphasis on the importance of the individual subject and of individual rights such as equality before the law, freedom of expression and freedom to participate in civil society. That Said, or anybody else, should endorse such values might seem to be unexceptionable. However, this set of values and ideas evolved in eighteenth- and nineteenth-century

European cultures that were both elitist and strongly hierarchical at home and imperialistic abroad. The stress on individual political and human rights was theoretically universal, but in fact applied only to a limited group: white Western middle- and upper-class men. In practice, it excluded all other men, and all women. Moreover, the idea of individual and social history and progress associated with these rights was based on a hierarchical view of cultures which tended to define European or Western culture as civilized and superior and other cultures as barbaric and inferior. Thus, when Said appeals to the tools of Western 'historical, *humanistic*, and cultural research' (*O*, p. 26, my emphasis), he is criticizing Orientalism on the basis of the value system and ideology which informed both anthropology, with its assumption of the possibility of objective and uninvolved description,[36] and Orientalism itself.

To say this is not to deny the contestatory current within Enlightenment and post-Enlightenment thought,[37] and it is within this contestatory or oppositional current that Said's version of Western humanism should be seen. He is aware and critical of 'the unpleasantly triumphalist freight' customarily associated with Western humanism, and also of its Eurocentrism.[38] Nevertheless he feels that, freed of these defects, humanism is still very valuable. More specifically, he wishes to complete the work of earlier European humanists such as Erich Auerbach and Theodor Adorno by extending Enlightenment concepts of human and political rights to the peoples of the non-Western world. That is, he is attempting to use the values of Western humanism against the imperialist tradition of Western culture and against its failure to acknowledge or value different cultures,[39] and to reassert the values of *truly* universal rights and freedoms. He seeks to modify the apparently universal but actually limited vision of Western humanism so that it can become what Kwame Anthony Appiah calls an 'ethical universal', that is, the idea of 'a *transnational* rather than a *national* solidarity' (emphasis in the original).[40] This is admirable, but it is not entirely unproblematic. As Audre Lorde has said, 'The master's tools will never dismantle the master's house.'[41] It is exceedingly difficult to free Western humanism from its Eurocentricity, from its assumptions of Western cultural superiority and from the idea of the civilizing mission which provided the rationale for colonial possession and imperial domination in the past and justifies neo-colonial economic inequality in the present.

In *Orientalism*, Said's discussions of the role of the individual writer can be taken as an example of his attempts to reconcile

Foucault, Gramsci and his oppositional version of Western humanism with its emphasis on individuals and their rights. Early in *Orientalism* he explicitly states his disagreement with Foucault's denial
of the significance of individual writers as determining influences
(*O*, p. 23). Later, though, he takes a more Foucauldian position,
arguing that it is the 'material presence and weight' of the discourse
and 'not the originality of a given author' which produces texts
(p. 94). Two later descriptions of the contributions of the individual writer try to reconcile Foucault's vision with Said's. The first
describes individual work as 'strategies of redisposing material
within the field'. This means that 'each individual contribution first
causes changes within the field and then promotes a new stability,
in the way that on a surface covered with twenty compasses the
introduction of a twenty-first will cause all the others to quiver, then
to settle into a new accommodating configuration' (p. 273). Another,
more instrumental, description of individual contributions soon
follows.

> And to a very large extent the Orientalist provides his own society with
> representations of the Orient (*a*) that bear his distinctive imprint, (*b*) that
> illustrate his conception of what the Orient can or ought to be, (*c*) that
> consciously contest someone else's view of the Orient, (*d*) that provide
> Orientalist discourse with what, at that moment, it seems most in need
> of, and (*e*) that respond to certain cultural, professional, national, polit-
> ical, and economic requirements of the epoch. (*O*, p. 273)

While the first description of the individual Orientalist's activities is ahistorical, the second makes specific reference to the Orientalist's historical situation. Both try to reconcile Said's view of the
importance of the individual author with Foucault's denial of it by
stressing the relationship between the individual, his scholarly field
and its historical location. Although Said does not explicitly refer
to Gramsci here, his statement that the Orientalist's representations
of the Orient correspond to the 'cultural, national, political and
economic' requirements of the period recalls Gramsci's vision of
culture as promoting hegemony by consent rather than by force.
The link between Foucault, Gramsci and an emphasis on the individual is successful to some extent. However, the fact that the first
of these descriptions recalls T. S. Eliot's famous characterization of
literary tradition as an 'ideal order' of monuments is worth pon-
dering. In a famous passage in 'Tradition and the individual talent',
Eliot says 'No poet, no artist of any art, has his complete meaning
alone'. He continues:

> The existing monuments form an ideal order among themselves, which
> is modified by the introduction of the new (the really new) work of art
> among them. The existing order is complete before the new work arrives;
> for order to persist after the supervention of novelty, the *whole* existing
> order must be, if ever so slightly, altered; and so the relations, propor-
> tions, values of each work of art toward the whole are readjusted
> [emphasis in the original] . . .[42]

Quite apart from the assumption made by both writers that all Orientalists or all artists are men, there are some striking similarities
between the two passages. Both are descriptions of discourse and
discursive fields as intertextuality, and although both evoke history,
they do so in a manner which effectively neutralizes it, since historical time is transformed into space in the metaphors of the compasses and the monuments respectively. Neither passage allows for
the political and ideological constraints that Foucault and Gramsci
both emphasize, in different ways, and that Said himself evokes in
the second description of the Orientalist's activities quoted above.[43]

Despite his criticism of 'Most humanistic scholars' who are
willing to admit ideas such as context and intertextuality, so long
as these are not given a political definition (*O*, p. 13), Said himself
appeals to several characteristics of Western humanism in *Orientalism*. He stresses the importance of the individual writer, uses
Auerbach and Curtius as role models and appeals to such notions
as 'the brotherhood of man' or 'the universality of certain principles
of human behaviour' (p. 261). These ideas occur not only in relation to such figures as Auerbach and Curtius, but also Burton, Massignon and Marx (pp. 197, 264, 154), or, conversely, in Said's
criticism of T. E. Lawrence for his inability to see Arabs as individuals with separate life stories (pp. 229–30). He also invokes categories such as 'human reality' in relation to some of the most
important general questions that he raises about one culture's perception of another. For example, he asks, in relation to what he calls
'the main intellectual issue raised by humanism': 'Can one divide
human reality, as indeed human reality seems to be genuinely
divided, into clearly different cultures, histories, traditions, societies, even races, and survive the consequences humanly?' (p. 45).
He also states, in the concluding paragraph of *Orientalism*, that 'I
consider Orientalism's failure to have been a human as much as an
intellectual one' in that it 'failed to identify with human experience'
(p. 328). Earlier, he evokes Yeats at least twice in order to characterize human experience as a whole as 'the human ground (the foul-

rag-and-bone shop of the heart, Yeats called it)' or 'ordinary human
reality, Yeats's "uncontrollable mystery on the bestial floor," in
which all human beings live' (pp. 110, 230). There are several problems with all these appeals to a universal type of human experience.
As James Clifford says, it is very doubtful whether the 'African pas-
toralist' and the 'Irish poet and his readers' share the same 'existential "bestial floor" '.[44] Moreover, the idea of universal experience
obscures the interrelations of power and knowledge that Foucault
emphasizes. It also seems to disregard the fact that Western imperialism and colonialism operated on the basis of hierarchies of race,
class and gender, all of which assumed the inherent superiority of
white, Christian, middle-class, Western men.

Gender in *Orientalism*: a neglected factor

In a conversation with Raymond Williams Said argued that 'in the
relationships between the ruler and the ruled in the imperial or
colonial or racial sense, race takes precedence over both class and
gender.' He added, 'I have always felt that the problem of emphasis and relative importance took precedence over the need to establish one's feminist credentials.'[45] As Ahmad notes, the phrase,
' "establish one's feminist credentials", takes care of gender quite
definitively, as imperialism itself is collapsed into a "racial sense".'[46]
Said's remark seems to imply only his – somewhat belated – awareness of the need for 'feminist credentials'. It does not suggest any
realization that, once gender is included as one of the defining parameters in any discussion of Orientalism, the terms of the discussion
are entirely changed.[47] The same might be said of class. As Fanon's
Wretched of the Earth demonstrates, in discussions of imperialism,
colonialism and postcolonialism it is necessary to differentiate
between various classes in relation both to the colonizing power
and to the colonized people. Fanon distinguishes between the government and the people in the case of the colonizing power (a distinction which, it might be argued, could be nuanced still further),
and between the 'national bourgeoisie', the 'militants' and the peas-
antry in the case of the colonized people.[48] The discussion below
will focus on the factor of gender, although a similar argument
could be made in relation to class.

Near the beginning of *Orientalism*, Said takes the famous example
of Flaubert and the Egyptian dancer, Kuchuk Hanem, as the proto-

type of the relationship between the Western colonizing power and the Eastern colonized people. He says, 'He [Flaubert] was foreign, comparatively wealthy, male, and these were historical facts of domination that allowed him not only to possess Kuchuk Hanem physically but to speak for her and tell his readers in what way she was "typically Oriental".' Said notes that the relation between them is 'not an isolated instance. It fairly stands for the pattern of relative strength between East and West, and the discourse about the Orient that it enabled' (O, p. 6). These statements suggest that Said will pay attention to gender and class, or at least economic position, as factors in 'the historical facts of domination'. Indeed, at a much later stage in the book, Said does comes back to his prototypical example, and its gender implications. Noting that 'latent Orientalism also encouraged a peculiarly (not to say invidiously) male conception of the world' and that as a field Orientalism was 'an exclusively male province', he says that this is particularly clear in travel writing and fiction, where 'women are usually the creatures of a male power-fantasy. They express unlimited sensuality, they are more or less stupid, and above all they are willing. Flaubert's Kuchuk Hanem is the prototype of such caricatures' (p. 207). Ironically, Said and I have reproduced in our texts one element of the unequal relationship between Flaubert and Kuchuk Hanem. The Egyptian woman is referred to by a name which, in Turkish, means 'little madam', but which is used by Flaubert himself and by others writing about him as if it were the woman's proper name. 'Kuchuk' in Turkish means 'small', while 'hanem' is an honorific title normally added after a woman's first name. 'Kuchuk hanem' would have referred to the unmarried daughters of a rich household. Egypt was a part of the Ottoman empire at the time of Flaubert's visit; hence the Turkish term.

Said's comments show that he is aware of the exploitative dimensions of Flaubert and Kuchuk Hanem's relationship and thus of the significance of gender for the analysis of Orientalism, but most of the time this awareness seems to forsake him. Identifying the connection between the Orient and sex as a staple ingredient of the relationship between the Western (male) writer and the Orient, Said singles out Flaubert as a particularly interesting example of the kinds of 'complex responses' which the association between sex and the Orient produced (p. 188). A little later he returns to the question of the Orient and sexuality, this time to 'the association . . . between the Orient and the freedom of licentious sex'. He sketches an explanation of this association, arguing that for nineteenth-century Europe, with its increasing *embourgeoisement*, sex had been institutionalized to a very considerable degree. On the one hand, there was no such thing as 'free' sex, and on the other, sex in society entailed a web of legal, moral, even political and economic obligations of a detailed and certainly encumbering sort. . . . the Orient was a place where one could look for sexual experience unobtainable in Europe. Virtually no European writer who wrote on or traveled to the Orient . . . after 1800 exempted himself or herself from this quest: Flaubert, Nerval, 'Dirty Dick' Burton, and Lane are only the most notable. In the twentieth century one thinks of Gide, Conrad, Maugham, and dozens of others. What they looked for often – correctly, I think – was a different type of sexuality, perhaps more libertine and less guilt-ridden; but even that quest, if repeated by enough people, could (and did) become as regulated and uniform as learning itself. In time 'Oriental sex' was as standard a commodity as any other available in the mass culture, with the result that readers and writers could have it if they wished without necessarily going to the Orient. (p. 190)

The description of European sexual behaviour at home and abroad is remarkable. In describing the nineteenth century's 'institutionalization of sex', Said declares that there was no such thing as free sex, that is what he calls 'sex outside society', while 'sex in society' was encumbered by 'a web of legal, moral, even political and economic obligations'. While this is true of middle- and upper-class marriage in the nineteenth century, it is scarcely true of working-class marriage or of prostitution, the other dominant forms of nineteenth-century heterosexual relations. In his relations with prostitutes, the nineteenth-century Englishman or Frenchman was almost totally unencumbered. Sex was (and indeed still is) a commodity easily available to the consumer, who is generally male, and involves no responsibility except the payment of a larger or smaller sum of money.

When Said goes on to comment on the European's search for 'a different type of sexuality, perhaps more libertine and less guilt-ridden' outside Europe, he makes two statements which are, at best, dubious. First he says that there was scarcely a single European traveller to the Orient after 1800 who 'exempted himself or herself from this quest'. Second, in an aside, he says that these travellers were 'correctly' looking for less encumbered sexuality outside Europe. The over-generalization in the first statement is obvious. Although this is one of the rare points in *Orientalism* where Said, by using the words 'himself or herself', implicitly registers the fact that there were female travellers to the Orient, he nonetheless asserts that their behaviour was exactly the same as that of their male counterparts. This is surely improbable, given the greater constraints on

European women's behaviour both at home and abroad; moreover, he also implies that the behaviour of all travellers, male and female alike, was the same, which is equally improbable. As for the second assertion, the reader is left wondering *why* Said thinks these European travellers were correct in supposing that they could find a 'more libertine and less guilt-ridden' kind of sexuality outside Europe. Here Said seems to be making the Orientalist statement that a freer kind of sexuality *was* available for European men and women in the Orient. The only plausible explanation for this would be that sex outside Europe was (and is) freer since the Europeans do not feel themselves bound either by the rules and conventions of their own society or by those of the society in which they are travelling; the first do not apply and the second have no relevance to them. If Said had identified this perverse and disrespectful way of thinking as typical of nineteenth- and twentieth-century Orientalism (whether in the form of the experience of the lone traveller or of the mass tourist, let alone the sex tourist), it would be hard to disagree. That he says that these travellers were 'correct' in thinking in this way is mystifying.

Elsewhere, sporadically, Said seems to see the gender implications of Orientalism in at least two forms: the West's feminization of the Orient in Orientalism and Western men's textual and real exploitation of Oriental women. He nonetheless fails to see that Orientalism was not an exclusively male province, although of course it was men who defined its dominant discourse. However, there were also women writers and travellers, and not all of these adopted what Said characterizes as the classic Orientalist approach, especially towards Eastern women. Some of them did, of course. As Sara Mills has noted in relation to Mary Kingsley, some women travellers adopted the flirtatious, bantering, masculine or masculinist tone more typical of male writers in describing the women they encountered.[49] Other Western women travellers, notably Lady Mary Wortley Montagu, among others, as Billie Melman and Lisa Lowe have demonstrated, had a very different attitude to the position and situation of Eastern women. They were often sympathetic, sometimes admiring, and sometimes identified with Eastern women to a certain degree or made comparisons which were not necessarily to Eastern women's disadvantage.[50] While some women writers and travellers did share the imperialist and masculinist philosophy typical of classic Orientalism, others did not. Some criticized both imperialism and patriarchy, like Annie Besant. Others adopted a version of the imperialist perspective while also maintaining a feminist critique of their own culture, such as May French-Sheldon or Flora Annie Steel.[51] Still others criticized particular versions or aspects of the colonialist project while not being opposed to imperialism *per se*, like Mary Kingsley.[52] There were also those who *did* adopt the masculinist and imperialist perspective more or less uncritically, such as Freya Stark or Gertrude Bell, although even writers like these were not slow to criticize what they saw to be errors or omissions in British government policy on occasion.[53] Said takes none of these multiple variations into account, he never discusses the position of colonized women, or considers that women on either side might speak for themselves.

Said constantly raises and then disappoints any expectation that he will pay attention to gender. When he says that 'as both geographical and cultural entities – to say nothing of historical entities – such locales, regions, geographical sectors as "Orient" and "Occident" are man-made' (*O*, p. 5), he is making a crucially important point. Such entities are man-made in the sense that they are non-natural ideological constructs; but they are also man-made in the sense that they are the products of male-dominated societies and their economic, political and cultural systems. This second aspect of the point constantly seems to escape Said's attention. This gender-blindness is, ironically, compounded by the fact that Said's diagnosis of the West's view of the Orient as something both desired and feared, as something relatively unfamiliar and therefore both attractive because exotic, *and* dangerous or repulsive because unknown and threatening, parallels the conventionally stereotyped view of women. It also parallels the oscillation in the Western stereotypes of the Orient which divide it into masculine and feminine sides. The male Oriental becomes the despotic male, to be both feared and despised, while the female becomes the exotic, sensual, penetrable odalisque or houri, to be desired and, arguably, also despised. For example, Said says that 'The Orient at large, therefore, vacillates between the West's contempt for what is familiar and its shivers of delight in – or fear of – novelty' (p. 59). The statement could just as well be rewritten to apply to male–female relations: [Women] at large, therefore, vacillate between [men's] contempt for what is familiar and their shivers of delight in – or fear of – novelty. For the West, the Other is embodied in the Orient; for men, the Other is embodied in women. For Western men, the images of women and of non-Europeans are conflated. As Helen Carr argues, the discourses of colonialism, racism and sexism 'continually reinforced, naturalized and legitimized each other during the process of European colonization'.[54]

Said's critique of what he identifies as the typically Orientalist move, whereby some human beings' experience is distorted or discounted altogether, can therefore be turned against his own analysis at various points. He criticizes Orientalism for having 'a *textual* attitude' to the Orient (p. 92, emphasis in the original), and he quotes Anwar Abdel Malek's summary of the dehumanizing and objectifying implications of Orientalism for the inhabitants of the Orient. Yet it could be said that, by neglecting the factors of gender and class, Said is making similarly distorting abstractions in relation to women and non-middle-class men. Abdel Malek notes that Orientalism as a discourse creates an ahistorical typology in which 'the normal man' is 'the European man of the historical period, that is, since Greek antiquity', and other types are seen as inferior and are categorized as 'homo Sinicus, homo Arabicus' and so on (p. 97). Neither Said nor Abdel Malek seems to notice that the exclusive emphasis on *male* and the corresponding exclusion of female experience (and textuality) implies a perspective which is just as distorting as the emphasis on European and the dismissal of non-European experience (and textuality). The 'typology' which Abdel Malek describes whereby one human being achieves transcendence and subjecthood at the expense of another who is objectified and confined to immanence has been famously and thoroughly explored in relation to man as the transcendent subject and woman as the immanent object by Simone de Beauvoir. The two types of objectification, and the two typologies, are eerily parallel, but there is no reference to this parallel.

Moreover, at other moments Said's own description of the Orient as seen by the West seems to reproduce unwittingly the sexual stereotyping which he criticizes. For example, referring back to his discussion in chapter 2 of nineteenth-century writers, Said observes that each of them 'kept intact the separateness of the Orient, its eccentricity, its backwardness, its silent indifference, its feminine penetrability, its supine malleability' (p. 206). Separate, eccentric, backward, silent, indifferent, penetrable, malleable: the list recalls Helen Carr's listing of the negative qualities associated with the 'woman' or 'the racial Other'.[55] It reminds the reader that the East is to the West what the woman is to the man, at least in the conventional view of the man. The added specification of 'feminine' in relation to 'penetrability' only rubs salt into the wound, as the classic Orientalist trope of the description of the unexplored land as 'virgin territory' to be penetrated and controlled resurfaces. Similarly, although Said criticizes Orientalism's opposition between Western strength and Eastern weakness as typical of any system that works on a binary model of 'what is believed to be radical difference' (p. 45), he himself reproduces a similar opposition in terms of gender.

This tendency to think in terms of binary oppositions is demonstrated elsewhere. Said criticizes the 'contemporary Orientalist attitudes [which] flood the press and the popular mind' as embodied in the stereotype of Arabs as 'camel-riding, terroristic, hook-nosed, venal lechers whose undeserved wealth is an affront to real civilization'. Said distinguishes the Eurocentric and ethnocentric assumptions of superiority which underlie the stereotype. He notes, 'a white middle-class Westerner believes it is his human prerogative not only to manage the nonwhite world but also to own it, just because by definition "it" is not quite as human as "we" are.' He adds, 'There is no purer example than this of dehumanized thought' (O, p. 108). As a man of Palestinian origin living in the West, Said is understandably and rightly sensitive to the West's dehumanization of Arab men. However, just as many Orientalists and many male and female consumers of Orientalist discourses and stereotypes dehumanize Arab men and women through their unthinking acceptance of these distortions, so Said dehumanizes both Western and Eastern women through obliteration. Western women have no place in his analysis of the 'white middle-class Westerner'. As a representative of imperial and postcolonial political and economic power, the latter is identified unambiguously as 'he'. Arab women are even more dramatically excluded from the Orientalist stereotype he quotes here and from the text as a whole.

There is also the unexpected use of the pronoun 'we' in the passage. Grammatically it would be more appropriate for Said to finish his sentence about the white middle-class Westerner by saying 'by definition, "it" [the non-white world] is not quite so human as "he" is' or 'as "his" is'. The unexpected use of the first person plural pronoun seems to place Said *in* the world of the white middle-class Westerner rather than in that of the 'non-white'.[56] This is true even if Said is using 'we' as a parodic illustration of the mindset he is criticizing. Yet it is perhaps scarcely surprising that Said should position himself like this, parodically or not. Although he insists on his experiential credentials as a Middle Easterner and a Palestinian in exile early in the book, Said is scarcely an exile in the privileged world of Anglo-American academia, but a full member of the club, although one who is always in opposition. This fraught membership of the very club which would seem to exclude him perhaps partly explains why Said is sometimes unable to see how other binary oppositions used in the Orientalist stereotyping of the East also occur in Eastern and Western men's stereotyping of women.

By almost totally ignoring both Western and Eastern women, Said misses the opportunity to make his approach more sensitive to various different historical specificities and thus more precise and complete as an analysis of the West's relationship with the East. Partly because he ignores the lives and works of those Western women who were involved in the Orient, Said fails to recognize that the West's Orientalist discourse about the Orient is in fact much less dominant and unified than he often states or implies. In particular, much travel writing by women may be seen to have a complex and variable relationship to the dominant discourse as Said identifies it.[57] For it is not only Western women who are obliterated in Said's account of East–West relations, but Eastern women too. The situation of Eastern women, after all, did not and does not merely duplicate that of either Eastern men or Western women and deserves some inclusion in the theorization of the framework of discussion of Orientalism. To be fair to Said, this is not easy, either in practical or conceptual terms. Evidence about non-Western women is less easily accessible than that relating to either Western men or women. Theorizing about non-Western women has also proved tricky for Western feminists, who have been accused by Gayatri Spivak and Chandra Talpade Mohanty, among others, of reducing them to the stereotype of the victim.[58] My own analysis here also marginalizes non-Western women to some extent. Finally, it should be remembered that Said's focus is on the analysis of Orientalist discourse and not on non-Westerners' responses to it.

Nevertheless, it might be of interest to consider one example of the use of race, class and gender stereotypes from contemporary advertising to suggest why these factors should be included. What is now happening in some Western advertisements shows a considerable advance in sophistication over the crude images of Arabs invoked by Said. It also demonstrates the ways in which, while certain advertisements have partially rehabilitated a certain eroticized version of the Arab man (in the admittedly still-stereotyped figure of the 'sheik'), they nonetheless still relegate both Western and Eastern women to their conventionally accepted stereotyped

roles as different kinds of sexual object. In a television advertisement for a well-known car, two blonde Western women rescue
two Arab men whose car has broken down in the desert. Overcome
with gratitude, one of the Arab men, the sheik, declares to the
women 'My house is yours'. The Western women are dazzled
by the opulence and luxury of the sheik's palace. However,
when they overhear him saying to his right-hand man, 'I want
them for my wives', they disguise themselves in the diaphanous
veils and other flimsy garments that the sheik's wives have
been glimpsed wearing, and escape from the house. As they drive
hastily away, the screen shows the sheik wondering, with a
knowing smile, 'Was it something I said?' Simultaneously, his wives
cluster admiringly round the new cars (of the same model, of
course, as the Western women were driving) which he has just
bought for them, thus revealing that the Western women have
completely misunderstood his words, interpreting them as referring
to themselves and not to the car. The advertisement plays know-
ingly on the stereotypes of Arab men, and of Western and Eastern
women. It first asserts the superiority of Western technology
and relegates the Arab man to second place (his car has broken
down). Yet it then shows the Arab man in a position of power and
authority. The Western women are revealed as possessing the
Western technology represented by the car, but as being trapped
in stupid and erroneous assumptions about Eastern life and
male–female relations, and in exaggerated notions of their own
attractiveness and desirability. The Eastern women represented in
the advertisement are figures of the background, flitting hither and
thither in the diaphanous clothing which has identified them as sex
objects for the male Western imagination for centuries. They neither
speak nor are spoken to, serving purely as signifiers of both the
power and the wealth of the Arab man. The advertisement as a
whole is directed, as it were, from the point of view of the Western
man who, as the supposed inventor of the technological achievement represented by the car, can look on all the participants in the
action from a position of superiority. Of course, both the sheik's
social status and the presumed wealth of the two Western women
fall into well-established patterns of advertising conventions,
whereby the lives and possessions of the wealthy and the leisured
are assumed to represent the aspirations of the many to the good
life. The Orientalist stereotypes used in television advertising are
created by and depend on interlinking factors of race, gender and

class, and these must be analysed jointly if these stereotypes are to
be demystified.

Conclusion: Said, *Orientalism* and the question of positionality

In an interview, Said describes his stance in *Orientalism* as that of
'an Oriental writing back at the Orientalists'.[59] This description
raises the issues of positionality and of audience. As James Clifford
has said, *Orientalism* ' "writes back" at an imperial discourse from
the position of an oriental whose actuality has been distorted and
denied'. It is thus clearly *'oppositional'* (emphasis in the original).
Nonetheless the book is still characterized by some aspects of the
Western humanism that it challenges, and which do not seem to
always be oppositional.[60] There is also the problem of the supposed
audience of the book. Zakia Pathak and her co-authors quote Said's
statement that he is writing for 'students of literature and criticism,
contemporary students of the Orient, the general reader and lastly
readers in the third world'. But they argue that 'This categorization
does not in effect reckon with [them]' as Indian women teaching
English to graduate students 'at a women's college in Delhi University', since they see the book as addressed to the Western reader.
Clearly Pathak and her co-authors do not recognize themselves in
the epithet 'readers in the third world' since the term is too undifferentiated and, perhaps, demeaning. Moreover, if Said's *Orientalism* is addressed to the Western reader, it is surely addressed to the
Western *male* reader, if only by default, since Said not only privileges 'racial markers to the exclusion of others',[61] but excludes the
notion of gender.

Said devotes the 1985 article, 'Orientalism reconsidered', and his
Afterword to the 1995 edition to a reconsideration of some of the
issues raised by the book and by its critical reception. 'Orientalism
reconsidered' reminds us that for Said, the literary and cultural
issues that made *Orientalism* such a contentious work cannot be
discussed in isolation from the larger political, ethical and intellectual matters with which he is concerned elsewhere. This is true
particularly of the Middle East situation, even if many critics of
Orientalism fail to take this fact into account, including those
who have offered the most detailed, perspicacious and illuminating
analyses of the book, such as Clifford, Bové, Young and Moore-
Gilbert.

In 'Orientalism reconsidered' Said begins by disclaiming any intention to answer his critics, although later, in fact, he does answer some of them specifically here and in the 1995 'Afterword'.[62] There seem to have been some developments in Said's thinking. He begins by reiterating that political interests are involved in Orientalism and noting the reluctance to discuss this fact in academic circles. He then goes on to ask how alternative, 'non-dominative and non-coercive', forms of knowledge can be produced in this context (OR p. 15). This is a question that he had already raised, but not answered, in *Orientalism* (*O*, p. 24). He refers to comparable issues raised by feminist, black and ethnic studies, and so on, and draws a parallel between Orientalism abroad and 'male gender dominance, or patriarchy', at home, even comparing Orientals to 'Victorian housewives'. He also acknowledges the work of non-Western thinkers who have dealt with the issues that are treated in *Orientalism* (OR, pp. 23–4). As Ahmad has observed, this acknowledgement contradicts other statements in the essay.[63] There is no such acknowledgement in *Orientalism* itself; neither is there any extensive development of the parallel between Orientalism and patriarchy. Finally, in 'Orientalism reconsidered' Said acknowledges that there is no 'Archimedean point outside the flux' for the commentator to stand in relation to the Arab-Islamic world (OR, p. 16). This statement seems to represent a change from the perspective offered by *Orientalism*, since that work often assumes that such a detached vantage point is indeed available to the disengaged critical consciousness.

Yet there are also continuities, such as the problem of representation and of Said's ambivalent attitude to it. At one point Said denies that his book was 'a defense of the Arabs or of Islam', adding that 'my argument was that neither existed except as ' "communities of interpretation" which gave them existence' (OR, p. 16). This seems to place an excessive emphasis on the construction of the Arab peoples and the Islamic religion by Orientalism, imperialism and colonialism. Moreover, 'Orientalism reconsidered' offers no modification of the hegemonic view of Orientalism. Power, speech and representation are still located exclusively with the colonizer, while the colonized are seen as powerless, silent and objectified. Equally, when Said notes that the history of resistance was left out of Orientalism (OR, p. 17), it is unfortunately true that the same 'repressed or resistant history' was also left out of Said's critique as well. Finally, Said gives a list of theoretical and analytical works by various writers as examples of the new, non-coercive knowledge he seeks, and describes them as positing 'new praxes of humanist (in the broad sense of the word) activity' (OR, p. 24).

Said's reference to 'new praxes' of humanism 'in the broadest sense' indicates once again that there is a danger that all of his adversarial or oppositional activity will simply be recuperated by the traditional praxes of Western humanism, a possibility on which Paul Bové has commented extensively.[64] Indeed, Said's comments on historicism in 'Orientalism reconsidered' offer a good example of the way in which the hegemony of the discursive field reasserts itself. Said's discussion of both European historicism and world history shows his awareness that they are still Eurocentric, and he concludes that 'the problem is once again historicism and the universalizing and self-validating that has been endemic to it.' He praises studies that help to discredit and disrupt 'essentialist universalism' (OR, pp. 22–3), without seeming to realize that *Orientalism* and indeed the two later essays periodically show a similar type of universalism, although he ends with a plea for a secular alternative approach. His attempt to forge such an alternative can be seen in his writings on Palestine and the Middle East, where the issues raised by contemporary forms of Orientalism take on more material, political and urgent forms.

2

Imperialism in the Middle East: Palestine, Israel and the USA

Introduction

Said analyses the political relationship between the West and the countries of the Middle East in a series of books and articles from the late 1960s onwards. Much of this work takes the form of essays linking polemical analyses of political events and situations with empirical historical narration and personal experience.[1] Said's Palestinian writings take a variety of approaches. The predominantly historical perspective of *The Question of Palestine* (1979) is complemented in *Covering Islam* (1981) by the analysis of the Western – primarily the American – media's representation of contemporary events in the Middle East, notably the fall of the Shah of Iran and the Iranian hostage crisis. *After the Last Sky* (1986) offers one version of the alternative narrative of Palestinian exile and dispossession in a combination of Jean Mohr's photographs and Said's text, with its mixture of commentary, autobiographical fragments and general philosophical reflections. *Blaming the Victims* (1988) is a collection of essays co-edited by Edward Said and Christopher Hitchens. Said's contributions develop his views on Palestinian history and his critiques of the American media's representations of the Middle East situation. There is also a more intensive analysis of American pro-Israeli historical studies and literary works related to the Palestinian issue. Said is careful to distinguish between uncritically pro-Israeli American historians and commentators, such as Joan Peters and Michael Walzer, and some of the younger generation of revisionist Israeli historians. He sees the latter as more scholarly and responsible and less biased in their treatment of Israeli and Palestinian history than the former (*BV*, pp. 9–10).[2] *The Politics of Dispossession* (1994) collects Said's essays on Palestine and the Middle East from 1970 to 1994. The essays are of three kinds: reviews of individual literary, journalistic and scholarly works on the Middle East; accounts of contemporary developments in the region; and general analyses of its politics and culture. *Peace and Its Discontents* (1995) focuses on the 1993 Madrid peace talks and the 1993 Oslo peace accord and their consequences, which Said sees as disastrous for the Palestinians. The interviews with David Barsamian collected in *The Pen and the Sword* (1994) offer an overview of Said's views on the Middle East and on other aspects of his work as well as more personal comments. There is also more directly autobiographical material: the memoir, *Out of Place*, published in late 1999, for example, or earlier articles like 'Reflections on exile' (1984), 'Return to Palestine-Israel' (1992), 'Lost between war and peace' (1996) and 'Between worlds' (1998). Finally, Said has made several television programmes, both in the USA and in Britain.[3]

This chapter will not try to discuss Said's writings on Palestine chronologically or exhaustively. Their sheer volume makes it impossible, and it would be unnecessarily repetitive; many of them cover the same ground, and Said's position on Palestine has not changed a great deal since the early 1970s. Instead, what follows will focus on two dominant concerns: first, the issues related to the question of writing a Palestinian narrative, and, second, Said's critique of all the major players in the Middle East and his search for a solution. Said sees the need for a Palestinian narrative to counter Zionist or pro-Israeli narratives of history in the Middle East, especially after the establishment of the state of Israel in 1948. He also examines the assumptions underlying the discursive frameworks governing the analysis of Israeli and Palestinian history, especially the construction in the American media of the Palestinian as terrorist and of Israel as the model of a democratic country. The second area of concern – the criticism of Middle Eastern regimes as well as of the American government – is very varied. It involves criticism of Zionism in Israel and of official Israeli government policy. Said also attacks the American government's apparently unqualified support for successive Israeli governments, and he sees Arab states, including the Palestinian Authority, as partly responsible for the plight of the Palestinians. Finally, Said attempts to offer alternative visions of Palestinian identity and destiny, of a Palestinian state and of Palestinian–Israeli relations.

It is important to note the anomalies of Said's own position in all this. As a Palestinian by birth and an American citizen he is both inside and outside the narratives he constructs. This can be enabling, but it is also at times problematic, especially when Said's position as a relatively privileged exile sometimes leads him to depict the Palestinians in Israel, the West Bank and Gaza, from an Orientalist perspective – the cruellest of ironies. Some of his versions of the Palestinian narrative assume the possibility of objective representation, a concept that he challenges elsewhere. There are also contradictions in his position on nationalism,[4] although it could be said that, to some extent, the contradictions are in the political context rather than in Said's response to it.[5]

Permission to narrate

Narrative is a key element in all of Said's work, as he says to Salusinszky.[6] For Said writing a narrative of Palestinian history means having 'Permission to narrate' (the title of a 1984 essay) in order to set the historical record straight. This involves a critical re-examination of the claims of Zionism and of Zionist and pro-Israeli historians, whose work Said sees as denying the Palestinians' very existence as a people and their right of return to their homeland. As he says, 'Facts do not at all speak for themselves, but require a socially acceptable narrative to absorb, sustain, and circulate them' (*PolD*, p. 254). Thus Said writes as 'a participant' or 'an engaged Palestinian' (pp. 386, 348), that is, as someone who sees such narration as part of the struggle for political and human rights for Palestinians.[7]

Throughout *The Question of Palestine*, Said repeatedly stresses that the Palestinians should be considered as a nation and not simply as a group of anonymous Arab refugees. He asserts the existence of the Palestinians as a nation linked by a 'Palestinian political identity' and their right of return to some part at least of their homeland of historical Palestine. Despite the facts of Palestinian dispersal and exile, he argues that it is possible to speak 'of a collective Palestinian position', and of the desire for self-determination, liberation and an independent state common to the vast mass of Palestinians (*QP*, pp. 118, 120). Said talks about 'the growth of a genuinely unified

Palestinian political self-consciousness' and 'national self-consciousness' (p. 141) after 1948 and especially after the 1967 war, when the PLO emerged as the body representing the majority of Palestinians and there was a growing demand for a Palestinian state. For Mark Krupnick, 'Said is *the* voice of Palestinian nationalism' as he is 'a westernized intellectual who has taken it upon himself to convey his people's cause to a North American and European public'.[8]

For Said, the primary purpose of the Palestinian narrative is the retelling of the story of the events in historical Palestine since the nineteenth century, which contradicts the pro-Israeli version which Said feels has had common currency in the West as a whole, at least until the 1960s. Ella Shohat has noted how this Palestinian narrative of exile and dispossession counters the Israeli claim to exclusivity in this respect. She also notes how Said's description of Israel as a colonialist state contradicts the usual version of the establishment of the state of Israel, since the latter belongs to both 'the meta-narrative of progress and the "civilized world" ', and the narrative of the Jew as victim.[9]

The most important pro-Israeli narrative that Said counters is the one that sees Israel as 'a land without people, for a people without land' (*QP*, p. 9). The corollary of this is that the creation of the state of Israel was the rightful compensation for the centuries of persecution of the Jews that culminated in the Holocaust. In *A Place Among the Nations: Israel and the World*, Benyamin Netanyahu quotes the works of eighteenth- and nineteenth-century European and American visitors to historical Palestine, such as Volney, Lamartine, Bovet and Twain, as reliable evidence that the area was an empty and desolate land (pp. 27, 30, 38–43). Said treats these texts as examples of Orientalist discourse for which, precisely, the 'natives' were seen as backward, uncivilized and primitive when they were visible at all, which means the authors of these works are totally untrustworthy guides to nineteenth-century Palestine (*QP*, p. 9). Right-wing Israeli commentators such as Netanyahu argue that the Arabs left Palestine in 1948 not because the Jewish authorities expelled them, but because they were ordered to do so by their leaders (*APN*, p. 228). Conversely, Said claims that there is absolutely no evidence that this was the case and that the Palestinian Arabs left to avoid Israeli persecution, hoping to be able to return later (*QP*, 101–2).[10] Netanyahu sees the Israeli occupation of the West Bank, Gaza and the Golan Heights after the 1967 war as justified recuperation of some of the land promised to the Jewish people by the

Balfour Declaration of 1917 but denied them by the British Mandate of 1948 (*APN*, pp. 50–90). For Said it represents the colonial occupation of yet more Palestinian land and the colonial domination of the Palestinian population (*QP*, pp. 14, 38–9, 106, 136–7, 205–6, 232). Netanyahu sees life on the West Bank as having considerably improved for the 'Arabs' after 1967 (*APN*, pp. 161–2). However, Said argues that both the West Bank and Gaza are examples of scandalous under-development, since their Palestinian Arab populations are provided with second- or third-class education and other social services and exploited as a cheap labour pool by the Israeli economy (*PolD*, p. xxxix; *PD*, pp. 45–52).[11] Netanyahu represents the Palestinian *intifadah* as a threat to law and order and describes Israeli army activity in the Occupied Territories as necessary to contain Palestinian unrest (*APN*, p. 163–7). Said sees the *intifadah* as a legitimate protest by a colonized population against the injustice of colonial domination and exploitation (*CI*, p. 377; *PolD*, p. xxvii).

The 1973 war and the events of 'Black September' in Jordan in 1970 are also represented from opposite perspectives, as are the 1978 and 1982 Israeli invasions of Lebanon and the later occupation of southern Lebanon. For right-wing Israelis the latter were justified in the name of Israeli security and as anti-terrorist operations. For Said they constituted unprovoked aggression against unarmed and innocent civilians.[12] More specifically, the deaths of hundreds of Palestinian civilians in the Sabra and Shatila refugee camps after the Israeli invasion of Beirut in 1982 are seen by Netanyahu as the responsibility of Lebanese Phalangists and nothing to do with the Israeli government or armed forces (*APN*, p. 384). For Said the actions of the Phalangists were clearly sanctioned and authorized by the Israeli government (*PolD*, pp. 72, 152, 247, 254).[13] Similarly, any official Israeli government narrative and Said's Palestinian narrative of the significance of Camp David, of the Gulf War and of the Madrid and Oslo agreements of 1993 take diametrically opposed but eerily parallel courses, continuing the seemingly endless dialogue of the deaf.

Modifying the discursive framework

Much of Said's writing, however, goes beyond this binary impasse, and he has tried to modify the discursive framework in which such exchanges take place by making two key moves. The first is to situate Israel in the context of European colonialism. This involves recognizing the irony that the state created for the people who suffered the Holocaust has now itself become the perpetrator of unjustified aggression and violence. The second is to argue that the construction of the Palestinians as terrorists is an ideologically motivated discursive strategy intended to render invisible the vast majority of Palestinians. Said contends that it should be seen as an example of contemporary popular Orientalist distortions of the East as 'Other' and as a technique for masking the much greater aggression of the Israeli military against Palestinian civilians and the other civilian inhabitants of Lebanon (*PolD*, pp. 249–50, 254–8).

Israel and European colonialism

In *The Question of Palestine*, Said claims that the philosophy of European colonialism provides both the historical context and the ideological basis for Zionism. He situates the origin of the state of Israel in the British colonial context of mandate Palestine, and sees British support for the idea of a Jewish national home embodied in the Balfour Declaration of 1917 as implying the 'doctrinal annihilation of the Palestinian people'. He further argues that the British colonial government was imposed against the will of the original Palestinian inhabitants and alienated them in their own land by authorizing Jewish immigration (*BV*, p. 242). The most telling specific example of Israel's colonialist policies relates to the Emergency Defense [*sic*] Regulations; these, Said says, were used 'by the British to handle Jews and Arabs during the mandate period from 1922 to 1948'. There were justified protests against them by the Jews, but 'after 1948 they were used, *unchanged*, by Israel against the Arabs', and 'forbade Arabs the right of movement, the right of purchase of land, the right of settlement, and so forth' (*QP*, pp. 103, 36, emphasis in the original).

However, Said also makes several distinctions between European colonialism and Zionism. First, he suggests that the society that the Zionists aimed to create in Palestine 'could never be anything but "native" (with minimal ties to a metropolitan center)', despite the settlers' disregard for the land's original 'native' inhabitants (p. 88). Second, he sees Israel as aligning itself with 'the West', but also notes that the Jews' history of persecution in Europe must be counted a mitigating factor in their occupation of Palestine. Third, stating that Israel is a country of 'settler colonialism', he begins by describing this as an 'absolute wrong', but then says it can be partially understood, if not excused, since it originated in a flight from European persecution. Finally, Said asserts that, however different the circumstances of the different types of settler-colonialism in Israel and South Africa, the effects on the victims who are 'wounded and scarred', are much the same (*QP*, p. 119). Said does not specify which 'West' Israel aligns itself with or which 'methods' it uses, although presumably he is referring to European colonialism. Elsewhere Said has warned against essentializing terms such as 'the West' since, as he says in 'The prospects for peace in the Middle East', 'There are many Wests' (*PolD*, p. 158). Ironically, he falls into an essentializing mode himself here.

Said's later works testify to his continuing attempts to describe the particular nature of Israeli colonialism. In *Covering Islam* (1981) and *After the Last Sky* (1986) he refers routinely to Israeli colonialism as an accepted fact (*CIs*, p. 41; *ALS*, pp. 110–12, 141). He also refers to it in *Blaming the Victims* (pp. 241, 243), *The Pen and the Sword* and *The Politics of Dispossession* (pp. 20–1, 68). In *The Question of Palestine*, Said compares Israel, South Africa and Algeria, since all are characterized by the unjust subjugation and exploitation of a majority by a minority, although he finds that, in the end, analogies between them usually break down (*QP*, pp. 163, 183–4). He argues that the Israeli state is colonialist because of the dispossession of the Palestinians in 1948 and thereafter, and because of the current status of Palestinians in Israel as second-class citizens. He adds that Zionism and the creation of the state of Israel must be seen as unique because they involve a victimized people transformed into victimizers.[14] As he says in *The Question of Palestine*, 'once victims themselves, Occidental Jews in Israel have become oppressors (of Palestinian Arabs and Oriental Jews)' (p. 69, and see also xxiv, 109, 119). This historical irony makes any defence of Palestinian rights and any criticism of Zionism vulnerable to the possible (if illogical) charge of anti-Semitism. Thus Said is forced to state openly in *The Question of Palestine* that 'To write critically about Zionism in Palestine has therefore never meant, and does not mean now, being anti-Semitic' (p. 59). As Said observes, these arguments about Palestinian dispossession and their current underprivileged situation in Israel are simple, apparently self-evident ones. Yet they must be made, since the version of Israel which is often projected in the United States is that of a modern Western-style democracy which offers all its citizens the political and civil rights associated with such societies.[15]

The rhetoric of terrorism

Said's challenge to the assumptions underlying the rhetoric of terrorism relate to the role of the media, primarily but not exclusively
in the USA. He sees the American media as a powerful influence
on public opinion and as both an expression of and an influence on
government policy in the Middle East.[16] He deconstructs the dehumanizing and over-generalizing image of Palestinians as terrorists,
and he argues that accusations of Palestinian terrorism are used to
conceal the much more extensive violence deployed by the Israeli
state against the Palestinians (*QP*, p. xxxx). He also attacks the more
or less total failure of the American media to report Israeli violence
against the Palestinians and other Arab Muslims in Lebanon and
elsewhere (*QP*, p. xxiv).[17]

In *The Question of Palestine* and elsewhere, Said first puts the
image of Palestinians as terrorists in perspective. Throughout
the book he notes and deplores the equation of Palestinians with
terrorists (*QP*, pp. xxxviii, xxxx, 6, 54, 112, 138, 211), and argues
that this equation obscures several facts: first, the majority of
Palestinians lack normal civil and political rights; second, they are
denied the right to fight for the recuperation of their homeland
because the 'terrorist' label obliterates both the fact of their dispossession and their right to struggle to regain what they have lost
(pp. xxii, 224). 'The essential terrorist' in *Blaming the Victims* analyses terrorism as a contemporary phenomenon in the USA and
reviews *Terrorism: How the West Can Win* by Benyamin Netanyahu,
at that time Israeli ambassador in Washington. As in *The Question
of Palestine*, Said disputes the way in which resistance to Israel is
equated with 'terrorism', 'communism' and 'anti-Semitism'. He
also notes that earlier Israeli tactics such as 'textual analyses of
documents like the Palestinian National Covenant or Resolutions
of the Palestinian National Council', which he sees as valid, have
now been replaced by a reliance on slogans or simple defamation
(*BV*, pp. 2–3, 15–16).

The essays in *The Politics of Dispossession* develop Said's dissection of the image of the Palestinians as terrorists. In 'An ideology
of difference' (1985) he argues that a philosophy of racial difference
is used to justify the unequal treatment of Israel's Arab population,
while 'Permission to narrate' (1984) explicates his view of the ideological function of the concept of terrorism in the American media.

Terrorism is always located in a context that helps reduce the world to the two competing realms of 'us' and 'them', and thus contributes to the dehumanization of the Palestinians by Israeli leaders (*PolD*, p. 257).

In 'Identity, negation and violence' (1988), Said notes that Islam, Arabs and specifically Palestinians are associated with terrorism (*PolD*, pp. 341–2). He asserts the need to contextualize 'terrorism' and deplores the fact that terrorism is frequently said to be 'endemic' in the Islamic world (pp. 345, and see 342–5). While it may be true that Islamic terrorist groups are the only ones currently engaging in terrorism outside their own societies, Said is surely right to argue that much media reporting of this terrorism suggests that it is typical of whole countries and not just isolated groups. He goes on to criticize once again the Israeli ability to justify 'what was a massive war against a sovereign country and a national liberation movement', that is, the 1982 Israeli invasion of Beirut and the rest of Lebanon, as 'a campaign against terrorism' (*PolD*, 348, and see 249–58). His conclusion is that the American mainstream media use the rhetoric of terrorism to disparage anything that does not meet the approval of the American government (p. 354; see also *PD*, pp. 132–43, 146–9, and *CIs*, pp. xxi–xxii, xliv–xlvii). Said often claims that this form of misrepresentation through racist stereotypes and comments exists in the West *only* in relation to the Arabs and to Islam (*PolD*, p. 99, *QP*, p. 26).[18] The uniqueness of such misrepresentations is perhaps doubtful: Salman Rushdie has identified similar systematically negative representations of Indians and Pakistanis in the British media, for example.[19]

In his analysis of the violence perpetrated on Palestinians by the Israeli state Said stresses the imbalance between the violence of the two sides and the hypocrisy of much of the American and Israeli media in reporting only one side of the story. He makes both points cogently in the 1979 and the 1992 Introductions to *The Question of Palestine* (pp. xxiii–xxiv, xxxviii). Elsewhere in the book, he comments on Israeli 'state terrorism', this time in relation to Golda Meir, Yitzhak Rabin and Menachem Begin (pp. 138–9). Said attacks the failure of the American media to report this Israeli state violence against Palestinian civilians inside and outside Israel, since this selective reporting obscures the fact that Palestinian violence is often a response to sustained Israeli actions. For example, Said sees the unsuccessful Palestinian attack on Maalot in Israel in May 1974 as a response to 'weeks of sustained Israeli napalm bombing of

Palestinian refugee camps in southern Lebanon'. He also argues that the bombs planted in Gaza and the West Bank were an answer to the 'day-to-day coercion and the brutality of a long military occupation' (*QP*, p. 172). He calls the American press's neglect of these Israeli actions 'one of the most scandalous omissions in the history of journalism'. He particularly condemns the hypocrisy and double standards of many American liberals, who fail to speak out about human rights' abuses in Israel although they are ready to condemn them elsewhere, comparing them unfavourably with their Israeli counterparts who do speak out (p. 42). However, Rashid I. Khalidi observes in a 1998 article that the coverage of Palestinian issues by the American media 'is not as abysmal as it once was'. His view is that it was the Israeli invasion of Beirut in 1982 and its repression of the *intifadah* that prompted the beginnings of a more critical media attitude to Israel in the USA.[20] Said's recurrent criticism of American intellectuals' cowardice, hypocrisy, and double standards may be related to his conception of the role of the intellectual whose duty it is to 'speak the truth to power' (*RI*, p. xiv) and not to be co-opted by the forces of conformity. It may also be taken as an example of Said's own tendency to criticize the main sides and players in the triangular relationship between Israel, the USA and Palestine.

The lonely critical voice and the search for an alternative

Said generally maintains a position of isolation from all of the power blocks and political and media elites in the USA and the Middle East, describing himself as being 'in the opposition in both places'.[21] He has said some very harsh if generally accurate things about Arab states, their totalitarian leaders, their lack of democracy, their repressive and anti-egalitarian regimes, their rhetorical rather than real or effective solidarity with the PLO and their harassment of the Palestinian populations in their own countries. He has also criticized Palestinian terrorism, the ineptitudes of the PLO and Arafat himself, especially since the Oslo peace agreement which he has called a 'Palestinian Versailles' (*PolD*, p. xxxiv),[22] and the mismanagement and corruption of the recently formed Palestinian Authority led by Arafat. However, the main target of his criticism has been American government policy, which he sees as bearing a large share of the responsibility for perpetuating the injustices from which the Palestinians suffer.

American government policy in the Middle East

For many years, Said was one of the few American intellectuals, along with Noam Chomsky and Christopher Hitchens, who took a courageously independent stand on Middle East affairs. His position is that successive American governments' generally uncritical attitude to Israel has meant the neglect of Palestinian rights. He sees the Middle East as an area of competition between the USA and the Soviet Union in the Cold War period, but argues that the role of the Soviet Union was a limited one compared with that of the USA. This was even truer after the demise of the Soviet Union as a global force from about 1990 onwards, when, as the remaining superpower, the USA had huge potential power and influence worldwide. Said sees its policy in the Middle East generally as an abuse of this power based on both profound ignorance about and prejudice against the Arab countries and peoples of the region, including the Palestinians, and unreasoning support for Israel.

Some of Said's criticisms of American government policy in the Middle East were first articulated in two articles written in the early 1970s, 'The Palestinians one year since Amman' (1971) and 'U. S. policy and the conflict of powers in the Middle East' (1973). In both, Said notes that American policy in the area is based on the need to maintain the supply of cheap oil and to protect American economic interests. The effect has been to disable any potential Palestinian revolutionary movement in the interests of maintaining the economic and political *status quo* in the region (*PolD*, pp. 25–6, 205–10). Both articles argue that successive American governments have seen the Palestinians' legitimate protest against Israel as an additional source of instability in an already unstable region, and as such something to be contained or defused. Palestinian rights take second place to economic and political imperatives.

A similar type of analysis is to be found in *The Question of Palestine*, where Said criticizes many aspects of US policy in the Middle East, including its opposition to real change. He notes the role of the American Jewish community in influencing American policy in the region (*QP*, pp. 50–1, 222, 228–9). He criticizes the US government's short-sightedness, and its tendency to focus on narrow issues such as the peace treaty signed by Israel and Egypt rather than on the attempt to create the conditions for peace in the region as a whole (pp. 170–1, 203–4, 215–17). He emphasizes American adherence to the principle of economic self-interest before anything else (pp. 188–9). Said sees the Palestinians and the ordinary people in many Middle Eastern countries as victims of American foreign policy as well as of their own oppressive regimes. Successive American governments support oppressive client regimes such as Israel and Iran under the Shah and oppose popular movements of liberation or resistance since these will threaten the *status quo*. Picking out the Camp David peace agreement between Israel and Egypt for particular criticism, Said notes that it entirely failed even to discuss the question of Israeli settlements in the West Bank, Gaza and the Golan Heights, let alone to consider whether Israel should relinquish these Occupied Territories (p. 192).

In *The Question of Palestine* and in other essays written between 1973 and 1980, American foreign policy in the Middle East is periodically situated in the context of the Cold War, although this is not Said's main focus. He argues that the Soviet Union had a generally peripheral role as an arms supplier to various Arab states. Despite the links between the Soviet Union and the PLO and Fateh, Said claims that the former neither exerted a determining influence on those organizations nor played the role of strategic ally for the Palestinians (*QP*, pp. 170, 160; *PolD*, pp. xviii–xix). Said sees the Soviet Union as a factor in US policy in the region in two main ways. First, American support for Israel is a means of 'holding Islam – and later the Soviet Union, or communism – at bay' and of negating Soviet influence in the Middle East (*QP*, pp. 29, 225). Second, the sale of American arms to Arab countries in the mid-1970s countered any excessive Soviet influence and maintained the *status quo* in the region, thus ensuring that the Palestinian problem would not be addressed (*PolD*, p. 215). However, Said admits that the success of this American strategy depended on most Arab governments' willingness to abandon the Soviet Union for American aid and friendly relations after the bilateral peace agreement between Israel and Egypt at Camp David in 1978 (*QP*, pp. 201–3).

Since the late 1970s the general lines of Said's critique have remained the same. In '"Our" Lebanon' (1984), Said describes American policy in that country as 'wilful and disingenuous' as well as 'lamentable', since it has helped to engender 'another cycle of violence and counter-violence' (*PolD*, pp. 269, 272). He compares American policy in Lebanon to those followed in Iran before the revolution and in El Salvador. Unconditional American support for Israel is viewed even more severely by Said after the beginning of the Palestinian *intifadah* in December 1987. In 'Sanctum of the strong' (1989), he criticizes American Secretary of State James Baker for his support for Israel after this new development. The speech given by Baker on 22 May 1989 to the American–Israeli Public Affairs Committee was held by some to be 'a new departure for U. S. Middle East policy'. However, for Said it was nothing of the kind, since Baker still opposed the creation of a Palestinian state, despite the 'significant changes in the Palestinian political position since the *intifadah*'. That is, Baker failed to take into account the concessions that the Palestinians had made since 1987 (p. 273).

For Said, the logical consequence of American policy is the peace proposal initially put forward by George Bush on 11 March 1991. Although the Americans were not involved in the Oslo negotiations until they were almost finished, Said describes the final agreement as 'an American show'. He sees the negotiations as disregarding the principle of Palestinian self-determination, since the Palestinians participated in the talks only as observers as part of the Jordanian delegation and Israel had a right of veto over the eventual Palestinian members of that delegation (*PolD*, p. xxxi). As Said says, it is scarcely surprising that, given these inequalities in the peace process, the Oslo agreement of 1993 should be favourable to Israel and immensely prejudicial to the Palestinians. However, these unsatisfactory arrangements reflected the unequal balance of power between the three parties involved, and the Palestinian leadership accepted them. This was probably because, after Arafat's support for Iraq during the Gulf War and Iraq's subsequent defeat, the PLO's bargaining position was weaker than it would otherwise have been. The Palestinians thus had less room to manoeuvre than they might have done, a point Said makes in *Out of Place* (p. 214). Moreover, the end of the Cold War weakened the PLO's position still further, since before 1989–90, the Soviet Union nonetheless acted as a counterweight to American influence on events in the Middle East.

The essays collected in *Peace and Its Discontents: Gaza–Jericho 1993–1995* (1995) articulate Said's critique of American government policy with specific reference to the situation in Jericho, the Gaza Strip and the West Bank, some of which is now under the control of the Palestinian Authority. Said criticizes America's continued provision of huge amounts of aid for Israeli security and its continued support for Israeli aggression against Lebanon in 1978 and 1982 and thereafter. Other targets are Israel's brutal military repression on the West Bank and in Gaza (*PD*, pp. 45–52, 121), especially during the *intifadah* (pp. 50, 147–50, 163–4). For Said, what this means is also implicit American support for new Israeli settlements on the West Bank and for the right-wing armed settlers, despite such events as the murder of several Palestinians in Hebron in 1994 by an armed Israeli settler (pp. 58, 126, 154–5, 161–3). The general tenor of Said's criticism of the USA and its financial and political support for Israel is clearly expressed in 'Who is in charge of the past and the future?', written in November 1993. His main points are that Israel's security is heavily dependent on US financial support ($80 billion over the twenty years up to 1995), support which the US government justifies as securing peace. However, Said sees it as enabling Israeli military dominance and acts of aggression in the region, despite the '29 UN Security Council resolutions censuring Israel for its illegal settlements, its deportations, its contraventions of the fourth Geneva Convention' and so on (p. 20).

Said also continues to castigate American hypocrisy and bias in administering the peace process and in failing to criticize Israel's economic 'de-development' of Gaza, noting the continuity and the success of America's policy of *realpolitik* in the area (PD, pp. 45–52, 84–90, 137–43). The articles in *Peace and Its Discontents* reveal Said to be continually at odds with American foreign policy in relation to Israel and the Palestinians. It makes no difference, for Said, whether the administration is Republican or Democrat, since he sees the policies of both as a continuation of American support for Israel at the cost of the Palestinian people.

Arab regimes and leaders

Said has often been unsparing in his criticisms of contemporary Arab regimes, notably because of their repressiveness, their failure to provide social justice and development for the majority of their peoples and their failure to provide real support for the Palestinians' struggle for self-determination. The 1971 essay 'The Palestinians one year since Amman' focuses on the split between Arab governments and their peoples (*PolD*, p. 26), while 'The Arab right wing' (1979) criticizes the repressive regimes of Arab states and their neglect of the development of their own societies. In the latter essay, Said deplores the fact that the power elite in wealthy Arab countries have spent their oil revenues on building luxury hotels and importing consumer goods and not on development, education or even the guarantee of their own survival (pp. 228, 229). There is some truth in his remarks about the neglect of democracy and education in many Arab countries, although it might be more accurate to talk about unequal educational opportunities and uneven development than a total lack of development. Said does not seem to see the irony of his position. His criticisms of the materialistic priorities of the Arab countries are justified, and his choice of US citizenship is not at issue. However, he seems not to understand the desire of the inhabitants of the Third World to share in some of those things that, as a relatively privileged American citizen, he can take for granted.

One criticism of Arab countries which remains constant is the complaint that the support which they give the Palestinians and the PLO is generally more rhetorical than real. In his comments on the relationship between Arab countries and the Palestinians in a 1980 essay, Said notes the 'obvious discrepancy between expressed and actual support' (*PolD*, p. 233). Ten years later, after the Gulf War, he says, 'Arab support for Palestinian self-determination was (as the history of the Gulf attests) *always* the result of popular pressure on the rulers, and not of their goodness of heart.' In November 1991 Said attacks the Arab world for its failure to offer the *intifadah* 'the financial and political support' it needed, while in an interview with Barbara Harlow in April 1991, he talks about 'the abandonment by the Arab regimes of the *intifadah*' (*PolD*, pp. 153, 160, 312).

'Behind Saddam Hussein's moves' (1990) provides a summary of the charges which Said levels at the Arab world as a whole. He describes that world as presenting a 'ghastly spectacle of corrupt and unjust regimes, massive social and economic inequities, horrendously backward educational and cultural establishments, overblown security apparatuses, and abrogated democratic freedoms'. Said lays the blame for this situation primarily on the Arab leaders themselves. However, at another point in the same article he attributes some of the responsibility to the countries of the West, since they have never taken Arab hopes and fears seriously or attempted to draw them into a real dialogue (*PolD*, p. 281).

This comment reveals the over-generalizing tendency in Said's writings about Arab countries. He is often critical of any essentializing Western discourse about Arab countries or Islam (*PolD*, pp. 16, 35, 385), but at times he himself uses essentializing expressions like 'the Arab genius' (*PolD*, p. 16). 'The Arab right wing' (1979) both shows the variety of Arab regimes and, somewhat paradoxically, uses the title phrase as a generalization to sum them up. In 'On Nelson Mandela and others' (1990), he talks about 'the Arab intellectual', while 'U. S. policy and the conflict of powers in the Middle East' (1973) talks about 'a seemingly ingrained Arab habit

of sheer stubbornness'. Even more alarmingly, 'A tragic convergence' (January 11, 1991) diagnoses 'an almost equally remorseless
Arab propensity to violence and exterminism' (*PolD*, pp. 216, 286,
371). These are expressions that it is hard to see Said accepting with
equanimity if they were used by American or European writers.
They demonstrate his tendency to fall into an esentializing mode of
which he is very critical in his other works, notably *Orientalism* and
Culture and Imperialism.

Sometimes, however, Said is more circumspect in his treatment
of the Arab world. In 'The other Arab Muslims' (1993), where he
counters the common Western perception that many Arab countries
are about to be overtaken by a wave of Islamic fundamentalism,
he is much less categorical. He is critical of the repressive nature
of the Egyptian, Lebanese and Jordanian regimes, and deplores
the lack of any alternative to repression by the state and the army
on the one hand and by religious fundamentalists on the other
(*PolD*, pp. 392–3, 398, 400). He is particularly scathing about the
'hypocrisy, unreality, [and] servility' surrounding Mubarak, in particular. But elsewhere in the essay his comments are less generally
negative, and he sees Egypt, in particular, as possessed of a hybrid
culture and civilization which resist both sorts of repression
(pp. 393, 395).

As the above comment on Mubarak shows, Said also finds specific Arab leaders unsatisfactory. In 'Behind Saddam Husssein's
moves' (August 1990), Saddam is described as 'an appalling dictator' and the enemy of democracy (p. 278). Said's conclusion after
the Gulf War is that 'The behavior of the Iraqi regime has been
disgraceful: repressive at home, mischievously adventurous and
violent abroad' (p. 157). Said's comments in a 1981 essay about the
assassinated Egyptian leader Anwar Sadat are more nuanced, but
ultimately negative. He sees Sadat as promising Arab countries
things which he could never deliver, and of working '*outside* Arab
history, society, and actuality, outside their rhetorical extravagances,
their infatuation with form, their dizzyingly collective incoherence'
(emphasis in the original). Towards the end of his time in office,
says Said, Sadat 'abused the Arabs mercilessly' and lost touch with
his people, so much so that his death was hardly mourned. Finally,
'The list of his recently jailed opponents is far from adequately
covered with a phrase like "Muslim fundamentalism," although his
was not an exceptionally repressive regime' (p. 244). To say that
Sadat's regime was not 'exceptionally repressive' is to damn him
with the faintest of faint praise, given Said's views about Arab

regimes. Said's later comments on Arafat follow the pattern of his criticisms of other Arab leaders, although in much of his writing in the 1970s and early 1980s he praised both Arafat and the PLO for their relative democracy (*QP*, p. xxxii). The fact that Said argues that Sadat abused 'the Arabs' as a whole and not just the Egyptians reflects a vacillation in his writings. At times he describes the Palestinians as a separate ethnic group, with their own history and culture, while at others he sees them as part of a group of Arab peoples, united by culture and religion. This vacillation is perhaps an involuntary reflection of Said's awareness of the difficult and far from harmonious relationship between the Palestinians and the other Arab peoples. It may also be linked to the variations in the way he positions himself in relation to America, Palestine and the Middle East, identifying himself as either a Palestinian or an Arab, or both, or, conversely, distancing himself from them, depending on the circumstances (see below, pp. 72–7).

Arafat, the PLO and the Palestinian Authority

Said's views of the PLO and of Arafat have changed, especially since the signing of the Oslo peace agreement in 1993 and the installation of the Palestinian Authority in the West Bank and Gaza, with Arafat at its head, in July 1994. Said has never been completely uncritical of the Palestinian leadership, but in his earlier writings he defends Arafat and the PLO as the legitimate representatives of the Palestinian people. There is little severe criticism of Arafat or of the PLO prior to the late 1980s, when Said's disagreements with PLO policy became more serious.[23] Since Oslo and the establishment of the Palestinian Authority, however, Said's view is that Arafat has betrayed both the interests of the Palestinian people and the goals of the PLO.

From the 1970s until the late 1980s, Said's position generally was one of support for both Arafat and the PLO. Although he was never a member of the PLO itself, he was a member of the Palestinian National Council (PNC) from 1977 to 1991. He attended its meetings in Cairo in 1977, Amman in 1984, Tunis in 1985 and Algiers in 1988 (*QP*, p. 178, *PolD*, pp. xxv–xxvi, *PandS*, p. 115). However, he never voted and was generally an observer rather than an active member, staying clear of factional fighting. As he says to Gary Hentzi and Anne McClintock, 'I've made it a point never to accept an official role of any sort.'[24] In his writings of the period he supports the PLO as the legitimate representatives of the Palestinian people and sees Arafat as the leader of a relatively democratic and successful liberation or independence movement (*QP*, p. 178).

In *The Question of Palestine* Said describes Arafat as 'a much misunderstood and maligned political personality', and he praises his understanding of 'all the major factors affecting the Palestinians everywhere' and 'the *detail* of Palestinian life' (emphasis in the original). Said commends the PLO's management of funds, although he also sees 'the dangerous prospect of Palestinian *embourgeoisement*'. Noting that contributions from wealthy Palestinians in exile helped to fill the coffers of the Palestinian National Fund, which was 'accountable to the Palestinian National Council', he nonetheless warns about the 'highly probable corruptions' of this wealth (*QP*, pp. 165–7). The warning about corruption is highly prescient, while Said's praise for the democracy and accountability of Arafat and the PLO leadership is ironic in view of his later criticism of their lack of political and financial accountability. As late as 1992, in the Preface to the new edition of *The Question of Palestine*, Said still asserts 'the air of relative democracy that characterized Palestinian political processes (when contrasted with the Arab environment)' and notes 'Arafat is the one leader who remains popular with his people' (p. xxxii). Despite this, the discussion which follows shows that Said holds Arafat responsible for continuing Palestinian losses on the West Bank and Gaza, in Beirut and Lebanon in 1982 and during and after the Gulf War in 1991 (pp. xxxiii–xxxiv). He refuses, perhaps surprisingly, to condemn Arafat unequivocally in relation to the losses he has described, and he praises the response of the PLO and Arafat to the *intifadah*.

In early essays like 'The Palestinians one year since Amman' (1971), Said criticizes the Palestinians' limited awareness of their revolutionary role, their inadequate political and military strategies and their lack of clearly defined goals (*PolD*, p. 27). However, by 1983, while Said still sees Arafat as 'personally incorruptible' and capable of keeping the Palestinian issue in the forefront of world affairs, his leadership is 'endlessly problematic'. This is because of 'His vacillations, his questionable involvements with extreme groups and nations, his legendary toleration of corrupt and incompetent subordinates, his frequent inability to seize political opportunities (some would say his incapacity for real leadership)'. Despite all this, however, Said concludes that there is no 'credible alternative' to Arafat's leadership (*PolD*, p. 102).

In essays written after the Madrid talks and especially after the Oslo peace agreement of 1993, any previous ambivalence disappears. Rashid Khalidi argues that Said's first public criticisms of the Palestinian leadership were made after his visit to South Africa and his meeting with Nelson Mandela in 1991.[25] After 1993, those public criticisms intensified. In an interview with David Barsamian given on 27 September 1993, Said gives a detailed critique of the peace agreement. He describes the accord signed in Washington on 13 September 1993 as 'an instrument of capitulation', signed at a 'tawdry' ceremony. He deplores the PLO's abandonment of 'all the other resolutions passed by the U. N. since 1948, including and above all, Resolution 194, which says that Palestinian refugees made refugees by Israel in 1948 are entitled to compensation or repatriation'. He also describes Arafat and the PLO as having a 'nigger mentality' (*PandS*, pp. 107–11).

In a historical overview in the same interview, Said argues that the Palestinian leadership lost touch with the majority of Palestinians in the 1980s, and he sees the Gulf War as a watershed. From that point on, the lack of any 'mechanism for accountability' in the PLO was clear, and after 1990 Arafat alone controlled the money. The very features of the PLO's accountability and Arafat's personal incorruptibility that Said had praised in the 1979 edition of *The Question of Palestine* have disappeared. Despite all this, however, he still asserts that 'the PLO is the only institution we have' and that the 1988 PNC meeting in Algiers which decided on support for the *intifadah* was the greatest achievement of the 1980s (*PandS*, pp. 114–16).

When he returns to the present (1993), Said deplores the total lack of parity in the Palestinian and Israeli positions. He sees this as exemplified by Israel's control over the land, security, foreign affairs and water and by the economic dependence of the West Bank and Gaza on the much stronger Israeli economy (*PandS*, pp. 120–7). This situation leaves the PLO as a 'municipal government' and 'an enforcer for Israel' (pp. 123, 125). All in all, Said sees the action of Arafat and the PLO in accepting the peace agreement as 'a betrayal of history' (p. 161). This sense of betrayal is reinforced by eyewitness reports from the West Bank and in Gaza that indicate that members of Arafat's Fatah group are now involved in the oppression and exploitation of their own people. Moreover, numerous newspaper articles from 1996 onwards have catalogued Arafat's dictatorial rule, the corruption of Arafat and his administration, and torture and other abuses of power.[26] It is not surprising, in the light of all this, that Said argues that Arafat should have asked for a mandate for the acceptance of the terms of the 1993 Oslo peace agreement from his people, and, if it was not given, should have stepped down (p. 135). Arafat did no such thing, and in July 1994 entered Gaza as the head of the new Palestinian Authority.

Since then there has been no improvement in the territories nominally controlled by the Authority and no let-up in Said's criticisms. In the Introduction to *Peace and Its Discontents*, written in July 1995, Said talks about Arafat's proliferating security services, and the torture, censorship and violent suppression of opposition he presides over (p. xxvii). In articles such as 'He won't gag me', 'Lost between war and peace' and 'Palestinians vent fury of the dispossessed', Said has continued to speak out against what he sees as Arafat's continuing abuse of power. 'He won't gag me' was provoked by the confiscation of Said's books from bookshops in the West Bank and Gaza, but is mainly concerned with Arafat's 'increasingly dictatorial, profoundly corrupt and visionless' rule. Said portrays him once again as an 'Israeli enforcer', a 'dictator and petty despot' who, like other rulers in the Arab world, refuses to allow any challenge to his authority.[27] 'Lost between war and peace' narrates Said's visit to 'Arafat's Palestine' in summer 1996 with his wife Miriam to visit his son, Wadie, who was working for the Jerusalem Media and Communication Centre. The article documents Arafat's total control of both the finances and the security services of the Palestinian Authority, although it also evokes the 'new spirit of resistance' to Arafat's authoritarian rule among the members of the Legislative Council.[28]

A significant recent example of Arafat's misrule is the imprisonment and torture of the Palestinian teachers who went on strike, criticized by Said in his conversation with Robert Marquand.[29] Said and various Palestinians whom he talks to in Palestine give the same explanation of at least some of these iniquities. Hassan Barghouti, the director of the Democracy and Workers' Rights Centre, an NGO, attributes many of the problems to 'the use of nationalist discourse to cover over social inequities, real economic injustices and the sorry state of our civil life generally'.[30] Said himself, in 'He won't gag me', says 'there has been an extraordinary Palestinian *trahison des clercs*, and I simply cannot understand why', although he suggests that the cause may be the resurgence of what he calls 'a primitive nationalism',[31] that is, nationalism as an end in itself.

Indeed, what seems to have happened is what Said foresaw in *The Question of Palestine*. A certain minority has profited from the situation in Arafat's Palestine as it has elsewhere in the Arab world, leaving the vast majority of Palestinians no better off. For Said, they are perhaps worse off because they have less hope than they did before. Whether the Palestinians as a whole are worse off than before is debatable. While it is true that money has gone into the West Bank and Gaza, the majority of Palestinians do not seem to have profited from what development there has been, as Rashid Khalidi argues and as several articles in the *Guardian* since 1997 suggest.[32] Said finds himself a very lonely figure, which is ironic, since the metaphor of the 'isolated voice' standing against injustice (*WTC*, p. 15) has long been one of his favourite characterizations of the intellectual's role and function. The metaphor in this case has become reality, and Said finds himself more isolated than before from the Palestinian community and its leaders.

The proposed alternative

Said nonetheless looks for alternatives, arguing, with an ironic echo of much recent feminist theory, that there is a need for 'a new logic in which "difference" does not entail "domination"'' (*PolD*, p. 100). The alternatives he puts forward involve a democratic and secular state in Palestine, non-nationalist and non-ethnic or sectarian visions of identity, and an alternative, non-totalitarian, non-fundamentalist form of government. The achievement of these depends on the exercise of the qualities of critical sense, memory and scepticism by intellectuals and others.

In the Introduction to *Covering Islam* in 1981 Said had declared: 'what I really believe in is the existence of a critical sense and of citizens willing and able to use it to get beyond the special interests of experts and their *idées reçues*' (p. lix). In the Introduction to *The Politics of Dispossession* (1994), the emphasis on the opposition between power elites and critical sense remains, but the latter is now embodied in the figure of 'the really independent critic or analyst', that is, Said himself. For this individual 'Memory and skepticism (if not outright suspicion) are requisites' (p. xli).

One of the things that the intellectual must reject is 'identitarian thought', a phrase which Said takes from Martin Jay's translation of Adorno. That is, the intellectual should reject values associated with 'stable identity as it is rendered by such affirmative agencies as nationality, education, tradition, language, and religion, on the one hand', and endorse those connected to 'marginal, alienated or, in Immanuel Wallerstein's phrase, antisystemic forces' on the other (*PolD*, p. 353). What this means becomes clearer in 'The other Arab Muslims' (1993), where Said gives the examples of two Arab intellectuals, Laith Shubeilat in Jordan and Nasr Hamid Abu Zeid in Egypt, who represent an alternative to totalitarian or identitarian thinking. Of Shubeilat, he says 'you notice not only the dedication to clear principles of human equality and real democracy, but an almost total absence of theoretical, religious, and sophistic rhetoric' (pp. 406–7).

In relation to the Israeli–Palestinian conflict, the search for an alternative means the search for a secular state, something which Said has emphasized in *After the Last Sky* (pp. 62, 146, 150–5), and in *The Politics of Dispossession* (p. xix). In a 1979 interview, and in articles written in the later 1980s and 1990s, he implicitly or explicitly suggests that 'a two-state solution' is inevitable and desirable.[33] Somewhat confusingly, he has also sometimes argued for 'the ideal of establishing a unitary secular democratic state in all of Palestine', with equal rights for Palestinians and Israelis.[34] In more recent articles, however, Said seems to implicitly acknowledge the utopian nature of such a prospect, although he still declares in 1998 that 'The only political vision worth holding on to is a secular bi-national one'.[35] The betrayal of this idealistic vision may be one of the reasons for Said's increasingly stern criticisms of Arafat and the Palestinian Authority, although there are others, like the corruption and brutality of its regime.

Said's proposed alternatives often seem more visionary than real. From one perspective, his insistence on the importance of rational discussion and of intellectual independence and resistance to conformism can be seen as a commendable attempt to maintain dialogue and open-mindedness. Yet it is hard to see the Middle East's problems being solved by 'the skills of a good critical reader' (*CIs*, p. lix). The public intellectual such as Said can articulate a principled critique and exercise some influence over public opinion, but he is unable to intervene directly or to effect any substantial change in the political domain. This is especially true if, like Said, he has always insisted on keeping his distance from official or institutional bodies. When it comes to the question of Said's own position in relation to the issues of representation, power, knowledge and objectivity, moreover, some troubling shifts and contradictions appear.

Questions of representation, position and objectivity

There is frequently a double focus in Said's writings on Palestine and the Palestinians. Said often seems to be obeying a potentially contradictory double imperative: to represent all Palestinians, and to offer a personal narrative that reflects his own position, inside and outside both the Palestinian community and the American intellectual and academic elite. This double imperative can be related to the split between his origins on the one hand and his country of adoption, his later education, social role and professional position on the other. Other complicating factors are the vacillations in his position on religion and nationalism, and on the question of truth or objectivity in relation to the Palestinian narrative.

Representing Others through universal values

The first imperative for Said is to represent all Palestinians. This can be seen as one example of his belief in a form of political universalism. In a 1993 interview with Joseph A. Buttigieg and Paul A. Bové in *boundary* 2, he said: 'it has to be universally accepted that certain democratic freedoms, certain freedoms from domination of one kind or another, freedom from various kinds of exploitations, and so on, are the rights of every human being – which is not the framework of the imperial world in which we live.'[36] For Said, it is a central part of the intellectual's function to defend these universal rights and speak for 'the poor, the disadvantaged, the voiceless, the unrepresented, the powerless' (*RI*, p. 84). In *Representations of the Intellectual* Said explains that universality in this sense means 'taking a risk in order to go beyond the easy certainties provided us by our background, language, nationality, which so often shield us from the reality of others.' More specifically, it means 'looking for and trying to uphold a single standard for human behaviour when it comes to such matters as foreign and social policy' (*RI*, pp. xii). This is what Said has tried to do in writing his various versions of the Palestinian narrative, and in criticizing the double standards of the American media and government in judging Israel and the Palestinians in terms of 'foreign and social policy'.

Yet, in the case of Said's Palestinian narratives, his own 'background, language, [and] nationality' do not provide any 'easy certainties'. Rather, it is precisely the complexity of his position that leads to the contradictions that emerge when he incorporates auto-biographical elements into the more generalized Palestinian narrative. These elements are most striking and important in the text accompanying Jean Mohr's photographs of Palestinians in *After the Last Sky* (1986) and in the second section of Said's Introduction to *The Politics of Dispossession*. They are also accompanied, in *After the Last Sky* and in some of his essays on the Gulf War, by a vacillation between the singular and plural first-person pronouns, the 'I' and the 'we', and between the referents for these pronouns.

These vacillations reflect the fractured and sometimes contradictory nature of Said's self-positioning in relation to religious and political realities. Discussing Said's work in general, Aijaz Ahmad notes the variation in the use of personal pronouns, and he argues that they are 'strategically' used 'to refer, in various contexts, to Palestinians, Third World intellectuals, academics in general, humanists, Arabs, Arab-Americans, and the American citizenry at large'.[37] While Ahmad seems to see a certain amount of bad faith in Said's varying use of 'we' and 'us', I would argue that these variations reflect the various constituencies for which Said is writing as well as the contradictions of his own position. It should be said, however, that Said does not always seem to be aware of the extent of these contradictions. JanMohamed has defined Said's position as one version of 'the *specular border intellectual*', and he sees this position as potentially productive of 'utopian possibilities of group formation'.[38] As regards Said's writings on Palestine, however, it might be argued that the border position leads more to contradictions than to utopian visions.

Inside and outside

In a 1998 interview with W. J. T. Mitchell, Said explains that *After the Last Sky* originated from three things: his realization of the absence of any 'personal dimension' in his writings about Palestine, his 'very strong feeling of exile', and his sense of the necessary fragmentation of any Palestinian narrative.[39] Both the autobiographical elements in *After the Last Sky* and the vacillation between 'I' and 'we' in the text may be considered as part of the fragmented and discontinuous nature of the work. Much of the time Said uses 'we' to link the personal and the collective in an apparently unproblematic way, as in this passage in the Introduction where he reflects on the obscurity surrounding Palestinians as a group. He says: 'It is certainly correct to say that we are less known than our co-claimants to Palestine, the Jews. Since 1948, our existence has been a lesser one. We have experienced a great deal that has not been recorded. Many of us have been killed, many permanently scarred and silenced, without a trace' (*ALS*, p. 4). Elsewhere, however, Said meditates on the distance between himself and the majority of Palestinians. Discussing the difference between his own family background and experience and those of most Palestinians in the Middle East who are peasants and farmers, he describes himself as 'an urban Palestinian whose relationship to the land is basically metaphorical'. As Glenn Bowman says, *After the Last Sky* exemplifies the point of view of the Palestinian bourgeoisie in exile, although he also notes that Said writes about other Palestinian communities both inside and outside Palestine.[40] Said gives details of his family background and of his life and education in the USA and concludes that he is far removed from the majority of Palestinians and that 'whatever tenuous childhood relationship I may have had with Palestinian village or farm life is pretty much dissipated. So even though I can still note the largely agricultural roots of our society, these have no direct personal immediacy for me. I continue to perceive a population of poor, suffering, occasionally colorful peasants, unchanging and collective.'

Said immediately goes on to recognize that 'this perception of mine is mythic' and 'further (de)formed by the specific inflections of our history and the special circumstances out of which my identity emerged' (p. 88). But he does not seem fully aware of the ironies of his depiction of rural Palestinians. For what he is doing is Orientalizing them, albeit sympathetically. The words Said uses to describe these people – 'essentially timeless', 'anonymously collective', 'unchanging and collective' – are the typical vocabulary of the eternalizing, objectifying, essentializing vision of the Orientalist tradition which Said diagnoses and discredits in *Orientalism*. Ironically, in *After the Last Sky*, Said's is the voice of the empowered metropolitan centre assessing the powerless rural periphery.

Somewhat later there are further reflections on the question of distance, this time in relation to narrative. Specifically, Said wonders whether his doubts as to the possibility and/or the adequacy of a coherent narrative are his alone because

I write at a distance. I haven't experienced the ravages. If I had, possibly there would be no problem in finding a direct and simple narrative to

tell the tale of our history. When I let myself go and feel as if everything
in the Palestinian situation flows directly from one original trauma, I can
then see a pattern emerging inexorably, as intertwined and as recount-
able as any other sequential tale of misfortune. What I have found is that
if you seize on all the evidence that appears intermittently – another massacre, one more betrayal, a damaging defeat – you can easily construct
the plot of a logically unfolding conspiracy against us. (p. 130)

Said begins by acknowledging his distance from the experiences of
most Palestinians, and observes that, if he had actually suffered 'the
ravages' suffered by many ordinary Palestinians in the Middle East,
he would probably be able to find 'a direct and simple narrative to
tell the tale of our people'. This suggests that it is his distance from
the experiences of the majority of Palestinians that determines his
earlier statement that the Palestinian story needs to be told through
a discontinuous and fractured narrative. However, Said then turns
this 'direct and simple narrative' of suffering into one of conspiracy
theory, apparently without noticing the logical leap he has taken.
He rejects this conspiracy theory narrative as a 'paranoid construction', but does not offer an alternative. He concludes that 'we
ourselves provide not enough of a presence to force the untidiness
of life into a coherent pattern of our own making.' Judging from
his own experience, he reads the Palestinians 'against another
people's pattern' where 'we appear as dislocations in *their* discourse' (p. 140, emphasis in the original). Here the doubt as to
whether the perception of a lack of coherence is Said's own or not
has disappeared behind the straightforward assertion that this lack
is general and completely disabling. Tellingly, by the end of the
passage, Said has slipped into the 'us and them' rhetoric which he
so often deplores and which his work generally opposes and
avoids.

On another occasion, grappling with the problem of his relationship to the majority of Palestinians, Said again falls into the
Orientalist trap. He distinguishes between the 'literary, entirely
bourgeois state' which exile typically represents for bourgeois intellectuals like himself, and the exile of the Palestinians in the Near
East who are 'almost by definition silent, indescribable, utterly
poignant'. This population, he says, 'survives with difficulty –
subject to the dictates of bureaucrats and soldiers, prone to disas-
ters and humiliations, more and more dependent on the whims and
internal politics of their host countries. Their history and actuality
cannot ever be recovered, but as a people, they can be represented,

and they can be connected to their more fortunate compatriots'
(p. 121). Said's assertion that the mass of Palestinians in the Middle
East are 'almost *by definition* silent, indescribable, utterly poignant',
and that although their history 'cannot ever be recovered' '*they can
be represented*' (my emphasis), is deeply problematic. For it ironically
reinscribes another classic Orientalist trope and one that, moreover,
Said foregrounds at the beginning of *Orientalism* in the epigraph
from Marx: 'they cannot represent themselves, they must be represented.' The fact that it is his own people whom Said is describing
in this way only adds to the irony.

Somewhat similar problems of positioning occur in Said's essays
on the Gulf War, primarily in 'A tragic convergence', 'Ignorant
armies clash by night' and 'The Arab–American war: the politics
of information', all written between January and March 1991. In
these, the split between his Palestinian origin (here represented
by his self-identification as part of the 'Arab' community) and
his status as an American academic and intellectual comes to the
fore in a series of statements which shows clearly his divided
allegiance and the difficulties of his situation. The first striking
characteristic of these essays is the prevalence of the singular first-
person pronoun, which, elsewhere, Said uses quite sparingly. This
in itself is perhaps not surprising, since the essays are very much
statements of personal position, called forth by exceptional historical circumstances. Even more interesting, however, are the variations in Said's use of 'we', 'our' and 'ours'. At times these are used
to refer to all or some Arabs; at others they are used to refer to all
or some Americans; at still others 'we' is put between double quotation marks. When it appears in this latter form, it seems to indicate either the American government or a version of American
(media-influenced) public opinion from which Said wishes to distance himself.

First of all, at the beginning of 'The Arab–American war: the politics of information', Said deals elegantly with the dichotomy and
the complexities involved in his own position. The article begins:

> The United States is at an extraordinarily bloody moment in its history
> as the last superpower. Perhaps because I come from the Arab world, I
> have thought often during the past few months and more anxiously
> during the past few days that such a war as we Americans are now
> engaged in, with such aims, rhetoric, and all-encompassing violence and
> destruction, could now have been waged only against an Arab-Islamic-
> Third World country. (*PolD*, p. 295)

Here Said locates his Eastern origin ('I come from the Arab world'), his American political and civil identity ('such a war as we Americans are now engaged in') and the ideological, political and racial underpinnings of the war itself. It could only have been fought against 'an Arab-Islamic-Third World country', that is, a country which is still perceived through what Said sees as the distorting tropes of contemporary Orientalism and the imbalance of power which inform the postcolonial situation. Later in the article, Said resorts to using ' "we" ', ' "our" ' and ' "ours" ', to express further splits. For example, castigating 'the academic experts on the Arab mind' for their reduction of Iraq to a demonized Saddam Hussein, Said says that it was 'as if all "we" were doing was fighting the one dreadful specter of evil. This enables us to bomb Iraq without a twinge of compunction, and to do it, indeed, with a horrific sense of righteous exhilaration' (p. 299). The passage shifts between "we" and 'us'. Said uses the first to apply to the manipulated and blindly patriotic 'public mood' created by the egregious 'experts on the Arab mind' whom he excoriates, and the second to refer to the mass of the American public who may or may not be so manipulated. Similar issues arise in a later passage, where Said asks 'What else [other than the failure to photograph the American bombing of Iraqi cities] in the many pictures we are getting is deliberately manipulative?' His reply focuses on what he sees as the distortion produced by the excessive coverage of Israeli losses and the relative neglect of Iraqi victims, especially civilian ones. He asks: 'why is it granted that only Israeli and Western affliction should be to this extent available – if not to maintain the fiction that Arabs are not equal with "our" side, that their lives and sorrows are not worth listening to?' The reference to ' "our" side' makes a clear distinction between that part of the American public that is manipulated by the media, and the American people as a whole. Said uses a similar strategy to criticize this hierarchical way of thinking a little later, when he concludes: 'It would therefore seem that the point of this war is to *prevent* lesser nations and subject peoples from enjoying the same privileges that "we" do' (pp. 300–1, emphasis in the original).[41]

It might be objected that Said seems to ignore the fact that one reason why the reporting of events in Iraq was limited is that many Western news teams were kept in Baghdad and away from the battlefields. Moreover, despite the restrictions imposed by the Iraqi government, there *was* coverage of Iraqi civilian deaths, notably of those of the women and children in the bomb shelter attacked by the American-led forces. However, there was much greater emphasis in both the British and the American media on deaths and other casualties suffered by the coalition forces. This has been a feature of most wars in the twentieth century and earlier. It is more or less inevitable, however inequitable, that a country's media will focus on the losses of its own forces and those of its allies, rather than on those of its adversaries.

Questions of religion and nation

These variations in Said's self-representation are also to be found in his position on his own religious background, and on questions of religion and nationalism more generally. Said's defence of universal human and political rights involves a corresponding rejection of ethnic or religious separateness, divisive forms of nationalism and rigid types of identity politics. His distaste for these is based on both his own experiences as a child and his later principles, as the 1991 interview with David Barsamian makes clear. Criticizing the idea of 'homogeneity', Said talks about his childhood: 'I didn't grow up that way. . . . When I was growing up it was possible to move from one country, Lebanon, Jordan, Syria, Palestine, Egypt, to go across them overland.' The schools, he says, 'were full of people of different races'. He goes on to express his hatred of 'The new divisiveness and the ethnocentrism' that exists and his distaste for 'national consciousness' as 'an end in itself' (*PandS*, pp. 59–61).[42] Ironically, the possibility of easy movement from one country to another and the mixed-race elite schools of Said's childhood were both products of British imperial domination, while the nationalism he is so ambivalent about is often part of the struggle against colonialism. Nonetheless, he rejects ideas of ethnic, racial or religious purity as unacceptable since, if put into practice, they would mean establishing a partitioned Palestine divided along ethnic lines, an idea that he has always opposed as 'totally inauthentic'.[43]

From a more personal perspective, Said has described himself and his family as 'members of a tiny Protestant group within a much larger Greek Orthodox Christian minority, within the larger Sunni Muslim majority'.[44] However, in 'The other Arab Muslims' (1993), he says that, 'as an Arab Christian', he sees himself as part of 'an Islamicate world, or culture', and not as 'a member of an aggrieved or marginal minority' (*PolD*, p. 389). While there is no reason at all to doubt Said's sincerity, such Christian sects as the one Said belongs to *are* marginal in the Islamic world, although this is perhaps less true in Palestine than elsewhere. On another occasion, Said claims to be 'really quite atheistic'.[45] Discussing Palestine as the site of Christianity, Judaism and Islam, he says: 'Lift off the veneer of religious cant – which speaks of the "best and noblest in the Judaic, Christian, or Muslim tradition," in perfectly interchangeable phrases – and a seething cauldron of outrageous fables is revealed, seething with several bestiaries, streams of blood, and innumerable corpses' (*ALS*, p. 152). The repetition of 'seething', the intensity of 'outrageous' and the wholly negative depiction of the three religions concerned are dramatic expressions of Said's antipathy to religious fanaticism. It is in order to avoid or minimalize such fanaticism that Said advocates a secular state for Palestine in the future. ' "There's room for all at the rendez-vous of victory" ', says Said, quoting C. L. R. James quoting Césaire, adding that this 'is a very important phrase for me'.[46] Indeed, Césaire's phrase recurs with great regularity in Said's work and symbolizes his inclusive communitarian stand.

The question of objectivity

In addition to these fractures in his political and religious allegiances, Said also takes two contradictory positions in relation to the narration of Palestinian experience and history. In relation to pro-Israeli versions of the history of Palestine, he argues that any claim to objectivity hides an ulterior motive: the defence of Zionism and Israel. Yet Said nonetheless offers his own version of the Palestinian narrative as a corrective to a distorted or false narrative, and thus as a true narrative in some sense. The underlying assumption of almost all Said's writings on Palestine and Israel is that it is possible to discern and to tell the true story, the story which reveals the truth about the Palestinians, their existence and their struggle for liberation and independence. Said refers constantly to archival work and other types of journalistic and historical research. As Griffin says, Said tends to see the operation of ideology in others' narratives and conceptions of truth, but not in his own. Griffin distorts Said's argument somewhat by oversimplifying it, but there is an element of truth in what he says. Said's response to Griffin shows the authoritative voice of the professor at the centre castigating the

unknown critic and even suggesting that he may be 'an ideological simulacrum' whose purpose is to prevent Palestinian
self-determination.[47]

Said's critique of the idea of the objectivity of Western scholarship and other writing about the Orient is one of the central ideas
of *Orientalism*, as the previous chapter has argued. Similarly, in
the Introduction to the 1979 edition of *The Question of Palestine*
Said questions any 'social science work that pretends to scientific
objectivity', since such work is inevitably compromised by its
political allegiances (p. xxxii). Elsewhere he denies the possibility
of objectivity, and argues that ' "Islam" ' is not a 'neutral object of
impartial research' (*PolD*, p. 402). Indeed, much of Said's writing
from *The Question of Palestine* onwards has focused on the ways in
which Islam and the Palestinian issue have been subject to biased
reporting.

Yet, while denying the possibility of objectivity, Said nonetheless
continues to write as if, once ideological constructions and miscon-
ceptions have been cleared away, it is possible to use the available
empirical evidence to write a true history. In *Blaming the Victims* Said
lists many of the current Zionist and pro-Zionist 'myths' about
Israel. He then counters them by arguing that: 'there was always
plenty of evidence to refute most, if not all these myths.' The types
of evidence he refers to are 'real, live Palestinians . . . census figures,
land-holding records, newspaper and radio accounts, eyewitness
reports, and of course the sheer physical traces of Arab life in Palestine before and after 1948' (p. 4). The last essay in the book, 'A
profile of the Palestinian people', purports to offer precisely this
type of unbiased political and socio-economic history of the Palestinians, as do *The Question of Palestine* and some of the essays in *The
Politics of Dispossession*. This should not be taken to indicate either
bad faith or naivety on Said's part about questions of representation. In a discussion with Eugenio Donato, he accepts Donato's
argument that ' "real history" ' and 'the problematics of representation of history' cannot be separated. Typically, however, he still
insists on imperial domination as a fact that affects events in history
and 'not simply representations which exist . . . in the discursive
history that we write as scholars'.[48] In the case of Palestine, however,
Said's involvement causes him to feel an understandable impatience with 'the problematics of representation' as an academic
issue, although elsewhere in his work, notably in *Orientalism*, it
emerges as a central issue.

Conclusion

Whatever the contradictions and inconsistencies in Said's self-representation and his representation of others, he has given Palestinians a presence and a voice in the West where they were, until relatively recently, absent or represented only through distorted stereotypes and discourses. He has fulfilled what he sees as the triple function of the Palestinian intellectual: bearing witness to injustice, acting as a kind of conscience and defending 'the identity which is under threat from many directions'.[49] He can also be seen as the embodiment of his own idea of an intellectual in an emerging nation as being both loyal to and critical of the group, and of the unco-opted oppositional intellectual 'speaking truth to power' (*RI*, pp. 29, 31, 63–75). In *Culture and Imperialism*, Said develops and extends the ideas he explored in *Orientalism*, but this time the emphasis is on the complicity of Western high culture in imperialism as well as resistance to it.

3

After Orientalism: Culture and Imperialism

Introduction

First published in 1993, *Culture and Imperialism* may be said to represent the culmination of much of Said's work in the years after the appearance of *Orientalism* in 1978. It links his writings on Palestine and the Middle East and his meditations on the role and function of the intellectual to the critique of the cultural and other forms of Western domination of the non-Western world which he had begun in *Orientalism*. *Culture and Imperialism* examines some works by canonical writers in a way that both emphasizes the privileged status of these works *and* at the same time reveals their imperial complicities. It also analyses certain models and types of cultural resistance to imperial and postcolonial power in the hope of proposing an alternative approach to the reading of literary texts and colonial history and their interconnections. Said has said that he thought of the book as 'a sequel to *Orientalism*', including the 'resistances . . . of European and American intellectuals and scholars', and based on both personal and historical experiences. However, he has also said that he tried to leave aside the issue of settler colonialism in Palestine since it was too personal.[1]

Nonetheless, there are important connections between *Culture and Imperialism*, *Orientalism* and Said's writings on Palestine and the situation in the Middle East. *Culture and Imperialism*'s inclusion of the culture of resistance and opposition to imperialism and neo-colonialism parallels Said's ongoing concern with a Palestinian narrative and Palestinian rights. Similarly, his insistence on the inextricably intertwined histories of the colonizers and the colonized and his explorations of the colonial complicities of some canonical narratives can be seen as a sequel to *Orientalism*. However, his analysis of actual and textual examples of past and present resistance to imperialism extends the scope of the earlier work, as he notes (*CI*, p. xii). Other important new departures include Said's model of cultures as inescapably hybrid, his model of contrapuntal reading as an alternative to the excesses of the '*rhetoric of blame*' of the formerly colonized as well as the conservatism or neo-imperialism of conventional, purely aesthetic literary criticism (p. 19). Finally there is his attempt to imagine new types of knowledge and new ways of thinking in order to challenge what he sees as the American neo-imperial domination of the contemporary world.

Culture and Imperialism is generally more coherent, methodologically explicit and consistent than *Orientalism*, although it is also less theoretically adventurous and demanding as well as less original. Indeed, Mary Louise Pratt has called it 'a decidedly untheorized book', while Jonathon Arac has said that it is not a narrative but 'an open set of variations on a theme'.[2] This is so, perhaps, partly because the scope of the work, although considerable, is less vast than that of *Orientalism*. Other factors which contribute to the coherence of the book are the clear delineation of the time-scale and the geographical area of reference, the consistent focus on the novel as the centre of analysis and the strong chronological line, at least until the final chapter. Moreover, the broad perspective offered in the Introduction and the first chapter frames the later discussions of individual texts, and the passages of recapitulation and synthesis also help structure the argument of the book. The one exception is to be found in the fourth and final chapter, which is the least clear and consistent (see pp. 88–9 below). There are also other significant differences between *Orientalism* and *Culture and Imperialism*. In the latter Said attempts to include, or at least mention, some elements that he had previously excluded. He mentions the factors of gender and class as elements influencing the relationship between culture and imperialism. He also moderates some of *Orientalism*'s more contentious statements about the impossibility of truthful representations, the relation between the individual work or author and imperialism, the inevitable racism of any nineteenth-century inhabitant of Europe and so on (*O*, pp. 204, 272–3). Inevitably perhaps, *Culture and Imperialism* has proved a much less ground-breaking and influential book than *Orientalism*. The latter has played a key role in the development of the field of postcolonial studies, but *Culture and Imperialism* asks to be seen as part of that field, and as a response to some of the other work which *Orientalism* may be said to have largely inspired. The references in *Culture and Imperialism* to works by Mary Louise Pratt, Peter Hulme, Homi Bhabha, Barbara Harlow and others may be seen as an indication of the interdependence of Said's work and that of other writers.

This chapter will first focus on the main themes of the book and its methodological framework, and notably Said's apparently paradoxical use of T. S. Eliot with Frantz Fanon, and Raymond Williams with Michel Foucault. Then it will analyse the three components of Said's search for a third way of approaching the relationship between culture and imperialism. These are the radical intentions and elements in Said's work, his contrasting conservative preferences and priorities, and the alternative mode of reading and interpretation which he offers. Finally, *Culture and Imperialism* will be examined as one embodiment of Said's views on the oppositional intellectual.

Overview

In the Introduction to *Culture and Imperialism* Said sets out the book's aims and summarizes many of its key ideas. He briefly states the links between culture and imperialism, and the dual meanings of culture as an autonomous realm of activity and also as, in Matthew Arnold's phrase, 'the best that has been known and thought'. He notes the centrality of narrative to the argument (*CI*, p. xiii), and emphasizes that the works analysed are, first, worthy of study in their own right, but also that they can only be completely understood in relation to imperialism (p. xv). Said's formulation of the relationship between writers and their historical and social milieux draws on such sources as Foucault without explicitly engaging with them, thus avoiding some of the theoretical problems of *Orientalism* (see pp. 89–90 and 96–7 below). Said focuses on the similarities between culture and imperialism in relation to Britain, France and the USA, although he also distinguishes between them (pp. xxv, 9, 350, 352), adding that he himself has personal experience of all three (p. xxvi).

Having set out the aims of the book, Said constructs the framework of ideas in which he situates the analyses of his chosen works. He uses T. S. Eliot's key essay, 'Tradition and the individual talent', as a way of linking past and present, and makes his central argument that nineteenth-century high culture supported the imperialist project (p. 12). The idea of the contrapuntal reading of history informs 'Discrepant experiences', where Said for the first time embarks on such a reading of two texts dealing with the Napoleonic conquest of Egypt: Jean-Baptiste-Joseph Fourier's General Introduction to the *Description de l'Egypte* and 'Abd al-Rahman al-Jabarti's *'Aja'ib al-Athar*.[3] Before doing so, however, he makes an important methodological point about his use of the word 'experiences' in the title of the section. He notes that it is not intended to sidestep the problem of ideology, but rather to enhance it, since experience is never unmediated and there is no 'Archimedean perspective' outside history or culture for the critic (p. 37).[4] He suggests a politicized version of comparative literature as a new approach to his topic, and sees it as in some way continuing the oppositional strand of the high humanistic tradition of nineteenth- and early twentieth-century comparative literature. Said has enormous respect for this tradition, although he has some reservations about its inevitable involvement in imperialism (pp. 50–6). He sees himself as part of a community of 'intellectuals and humanists and secular critics' (p. 65) whose duty is to speak out clearly about the imperial past, the neo-imperial present and the interconnections between literature and politics in opposition to those who ignore or obscure these issues.

In 'Consolidated vision', Said returns to the nineteenth century. He begins by tracing the evolution of imperial philosophy from the beginning of the nineteenth century to the early years of the twentieth, commenting on the evolution of the relationship between the English novel and the imperial project in the course of the century. He traces this process by mixing general and specific analyses and by paying attention to both imperialism and resistance to it. He relates the individual works that he discusses to the key idea of the general 'structure of attitude and reference' of imperialism (p. 73), and argues that the nineteenth-century novel in Britain and France would never have developed as it did without the phenomenon of European imperialism (p. 82). This is a huge generalization that can hardly be substantiated by the book, as Bart Moore-Gilbert, Peter Childs and Patrick Williams, and John M. MacKenzie all note.[5] The other sections of the lengthy second chapter are of two kinds. First, there are case studies of works of art which demonstrate Said's general argument about the interdependence of imperialism and cultural forms such as fiction and opera, for example the analyses of *Mansfield Park*, *Aida*, *Kim*, and Camus's short story 'La femme adultère'. Secondly, there are passages of synthesis that deal with the development of the cultural discourses of imperialism in the nineteenth and twentieth centuries. Both the specific analyses and the passages of synthesis elucidate the 'structures of attitude and reference' which Said sees as underlying the relation between culture and imperialism. The concept, which draws its inspiration from Raymond Williams's idea of 'structures of feeling', is a key one for Said and will be discussed in more detail below (see pp. 94–5).

With the move to 'Camus and the French imperial experience' the generally chronological arrangement of the material breaks down. In his discussion of Camus's work Said moves forward into the middle of the twentieth century, only to move back again, in the final section of chapter 2, to the early twentieth century with his 'Note on modernism'. Like the sections on *Aida* and *Kim*, the analysis of Camus succeeds in linking culture and imperialism by demonstrating the connections between textual analysis, the political and economic realities of the life of the author and the history of the colonized country (pp. 211–24). Said concludes by commenting on the 'waste and sadness' and the 'negative vitality' of Camus's narratives. He argues that, since Camus's work is characterized by the contradiction between his loyalty to France and his understanding and sympathy with Algerians as people, but not as a people demanding independence, his 'limitations seem unacceptably paralysing' (p. 224). It is noteworthy that Said criticizes Verdi, Camus and Kipling for their complicity in the imperial process; however, he does not seem to find the compensatory pleasures in Verdi's and Camus's works that he does in the English author's.[6]

The final section of chapter 2, 'A note on modernism', is the most compressed, and, initially at least, the connections which Said establishes between modernism and European imperialism seem rather obscure. Said compares modernism to the 'ironic disillusion' in the mainstream nineteenth-century novel and contrasts it with the 'infection of excitement' of the colonial experience via late nineteenth-century travel narratives and adventure novels. Specifically, he contrasts the latter with the modernist anxiety of the narratives of Conrad, Forster, Malraux, T. E. Lawrence, Eliot, Yeats and Joyce, and sees the anxiety as having an imperial source (pp. 226–9). Having identified, somewhat schematically, the imperial sources of modernist anxiety, Said identifies three strategies in modernist texts for dealing with it: the use of circular structure, the novelty of the juxtaposition of divergent fragments, forms, and modes, and the irony of form as the only source of unity in reality. The whole treatment of modernism and imperialism is so brief that any judgement must be suspended, since the lack of any detailed theoretical or practical exploration of the ideas means that they seem to be exciting speculation rather than convincing demonstration. It is noticeable that Said's analysis thus far pays no attention to the factors of either gender or, except for his analysis of *Mansfield Park*, class. Yet gender is a central factor in all these works. The protagonist of Austen's novel is a young woman, Verdi's opera is named after a female slave, the protagonist of the short story by Camus is the wife of a *colon*, and *A Passage to India* has a rape at the centre of its action. While Said meticulously includes references to class and gender in his passages of synthesis and general discussion, such factors are not integrated into the detailed analyses of individual works in any meaningful way.[7]

Said next moves to 'Resistance and opposition' to imperialism. The chapter opens with a discussion of resistance and liberation movements between World Wars I and II and afterwards and demonstrates some of its general points through analyses of E. M. Forster's *A Passage to India* and works by Gide and Malraux. Here, as elsewhere, the emphasis is on British culture and imperialism, and the French experience is relegated to second place. Yeats's work is discussed at some length, and the rest of the chapter deals with the emergence of narratives of opposition and their themes, which are related to alternative visions of history and an integrative view of human community and liberation rather than a narrowly nationalistic one. The concept of nationalism poses problems for Said. Like Fanon, he considers nationalism as an essential transitional stage in the evolution from the primary political type of resistance to imperialism to the secondary ideological type that leads to the establishment of new states (p. 258). However, Said is opposed to nationalism when it is 'exclusivist'; he calls for it to be self-critical and praises those like C. L. R. James, Neruda, Tagore, Fanon and Cabral, whose nationalism is of a less exclusive and simplistic kind (pp. 263–4).

'Yeats and decolonization' takes Yeats as an exemplar of both the national and the nationalist poet opposing imperialism. Placing Yeats in the context of Irish nationalism causes Said to return to the problems caused by the collaboration of what Fanon calls the nationalist bourgeoisie with the colonial powers and by the 'patriarchal cast' of most versions of nationalism (pp. 268–70). Anti-imperialist cultural resistance is seen to entail a geographical priority to 'reclaim, rename, and reinhabit the land' (p. 273). Yeats is mentioned along with Neruda, Césaire, Faiz and Darwish as embodying a particularly interesting case of the writer who sought to recreate not only the land but the heroes, mythology and the language of Ireland in his poetry. As Moore-Gilbert has remarked, Yeats is a problematic choice as an anti-imperialist poet, given the ambiguity of his location and his loyalties.[8]

In 'The voyage in and the emergence of opposition', for the first time, Said focuses on the work of four writers from the peripheries: C. L. R. James and George Antonius from one generation of scholars, Ranajit Guha and S. H. Alatas from another (pp. 295–313). These four writers and more specifically their works, *The Black Jacobins*, *The Arab Awakening*, *A Rule of Property for Bengal* and *The Myth of the Lazy Native*, are taken as examples of what Said calls 'the voyage in'. This involves the 'extension into the metropolis of large-scale mass movements' in the form of 'anti-imperialist and scholarly work done by writers from the peripheries who have immigrated to or are visiting the metropolis' (p. 294). Said's comparison of James and Antonius with Guha and Alatas reveals his view of the progression of anti-imperialist writing from the middle to the late twentieth century. While he argues that all four are examples of the literature of resistance to imperialism, he seems to prefer the strong narrative lines of James and Antonius to the irony and hermeneutical suspicion which characterize Guha and Alatas's more specialist works (pp. 311–12). Pratt also notes Said's nostalgic preference for the two earlier writers, and attributes it partly to the fact that they synthesize Western and 'native' cultural traditions.[9]

In the final section of this third chapter, the focus remains on the peripheries and specifically on Frantz Fanon's *The Wretched of the Earth* as a central text in resistance literature. Narrative is again a central issue. Said argues that the fact that conventional narrative is central to imperialism means that it cannot be taken over unproblematically by nationalism and must instead be replaced by 'lateral, non-narrative connections among people whom imperialism separated into autonomous tribes, narratives, cultures' (p. 330). This should not be taken to mean that Said sees all narrative as tainted by its connections with imperial domination. As his discussions of Fanon in *Culture and Imperialism* and his writings on Palestine show, he also believes in the possibility of a counter-narrative, that is, narrative used as a tool of liberation and self-assertion by previously oppressed and colonized peoples.[10]

Culture and Imperialism's final chapter differs from those preceding it in several ways. First, it pays less attention to literary works and more to political events such as the Gulf War; second, the chronological pattern more or less completely disappears; third, the argument is less clear and coherent, the tone less urbane and composed. In a 1993 interview with Joseph A. Buttigieg and Paul A. Bové, Said explains the change in tone by saying that during the writing of the chapter he discovered he had a chronic blood disease and was worried about not finishing the book, adding that he was also very disillusioned about the political situation, especially the Madrid peace talks.[11] Said passionately denounces American policy in the Middle East and elsewhere, the failure of American intellectuals to oppose their government's neo-imperialist policies, and finally the failure of Western humanist academics to engage with the real world instead of the purely theoretical hinterland which they have come to inhabit. This is in section I; the second and third sections offer analyses of the political and cultural system of American neo-imperialism and suggestions as to how it might be opposed and, eventually, overcome. There are many themes and ideas in the final chapter of *Culture and Imperialism* that link it both to Said's writings on politics and to his more general discussion of the role of the intellectual. In addition to this, the potential contradictions in his approach to literary works emerge more strikingly than before. The primacy of great works and of the Western canon seems to be reasserted, while much literature from the peripheries is seen to have too close or direct a connection with political matters to be worthy of sustained attention purely *as* literature.

Said sees American imperialism and neo-imperialism as both similar to and different from their British and French imperialist counterparts. They resemble them in justifying the exercise of power by spurious appeals to moral legitimacy, but are different from them because of the media and information technology explosion. Said analyses America's role in the Gulf War and in the Middle East more generally. To readers who know his writings on the Middle East, the topics are familiar. Said attacks the irresponsibility and distortions of the American media and its effects on public opinion inside and outside the USA, America's irresponsible and opportunist role in Middle East politics and the failure of American intellectuals to challenge any of this (pp. 352–67). 'Challenging orthodoxy and authority' describes American imperialism as oppressive, undemocratic and culturally impoverished in the extreme. To this, Said opposes his oppositional version of Western humanism and of the role of the secular critic. He argues that intellectuals have a role to play in formulating new kinds of research in the humanities, and he cites the *Subaltern Studies* group and works by Samuel, Bernal and others as examples (pp. 377–8).

Like the second section, the third, 'Movements and migrations', might be said to contain three different types of ideas. There is, first, an attempt to describe the contemporary global situation, which Said sees as characterized by unstable patterns of domination and interdependence, where both theory and real life embody migrancy and exile. Readers of Said's writings on the role of the intellectual find themselves in familiar territory. Said regrets the disappearance of the 'general secular intellectual' exemplified by such figures as Jean-Paul Sartre, Raymond Williams, Roland Barthes and Michel Foucault (p. 398), and he calls for a new awareness to change things (p. 401). Finally, in a move as initially startling as it later seems perfectly in character, Said returns to a medieval text as a means of conceptualizing his vision of such a non-coercive community. He quotes a passage by Hugo of St Victor, a twelfth-century monk from Saxony, which argues that 'The tender soul has fixed his love on one spot in the world; the strong person has extended his love to all places; the perfect man has extinguished his' (p. 407). Said interprets this to mean that we should work through individual and specific attachments to an all-embracing and undifferentiated universalism. That is, he appeals for a transcendence of national boundaries and separate traditions.

The methodological framework

Culture and Imperialism is more accessible than *Orientalism* partly because it is less overtly theoretical. Whereas *Orientalism* tried to link the three ultimately irreconcilable positions of Foucault, Gramsci and Western humanism and to resolve such questions as whether there can or cannot be such a thing as true representation, *Culture and Imperialism* sidesteps such theoretical problems. Foucault and Gramsci are vital to the implied framework of ideas of the book, but there is much less explicit engagement with their theories, and the literary and humanist dimension of Said's approach is very obvious in his use of T. S. Eliot and, to some extent, Raymond Williams. Said uses Eliot's essay, 'Tradition and the

individual talent' as a framework for his discussion of the interre-
lationship of the past and the present, while Williams's concept of
'structures of feeling' provides the inspiration for Said's 'structures
of attitude and reference'. Foucault's notion of the 'microphysics of
power' is contrasted unfavourably with Fanon's theorization of the
power relation between colonizing powers and colonized countries
(pp. 335–6). Gramsci's early essay 'Some aspects of the Southern
question' is the source of one of Said's key motifs: the analysis of
culture and imperialism in geographical, spatial terms as well as
historical, temporal ones (pp. 56–9).

The lack of explicit theoretical discussion in the book does not
mean that the methodological framework of *Culture and Imperialism*
is entirely unproblematic. While T. S. Eliot provides a key reference
point, then so also does Frantz Fanon, especially *The Wretched of the
Earth*. T. S. Eliot and Frantz Fanon are an unlikely pair, and they are
deployed alongside Raymond Williams and Michel Foucault. Said
combines elements of all these writers' ideas in order to construct
his own distinctive approach. He leavens the idealism of Eliot with
the political radicalism of Fanon, and finds some of Williams's and
Foucault's ideas indispensable as starting points for his own model,
even if they fail to take imperialism into account in their analyses
of English or European culture and history.

T. S. Eliot and the relationship between
the past and the present

For Said, the key text by Eliot is 'Tradition and the individual
talent',[12] and notably the concept of the 'historical sense' and its
importance for the individual writer. For Eliot, tradition is an
entirely positive value. The writer needs to possess an awareness of
the interrelation and of the mutual influence of the past and the
present. Eliot develops these ideas purely with reference to literary
works, notably in his famous image of literary tradition as an 'ideal
order' of monuments. Said praises Eliot's conception of tradition as
a matrix linking the works of individual writers. He does note that
'Eliot's synthesis of past, present, and future . . . is idealistic' and
that it leaves out the 'combativeness' inevitably involved in the
establishment of a tradition or a literary canon. Said focuses especially on Eliot's idea of the 'historical sense', which he restates as
the idea that 'how we formulate or represent the past shapes our
understanding and views of the present', but gives an example that

is far removed from Eliot's literary and idealist model. Said argues that the Gulf War of 1990–91 is best understood if it is seen as a conflict not only between two states but also between two histories, each with its own ideological imperatives. For Iraq the Gulf War represented an attempt to right Arab wrongs, notably the 'unrealized, unfulfilled promise of Arab independence', betrayed by the West and others; for the USA the war was a defence of freedom and democracy (pp. 2–3). Said's example here and his suggestion that Eliot's ideas are especially useful in relation to the phenomenon of imperialism are ironic, since it is precisely the political and ideological dimensions of history which are excluded from Eliot's abstract and idealist model. As Bogumil Jewsiewicki and V. Y. Mudimbe note, 'Nothing better expresses the necessary ambiguity in Said's procedure than the insistent aspect of his recourse to Eliot's.'[13] Other examples of Said's politicization of Eliot relate to the post-World War II period, in which Said sees the consequences of nineteenth-century imperialism. Even though the imperialist period is over, its effects remain, both for the former rulers and for those they ruled (p. 11). Similarly, in relation to contemporary American neo-imperialism, Said asks whether it is not repeating the past experiences of the European imperial powers (pp. 64–5).

Fanon: from imperialism to liberation

Eliot thus contributes an idealist, literary version of the interdependence of past and present to Said's conceptual framework in *Culture and Imperialism*. To further theorize the political dimension of this interdependence, Said turns to Frantz Fanon. Fanon is first invoked as representing the justified 'anger and resentment' of formerly colonized peoples (p. 12). Indeed, Fanon is present in *Culture and Imperialism* primarily as the author of *The Wretched of the Earth*, and as the representative of the philosophy of resistance and liberation. Fanon's famous declaration that 'For the native . . . objectivity is always directed against him', is quoted twice as Said explains the distorting power of the imperialists' and natives' visions of each other (pp. 196, 312). Said also uses Fanon in one of the examples he gives of contrapuntal reading, where he argues that Austen should be read alongside Fanon and Cabral (p. 71). Even more importantly, however, Fanon functions as the critic of European imperialism and colonialism, and of the creation of modernity in the West at the expense of colonized peoples. Said says, quoting Fanon with obvious approval, 'Europe is literally the creation of the Third World' (p. 237). Said also takes over Fanon's critique of the 'nationalist bourgeoisie' and its specialized elites, who replaced colonial rule with a type of neo-colonialism based on class differences, which was equally exploitative (pp. 20, 269). In Said's analysis of Yeats, Fanon plays a dual role. He represents the discourse of liberation as opposed to Yeats's discourse of nationalism (p. 283). In addition, in relation to Yeats, Said invokes Fanon's analysis of how colonialism 'distorts, disfigures and destroys' the past of the colonized people and separates the colonized individual 'from his or her own instinctual life', thus disrupting the formation of national identity from one generation to another (p. 286).

Fanon is most important for Said, however, because of his argument that liberation must succeed resistance, and that national consciousness must be replaced by social consciousness in the newly independent country (p. 323). As Henry Louis Gates, Jr has said, Fanon functions as Said's 'own counternarrative, in the terrain of postcolonial criticism'.[14] For Said, Fanon's argument represents 'the immense cultural shift from the terrain of nationalist independence to the theoretical domain of liberation'. For both Said and Fanon, politics and culture are inevitably interrelated. Introducing Fanon's description of how the European settler sees his own arrival in the colony as the beginning of that country's history, Said notes 'Fanon penetratingly links the settler's conquest of history with imperialism's regime of truth, over which the great myths of Western culture preside' (p. 324). The statement provides a striking demonstration of Said's method in *Culture and Imperialism*. Said adopts Fanon's analysis of the interdependence of politics and culture, and articulates it in Foucauldian terms. The reference to 'imperialism's regime of truth' unobtrusively provides the connection between culture and politics, since the 'regime of truth' in Foucault's model of discourse consists of the unspoken assumptions that determine the kinds of statements that can be made in both the political and the cultural contexts.

In his extended analysis of Fanon's *The Wretched of the Earth*, Said returns to one of his central concerns: narrative. He argues that to write a conventional narrative of a nationalist movement is to follow the same road of identitarian politics that characterizes both imperialism and nationalism. For Said, Fanon's work should be read as 'a surreptitious counter-narrative' to the power of the colonial regime (p. 283), not least because of its ability to include 'conflicting narrative and historical patterns' derived from the splits and conflicts in nationalist movements (p. 328). It can be argued that Said sees himself as writing the counter-narrative whose 'complexity and anti-identitarian force' he feels Fanon himself could not make explicit at the end of *The Wretched of the Earth* (p. 331).

Generally, Said quotes Fanon with approval, although he occasionally strikes a critical note. One example of this is the way Said sees Fanon's use of certain aspects of European thought for the elaboration of his ideas. When he discusses Fanon's reinterpretation of Hegel in the colonial situation, he describes it as 'the partial tragedy of resistance' since it must work with the colonizers' theories (p. 253). Elsewhere, he is less pessimistic, and sees both Fanon's and Césaire's use of the French language and European theories positively, as acts of defiance of the colonizer and as an assertion of independence (pp. 323–5). Said's reading of *The Wretched of the Earth* is one of the few examples in *Culture and Imperialism* of a sustained engagement of a work by a non-Western writer.

On one occasion, Said's reading of Fanon seems more contentious. He quotes Fanon as saying that the task of formerly colonized peoples in the postcolonial period is that 'of re-introducing mankind into the world, the whole of mankind'. He argues that this task 'will be carried out with the indispensable help of the European peoples, who themselves must realize that in the past they have often joined the ranks of our common masters where colonial questions are concerned'. Said sees this as an appeal to 'a trans-personal and transnational force' (p. 325), and he says a few pages later that 'Fanon wants somehow to bind the European as well as the native together in a new non-adversarial community of awareness and anti-imperialism' (p. 331). This formulation is problematic since it completely obliterates the distinction which Fanon clearly makes between 'European *peoples*' and 'our common *masters*', that is, the ruling class both in Europe and in the colonies (my emphasis). Fanon clearly distinguishes between the two; Said does not. He also ignores the several occasions at the end of *The Wretched of the Earth* on which Fanon rejects Europe as a model to be followed for the creation of the new world he envisages.[15]

Raymond Williams and Michel Foucault

If both T. S. Eliot and Frantz Fanon are key figures, then the work of Raymond Williams and Michel Foucault is both praised and ultimately found wanting. Early in the book Said pays tribute to

Williams and Foucault as two theorists who have offered models of 'the development of dominant discourses and disciplinary traditions' which he wishes to trace in relation to culture and imperialism, although he reproaches them for their neglect of imperialism (p. 47). Both are essential to Said's method and approach. Williams's notion of 'structures of feeling' is central to Said's analysis, and Foucault provides such vital ideas as discourse, discipline and surveillance. As Radhakrishnan has noted, it is the precise nature of Said's engagement with Foucault and others that is interesting.[16] The same is true of his attitude towards Williams.

Said derives his central concept of 'structures of attitude and reference' from Williams's idea of 'structures of feeling'. Both Said's and Williams's concepts are complex, to some extent problematic and yet also immensely suggestive. Williams uses the phrase '*structures of feeling*' to describe changing patterns of experience in a given social group, or class, or generation, or period within British, usually English, culture (emphasis in the original).[17] Admitting that the combination of 'structure' and 'feeling' is paradoxical, he uses it nonetheless to suggest that such changes are matters of both individual variation and social pattern. They are related to changing individual feelings and so they cannot be equated with 'more formal concepts' such as ' "world-view" or "ideology" '. Yet they are also social in that they are 'a set, with specific internal relations, at once interlocking and in tension' and 'a social experience which is still *in process*' (emphasis in the original). Literary works play a key role in Williams's articulation of the concept. He explains that it was originally drawn from his study of literary texts, and that a new structure of feeling is often first seen in the 'forms and conventions' or 'semantic figures' in art and literature.[18] Furthermore, Williams's examples are often literary: the work of Hobbes and of Jacobean dramatists such as Webster and Tourneur, the novels of the 1840s or the young writers of the 1930s are used to document the structure of feeling of their respective periods.[19]

Said broadens Williams's term by giving it geographical and political dimensions. Although he regards Williams as a 'great critic' from whom he has learned a great deal, he cannot understand how Williams can discuss Dickens's *Dombey and Son* and the 1840s without reference to Britain's imperial possessions and relations (p. 14).[20] He explains that his own phrase, 'structures of attitudes and reference', refers to both the geographical realities of British, French and American imperialism and also 'Raymond Williams's seminal phrase, "structures of feeling" '. Said defines his own 'structures of attitude and reference' as 'the way in which structures of location and geographical reference appear in the cultural languages of literature, history, or ethnography, sometimes allusively and sometimes carefully plotted, across several individual works that are not otherwise connected to one another or to an official ideology of "empire"'. The statement is explicated in relation to nineteenth-century English novels. In many of these, Said argues, 'socially desirable, empowered space' is located in 'metropolitan England or Europe', and it is connected to 'distant or peripheral worlds . . . conceived of as desirable but subordinate'. With these geographical references come certain attitudes 'about rule, control, profit, and enhancement and suitability', which develop from the seventeenth century to the end of the nineteenth. Like Williams, Said depends on literary works for the elaboration of his idea. Like Williams, he suggests that one particular set of structures of attitude and reference dominated in the nineteenth century, that is, the imperial set. Like Williams, Said sees individual variation within this general pattern and rejects any idea that there was a 'pre-existing (semi-conspiratorial) design' manipulated by the writers (p. 61).

Said's approach to Williams in relation to 'structures of feeling' is typical of his approach to him throughout *Culture and Imperialism*. He frequently refers to his comments on a particular text, only to modify what he says so that the approach is completely transformed. For example, in discussing Williams's analysis of *Mansfield Park* he disagrees fundamentally with Williams's assertion that the novel is concerned with only one class. On the contrary, he shows how the Bertrams' life-style is dependent not only on the labour of Fanny Price and her family but also on the slave labour of the Antigua estate (pp. 100–6). Although Said refers to Williams, not surprisingly, much more often in those parts of the book which deal with the imperial complicities of Western literary works than in those parts which analyse the resistance to imperialism, there is one exception. In his discussion of what he calls 'the voyage in', Said refers to Williams's *Culture*, and specifically to the chapter on 'Formations'. Said is particularly interested in Williams's comments on the role played by immigrants in the creation of 'new [avant-garde] international or para-national formations . . . in the metropolitan centre'. Said argues that Williams's argument needs to be put 'into the historical setting of imperialism and anti-imperialism' so that it can clarify the situation which he wishes to analyse (p. 294). This is in fact what Said has been doing throughout the book.

Like Williams's, Foucault's ideas are vital to *Culture and Imperialism*. The ideas of discourse, of areas of disciplinary knowledge and of the different types of surveillance are so much a part of Said's way of thinking that they seem to be taken for granted rather than explicitly discussed. Thus in commenting on the 'scope and *authority*', and the 'great creative power' of the cultural effects of imperial attitudes, Said notes that 'Foucault's ideas about *discourses* are apt here' without further comment (p. 132, emphasis in the original). Foucault's analysis of the movement from ' "sovereign" to administrative surveillance' in *Discipline and Punish* is related to British imperial policy in India in the nineteenth century, and more particularly to the work of Sir Henry Maine on the law (pp. 198–9). Similarly, Foucault's concept of 'subjugated knowledges' is evoked with reference to contemporary literature and scholarship from the postcolonial world (p. 293). His work on disciplinary systems is used to explicate the challenge to 'the principle of confinement' represented by contemporary mass protest movements such as the Palestinian *intifadah* (p. 396). In a passage towards the end of the book, Said compares Fanon and Foucault. He dismisses the latter as a sufficient guide to the analysis of the links between culture and imperialism since his work came to concentrate more and more on the 'microphysics of power', avoided considering whole societies, and finally left both resistance and politics behind (pp. 335–6).

Elsewhere, the influence of Foucault's thought can be felt behind much of the book, but Said avoids the complex issues of the status of the individual work of art, representation and the significance of the individual author that proved so problematic in *Orientalism*. Thus, when he stresses his focus on individual works in the Introduction, Said is saying that he does not believe that 'authors are mechanically determined by ideology, class, or economic history' but that he does believe them to be 'very much in the history of their societies' (p. xxiv). The formulation neatly sidesteps the contradictory formulations into which Said was forced in *Orientalism* when he tried to reconcile T. S. Eliot and Foucault's views of the relationship between the individual writer, the work and the discursive field (*O*, p. 273, and see chapter 1). In *Culture and Imperialism*, in the course of the discussion of the post-imperial world in the first chapter, Said asserts the political implications of cultural representations and deplores the separation of the spheres of politics and culture (pp. 66–7). The thorny issue of the truth-value of representations is not touched upon, but the question of the status of the individual work of art provokes a more extended discussion. Said defines a novel 'first as a novelist's effort and second as an object read by an audience'. He continues by relating individual novels to other novels and to the community of readers and other writers, but he insists that novels are neither purely sociological symptoms nor works of genius alone (p. 87). He argues for a middle-of-the-road position that tries to encapsulate both the political and social dimensions of novels and the fact that they are primarily aesthetic works. He avoids the theoretical question as to how precisely the political and the aesthetic are intertwined, although his detailed analyses of individual works offer impressive practical demonstrations of the connections between the two.

The search for an alternative

Culture and Imperialism may be said to show, perhaps more clearly than any of Said's other books, his search for an alternative to both radical and conservative orthodoxies. This search is apparent in his dual approach to great works of art as both worthy of attention in their own right *and* as symptoms of imperialism. It also determines his espousal of the notion of cultural hybridity and of the technique of contrapuntal reading, his revision of the concepts of nationalism and humanism and his attempt to demystify the system of American neo-imperialism. Yet this search for an alternative approach is characterized by two contradictory tendencies: the radical impulse to link literature, politics and culture on the one hand, and the fundamental conservatism of Said's literary tastes and loyalties on the other.[21] The first is clearly discernible in his analysis of culture and imperialism and of resistance to imperial and neo-imperial domination. Conversely, his literary conservatism appears in the primarily Eurocentric and canonical texts chosen for analysis, his occasional apparent odd complicity with textual imperial attitudes, the general lack of sustained attention to non-Western writers and works and his somewhat problematic concept of oppositional humanism.

Radical intentions

The most radical move in *Culture and Imperialism* lies in Said's insistence on linking high culture and British, French and American imperialism. Said argues that there are connections between culture, imperialism and national identity which have been neglected by scholars. Equally radical in intention are Said's desire to give a hearing to the voices of resistance and opposition, his opposition to any ideas of purity or priority of race or voice and his critique of American neo-imperialism, along with his attempt to formulate effective ways of opposing such domination.

These radical intentions are first articulated in *Culture and Imperialism* in the form of Said's challenge to 'the universalizing discourses of modern Europe and the United States' because they 'assume the silence, willing or otherwise, of the non-European world' (p. 58). Furthermore, a few pages later Said acknowledges that these dominant discourses also silence the 'minority and "suppressed" voices within the metropolis itself: feminists, African-American writers, intellectuals, artists, among others' (p. 63). He criticizes the New Historicists for being ahistorical and failing to address imperialism as a factor in the areas and periods they study (pp. 66, 70), and also the critical neglect 'of the enormously exciting, varied post-colonial literature' (p. 71) produced by resistance to imperialism.

Such is the project, and much of the book does suggest new perspectives on literary texts from Austen to Camus. The book also documents the fact that much nineteenth-century English high culture – the cultural and aesthetic theories of Carlyle, Ruskin, Mill, for example – failed to resist imperialist philosophies and, indeed, sometimes helped to create them. Said demonstrates that this was at least partly because imperialism, culture and national identity were all bound up together, and that the very definition of Englishness came to involve a sense of superiority to other, especially non-European, nations, of power over them and of the legitimacy of that power. As well as criticizing the complicity of the theorists of high culture, and, indeed, the British population as a whole in the philosophy of imperialism, Said also deplores the way these facts are neglected in modern criticism of literature (pp. 10, 121–9).

Said also raises the issues of resistance and opposition to imperialism, both on the peripheries and in the metropolis, and urges that such resistant and oppositional writing be given the attention which it deserves. On several occasions Said offers a counterpoint to his analysis of a Western work by providing some discussion of a resisting or oppositional work. One example is the contrast between Fourier's General Introduction to the Napoleonic *Description de l'Egypte* and al-Jabarti's *'Aja'ib al-Athar*. Another is the comparison between Conrad's *Heart of Darkness*, Ngugi's *The River Between* and Salih's *Season of Migration to the North* (pp. 254–6). Moreover, the chapter which deals with resistance and opposition includes analysis of specific works by C. L. R. James, George Antonius, Ranajit Guha and S. H. Alatas, of Fanon's *The Wretched of the Earth*, and scattered references to the work of Aimé Césaire and Partha Chatterjee. There is a discussion of Yeats as an anti-colonial poet and a comparison between aspects of his work and that of Neruda and Darwish. In the final chapter of the book Said expresses his desire to help to create 'new and innovative paradigms for humanistic research' (p. 377) in the hope of combating the distortions and manipulations of the Western news and other media. He pays tribute on numerous occasions to scholars from the West and elsewhere who have participated or who are participating in this effort to challenge what he calls the 'gigantic reductions' (p. 375) of the West's misrepresentations of its adversaries. He mentions Adonis, the *Subaltern Studies* group and 'many Caribbean intellectuals and artists whose heritage is traced to C. L. R. James (Wilson Harris, George Lamming, Eric Williams, Derek Walcott, Edward Braithwaite, [and] the early V. S. Naipaul)' (p. 379). Finally, he refers to Eqbal Ahmad, Faiz Ahmed Faiz, Ngugi wa Thiongo and Abdelrahman el Munif as 'major thinkers and artists', as well as intellectuals defending political and literary freedoms (p. 19).

Conservative preferences and priorities

Yet, despite the radical moves which Said makes in linking politics and literature, or culture and imperialism, it is the conservatism of his literary tastes and values that gives the book much of its distinctive character. After having emphasized the articulation of previously silenced voices, and the extension and rethinking of the canon, *Culture and Imperialism* focuses primarily on the canonical texts of Western literature by European, primarily anglophone, male writers, very occasionally showing an apparent complicity with some of their imperial attitudes and values. As Pratt says, Said 'starts (typically, infuriatingly) in the canon', and 'the point of reference . . . is still the metropolis'.[22] Moreover, the resisting and oppositional voices from the peripheries or the metropolis are more often evoked rhetorically than heard speaking for themselves, and the focus on the First World is maintained at the expense of the Third.

The focus of the book is on Western, often English, canonical texts. After evoking Dickens's *Great Expectations* and Conrad's *Nostromo* in his Introduction, Said opens his discussion of 'Empire, geography, and culture' by quoting T. S. Eliot's 'Tradition and the individual talent'. He ends his book, over four hundred pages later, with Hugo of St Victor, the twelfth-century monk from Saxony, Erich Auerbach (Said's preferred exile-figure) and, once again, T. S. Eliot. In between, the texts on which Said focuses in the second chapter are Conrad's *Heart of Darkness*, Jane Austen's *Mansfield Park*, J. S. Mill's *Principles of Political Economy*, Carlyle's *The Nigger Question*, Ruskin's 1870 Slade lectures, Verdi's *Aida*, Kipling's *Kim*, Camus's fiction and various canonical modernist works. Chapter 3 continues with Forster's *Passage to India*, Malraux's *La voie royale* and the poems of Yeats. Said pays no sustained attention to the voices from the periphery until the fourth section of this third chapter, where he discusses C. L. R. James's *Black Jacobins*, George Antonius's *The Arab Awakening*, Ranajit Guha's *A Rule of Property for Bengal* and S. H. Alatas's *The Myth of the Lazy Native*. Even here the anti-colonial poet whose work is examined at length is W. B. Yeats, a somewhat problematic choice. It is true that many other post-colonial and anti-colonial writers are mentioned and praised in passing. Achebe, Ngugi, Salih, Fanon, Rushdie, Tagore, Cabral, Césaire, Du Bois, Abdel Malek, al-Afghani, al-Jabarti, Kincaid and Morrison all appear briefly in Said's text, and Fanon is a key reference throughout. But these writers never occupy centre stage. Said's technique is generally to assert the importance of 'post-colonial writers', and then give a list of them: 'Rushdie, Derek Walcott, Aimé Césaire, Chinua Achebe, Pablo Neruda, and Brian Friel' (pp. 34, 35). Alternatively, he mentions some important 'revisionary works' which are then very cursorily discussed (pp. 48–9). Or again he will speak admiringly of the attention now paid in universities to 'African literature', or speak of 'the remarkable outpouring of first-rate literature and scholarship emanating from the post-colonial world'. These types of statement are generally followed by a list of names: 'Gabriel Garcia Marquez, Salman Rushdie, Carlos Fuentes, Chinua Achebe, Wole Soyinka, Faiz Ahmed Faiz' and so on (pp. 288, 293).

Typical examples of the book's bias towards the traditional Western canon can be found in Said's references to Achebe's novels and criticism and in his comparison of *Heart of Darkness* to Tayib Salih's *Season of Migration to the North* and to Ngugi wa Thiongo's *The River Between*. Said invokes Achebe's critique of *Heart of Dark-*

ness on two separate occasions (pp. 91, 200). But he never directly challenges Achebe's reading of the novel or compares it to his own. Said refers to *Things Fall Apart* as Achebe's 'great novel', but says no more (p. 284). Similarly, in discussing the crisis of neo-imperialism in many now-independent countries, he mentions 'Achebe's most recent novel, *Anthills of the Savannah*' as 'a compelling survey of this enervating and dispiriting landscape', without paying any further attention to it (p. 372). Conrad's *Heart of Darkness* receives over twenty pages of analysis in the course of the book, but the comparisons with Salih and Ngugi take up only a few lines (pp. 254–5).

Moreover, among the lists of works given above, only one work by a female author – Jane Austen's *Mansfield Park* – receives extended analysis, and only two contemporary women writers are mentioned: Toni Morrison and Jamaica Kincaid. Said makes gestures towards including non-Western writers and women in the metropolis in his analyses; however, as in *Orientalism*, in *Culture and Imperialism* it is primarily the non-Western man who is to be rescued from oblivion; other 'Others' remain in the shadows. An exchange between Said and a 'professor of history, a black woman of some eminence . . . but whose work was unfamiliar' to him, which he reports in 'The politics of knowledge' (1991) is enlightening in this context.[23]

Describing some hostile elements of the reception of a preliminary version of the Introduction to *Culture and Imperialism*, Said gives an account of the exchange between himself and the black woman historian. The latter criticizes Said for his focus on 'white European males', a criticism which he finds absurd and inappropriate, since he 'was discussing European imperialism, which would not have been likely to include in its discourse the work of African-American women'. Said ends his presentation of the exchange by writing what he 'had wanted to say [to the woman professor], but didn't, "Is all that matters about the issue of exclusion and misrepresentation the fact that *names* were left out? Why are you detaining us with such trivialities?" '[24]

Said's response to this criticism is interesting. He justifies his choice of canonical Western male writers by the fact that he is writing about European imperialism: since these writers were intimately involved with imperialism, it is logical to focus on their work. Yet what the black woman professor is suggesting is that it is possible to take an approach to the topic that is less identified with the metropolitan centre. For in limiting his discussion of culture and imperialism to the works and actions of predominantly Western male writers, Said loses an opportunity to look at Western imperialism in a radically different way. A consideration of the works of non-canonical writers, both men and women, Western and non-Western, would give a very different view of the imperialist project from the peripheries rather than from somewhere near the centre. It is also symptomatic that the black woman history professor has read (or at least has listened to a presentation of) Said's work, but he does not know hers.

The incident is revealing in terms of the authority structures of Western academia. It is Said who is at the centre, the black woman professor (whatever her relative eminence) who is on the periphery. Said expresses surprise and discomfort 'not because I was being attacked, but because the general validity of the point made in *Orientalism* still obtained and yet was now being directed at me'.[25] Said seems unable to see that in both *Orientalism* and *Culture and Imperialism* non-Western men are partially empowered, but women and most non-canonical writers and their work(s) are marginalized if not excluded altogether. While it is true that it is not Said's project to examine these writings, and that it may be somewhat unfair to criticize him for failing to do something he has no intention of doing, the 'general validity' of the point about exclusion does still obtain.

Moreover, there are, ironically, times when Said as a reader seems to fall into a position of complicity with certain imperialist literary tropes or metaphors, the African darkness of Conrad, for example, or the imperial pleasures of Kipling's *Kim*. The title of Conrad's book is an obvious imperial allusion. As Patrick Brantlinger has said, 'The myth of the Dark Continent' was 'a Victorian invention', a staple of nineteenth-century imperial ideology in the form of the idea of the civilizing mission.[26] Said's approach to *Heart of Darkness* throughout *Culture and Imperialism* is generally one of studied moderation; he does not neglect its imperialistic perspective (pp. 24–9, 32–4, 81–2, 197–201), and yet he stops well short of Chinua Achebe's indictment of Conrad as racist (p. 200). Said's discussion of Conrad's use of the metaphor of darkness is interesting. Occasionally he writes as if the metaphor of darkness were an unproblematic descriptive trope, as when he says:

> Conrad's genius allowed him to realize that the ever-present darkness could be colonized or illuminated – *Heart of Darkness* is full of references to the *mission civilisatrice*, to benevolent as well as cruel schemes to bring

light to the dark places and peoples of this world by acts of will and
deployments of power – but that it also had to be acknowledged as independent. (p. 33)

Said's use of the expressions, 'the ever-present darkness' and 'the
dark places and peoples', seem to bring together the condescend-
ing attitudes of those originally involved in imperialism and the
critic reading Conrad's novel. However, they are immediately distinguished from each other in the following sentence. Here Said
says that Kurtz and Marlow '(and of course Conrad) are ahead of
their time in understanding that what they call "the darkness" has
an autonomy of its own, and can reinvade and reclaim what imperialism has taken for *its* own' (emphasis in the original). Indeed,
from this point on, Said takes up a more radical perspective, arguing
that both characters and author were products of their time and
could not see that the darkness was a world resisting the empire.
Marlow and Kurtz are described as seeing Africa 'disablingly
and disparagingly' through the metaphor of darkness, and
Conrad's inability to envisage African independence despite his
awareness of the true dominating and exploitative nature of imperialism, is now seen as a 'tragic limitation' (pp. 33–4). The reader
might be tempted to think that the temporary lapse in critical perspective was a dream, except for another example, much later in the
book. On this later occasion Said invokes the way in which Conrad's
narrative 'is preoccupied with what eludes articulate expression –
the jungle, the desperate natives, the great river, Africa's magnifi-
cent, ineffable, dark life' (p. 199). Here the use of adjectives is so
Conradian as once again to suggest the blurring of the perspectives
of critic and author.

Said's reading of Kipling's *Kim* shows a similar ambivalence.
Said vacillates between a recognition of the effects of Kipling's pro-
imperialist views in the novel and an evocation of what he calls 'the
pleasures of imperialism' (p. 159) which seem to exist for the protagonist, the author and the reader, as long as the reader is male or,
at least, male-identified. Said begins by arguing that Conrad, like
Kipling, expressed 'the colour, glamour, and romance of the British
overseas enterprise' (p. 160). He argues that it offers its protagonist
(and, by extension, its male-identified reader) the fictional fulfilment
of the 'dreams of passion, success, and exotic adventure' which is
denied the protagonist and the reader of the European novel of the
period. After all, as Said says, 'Isn't it possible in India to do everything? Be anything? Go anywhere with impunity?' – if, that is, you

are a 'white Sahib' (p. 192). Yet from time to time the analysis seems to disregard the imperial framework and takes off into the world of the 'boyish pleasures', even as the component of pleasure in (the reading of) imperial texts such as *Kim* and in imperialism itself is reasserted. Said seems to be seduced by the practically all-male, celibate world of the novel. He celebrates the 'two wonderfully attractive men at its centre', the hero's 'boy's passion for tricks, pranks, clever wordplay, resourcefulness', his defiance of 'domineering schoolmasters and priests' and his ability to go anywhere and do anything, and so on (pp. 165–6). Said ultimately affirms that in *Kim* we see 'a great artist in a sense blinded by his own insights about India'. Still, his evocation of the pleasures of the reading of a text as 'a wish-fantasy of someone who would like to think that everything is possible' (pp. 196, 194) would seem to suggest that, at times, the 'wish-fantasy' is very appealing to him too.

Moreover, in relation to the effect of the interdependence of culture and imperialism in literary texts, something like a double standard seems to operate. When Said discusses Jane Austen, Rudyard Kipling, E. M. Forster, W. B. Yeats or Albert Camus, he asserts that their inevitable involvement in imperialism does not detract from the value of their works but rather makes them '*more* interesting and *more* valuable' (p. 13, emphasis in the original). He is also at times at pains to assert specifically that it is not a question of blaming writers like Jane Austen or Albert Camus for failing to take a more radical stance in relation to the colonial and/or imperial situation (pp. 115–16, 212–13). However, at the end of the analysis of *Mansfield Park*, Said notes that whereas Austen's novel 'encodes experiences and does not simply repeat them', a 'lesser work wears its historical affiliation more plainly: its worldliness is simple and direct' (p. 116). It is clear that on this occasion the word 'worldliness', so often a positive one for Said, has negative connotations: great works are worldly, but indirectly; lesser ones are more directly involved in the world and are, it is implied, less worthy of the reader's careful attention as a result. This elitist position is reasserted when Said discusses the connection between politics and literature in relation to 'the art of the post-colonial era'. He takes the case of Salman Rushdie and *The Satanic Verses* as an example. While he states that Rushdie's work is to be admired 'as part of a significant formation within Anglophone literature', he also says that it reminds us 'that aesthetically valuable work may be part of a threatening, coercive, or deeply anti-literary, anti-intellectual formation'. By this, Said seems to mean that Rushdie's reputation among many

Indians and Pakistanis changed from that of a 'champion of immigrants' rights and a severe critic of nostalgic imperialists' to that of a traitor to both Islam and India after the publication of *The Satanic Verses*. Said sees this change as a sign that 'the urgent conjunction of art and politics . . . can be explosive'. He adds, 'Those darker connections are where today's interesting political and cultural conjunctures are to be found.' Moreover, he argues that these 'affect our individual and collective critical work no less than the hermeneutic and Utopian work we feel easier about when we read, discuss, and reflect on valuable literary texts' (pp. 373–4).

These comments merit analysis. First, the phrase, 'darker connections', seems to echo such images as 'the Dark Continent' or 'the heart of darkness', with all their imperialist implications. Second, the distinction between the two types of work made in the final sentence seems to go against the prevailing argument of the book which is precisely to bring together the 'individual and collective critical' and the 'hermeneutic and Utopian' modes of reading. Third, by the end of the passage it is not at all clear whether or not Rushdie's novel fits into the category of 'valuable literary texts' any longer, despite the admiration which Said has expressed both for its author and the work itself earlier on.

A similar inconsistency emerges a little later in the discussion of 'non-European literatures'. Students and teachers must take account of the politics of these literatures, Said argues, and of the question of their position, both in the postcolonial countries in which they originate, and in the metropolitan centres in which they are studied. He then continues: 'it is a mistake to argue that the "other" non-European literatures, those with more obviously worldly affiliations to power and politics, can be studied "respectably", as if they were in actuality as high, autonomous, aesthetically independent, and satisfying as Western literatures have been made to be' (p. 383). Aijaz Ahmad takes Said to be saying that, unlike 'Western literatures', the '"other" non-European literatures' are not to be considered as 'high, autonomous, aesthetically independent, [or] satisfying', since they are too closely connected to issues of politics and power.[27] However, it might be more accurate to interpret Said as saying that, in both Western and non-Western contexts, there are literary works that transcend their social and political contexts and are thus 'high, autonomous, aesthetically independent, and satisfying', and there are 'other', lesser works, which are not. Moreover, works of Western literature do not necessarily transcend their social and political contexts, although they

have been 'made' to do so. Thus the distinction between great
works and lesser ones re-emerges, as does the opposition between
European and non-European literatures. The reader might wonder
what has happened to the model of 'overlapping territories' and
'intertwined histories', to the interdependence of the colonizers and
the formerly colonized in terms of history, politics, cultures and literature. What has happened to the contrapuntal reading and
hybridity that Said has been at pains to stress so far? In fact, they
immediately reappear, as Said rejects the word 'contamination' to
describe the relation between politics and literature in relation to
the types of works he has been discussing. He chooses instead
'some notion of literature and indeed all culture as hybrid (in Homi
Bhabha's complex sense of that word) and encumbered' (p. 384).
It is clear, however, that some works are more encumbered
than others, and in ways which for Said detract from their value as
literature.

The alternative: hybrid cultures and contrapuntal reading

In *Culture and Imperialism* it is Said's avowed intention to articulate
an alternative to what he sees as the critical equivalent of 'tribalism'
(p. 21). He proposes a view of cultures, histories and literatures
as 'hybrid' (p. xxix) or overlapping and interdependent, which
requires a technique of contrapuntal reading, a dual approach to literary texts, the transcendence of nationalism and the redefinition of
Western humanism. Together, he argues, these strategies of reading
and interpretation allow us to see the past and present of imperial
domination differently, that is, resistingly (p. 58).

Said relates the concept of contrapuntal reading to the vision of
culture as hybrid; moreover, hybridity is viewed as a characteristic
of culture (or cultures) and of individual works of art. Said makes
the point first of all in the Introduction, arguing that a 'contrapuntal and often nomadic' perspective or historiography is necessary
since, 'Partly because of empire, all cultures are involved in one
another; none is single and pure, all are hybrid, heterogeneous,
extraordinarily differentiated, and unmonolithic' (p. xxix). Here the
word 'hybrid' seems to mean little more than varied or heterogeneous, although on other occasions there are indirect references
to the influence of the imperial past on this heterogeneity. The
concept becomes a little clearer later when, in connection with the
statement that 'Cultural experience or indeed every cultural form is

radically, quintessentially hybrid', Said talks about the need to rejoin the 'cultural and aesthetic realms' with 'the worldly domain' (p. 68). Hybridity at this point seems to mean the worldliness of texts, that is, their involvement in the social and political complexities of their historical moment that Said first proposed in *The World, the Text, and the Critic*. The connection with imperialism is made plain when Said describes *Heart of Darkness* as a 'hybrid, impure and complex' text because of its depiction of 'a politicized, ideologically saturated Africa' (p. 80). Similarly, he says that Verdi's *Aida* is 'a hybrid, radically impure work that belongs equally to the history of culture and the historical experience of overseas domination' (p. 137). Hybridity thus means the recognition of the involvement of culture and specific literary works with imperial and colonial history. The only time that Said comes close to offering a definition or explanation of what hybridity might mean comes towards the end of the book when he refers to Homi Bhabha's use of the word, mentioned above. Said does not expand on what Bhabha's 'complex sense' of hybridity is, although he refers in a footnote to the 'extraordinary subtlety' of Bhabha's exploration of the term in two of his essays (p. 431, n. 39, and see chapter 4, pp. 118–23 below).

For Said, hybridity ultimately seems to refer to a relatively untheorized but productive idea of the interrelation of culture and politics, especially the politics of colonial and imperial domination. Similarly, his concept of contrapuntal reading is more successfully embodied in his textual analyses than in theoretical exposition. Pratt sees it as 'the chief methodological proposal' of the book, and as involving reading back and forth 'across the "activated imperial divide" '.[28] While, as George M. Wilson says, Said does not explain in any detail what exactly the process involves, and what the constraints or conditions of such reading are or should be,[29] he does explain how he came to propose the technique of contrapuntal reading. He sees himself as occupying an intermediary position between theorizing Western intellectuals and formerly colonized people suspicious of these theories, since in a sense he might be said to belong to both groups. He offers a 'broad perspective' of the contrapuntal reading of literary texts and their entanglements with imperialism as a 'homespun resolution of the antitheses' in which he finds himself (*CI*, p. 234).

He also explains that the term 'contrapuntal' is derived from the idea of counterpoint in Western classical music, and relates musical structures to the relationships between narrative, especially novels, and colonialism, imperialism and resistance.[30] In counterpoint in

Western classical music, he says, 'various themes play off one another, with only a provisional privilege being given to any particular one.' The polyphonic 'concert and order' which results is derived from the themes, and 'not from a rigorous melodic or formal principle outside the work'. If music should be analysed in terms of its themes, so, similarly, English novels should be read in terms of their (usually suppressed) engagement with imperial possessions, an engagement that is itself 'shaped and perhaps even determined by the specific history of colonization, resistance, and finally native nationalism'. This means that contrapuntal reading involves a re-reading of 'the cultural archive' in terms of 'the metropolitan history that is narrated' and 'those other histories against which (and together with which) the dominating discourse acts' (pp. 59–60). Thus nineteenth-century English coronation rituals should be seen in relation to Indian durbars, and *Aida* and the works of Camus need to be situated in relation to colonial history (pp. 36, 137, 216). Texts from the metropolitan centre should be read along with those from the peripheries, Austen with Fanon and Cabral, for example (p. 71). Contrapuntal reading must encompass both imperialism and resistance and adopt a global perspective (pp. 79, 312). For Jewsiewicki and Mudimbe, this technique is 'probably the only way to subvert the recurring metaphor of paternal authority so central to the postcolonial world', and thus allow new narrative forms to emerge.[31] The emphasis throughout the book remains overwhelmingly on the texts of the Western canon, although with the admittedly highly significant difference that they are resituated in the history of imperialist and colonialist culture.

Both the view of culture and cultural works as hybrid and the principle of contrapuntal reading depend on the transcendence of nationalism and the redefinition of Western humanism as oppositional. Like Fanon, Said sees nationalism as essential as a first step to resistance to imperialism (pp. 258–62), but he criticizes it as 'separatist, even chauvinist and authoritarian', and 'exclusivist' (pp. 262–3, and see 371–2). He mentions two very different examples of the transcendence of nationalism. The first is that of the internationalist vision of such literary comparatists as Curtius and Auerbach, two of his preferred father figures, or of 'Goethe's idea of *Weltliteratur*' (pp. 51–2). The second is represented by the 'oppositional' work of 'many Third World scholars and intellectuals, particularly (but not exclusively) those who are exiles, expatriates, or refugees and immigrants in the West' (p. 63).

If there is a vision of nationalism transcended, there is also a redefinition of Western humanism and of universalism. In his

analyses of Carlyle, Mill, Ruskin and others, Said criticizes traditional European humanism for its failure to resist imperialism and
for its complicity in the imperial enterprise. Instead of this he proposes a version of humanism derived from Fanon 'free from the
narcissistic individualism, divisiveness, and colonialist egoism' of
imperialism (p. 325). He is aware of the pitfalls of the traditional
definition of universalism and sees it as a factor in the silencing and
oppression of the non-European world, and as invariably tainted
with its imperialist heritage, even in recent theoretical work (pp. 58,
66). Nonetheless he feels that Western humanism without 'the
unpleasantly triumphalist freight that is carried with it' is 'very
much worth saving', since it can offer the intellectual a means of
articulating and defending the human and political rights of previously oppressed peoples.[32] This means that figures like Yeats,
Tagore, Senghor or Césaire rise 'out of [their] national environment
and [gain] universal significance' (p. 281). This oppositional version
of humanism can be related to Said's vision of the secular intellectual as an opponent of both American neo-imperialism and certain
types of critical discourse.

Conclusion: the oppositional stance of
the secular intellectual

Towards the end of the Introduction to *Culture and Imperialism*, Said
observes that 'this book is an exile's book' because he 'grew up as
an Arab with a Western education' and has always felt that he
'belonged to both worlds without being completely *of* either the one
or the other' (p. xxx, emphasis in the original). For him, exile is not
a state of deprivation but a privileged condition since it enables him
to understand the two sides better. It is partly in his intimate knowledge and understanding of more than one culture that his desire
for synthesis and compromise originates. The political awareness
which exile gives may also be seen as one source of Said's belief that
the critic or intellectual should seek both to unify aspects of one or
various cultures, and to oppose elements in them which are inimi-
cal to principles of freedom and self-expression. *Culture and Imperialism* tries to do both these things.

  In the book's final chapter, Said deplores the lack of any effective
oppositional discourse (p. 347) and offers some suggestions as to
what it might consist of. He attributes the lack of opposition partly
to the compartmentalization of professional academic life and the
separation of theory from practice, and partly to the immense

power of the dominant discourse and its diffusion through the media (pp. 352–7, 387). As a potential source of effective opposition, Said appeals to the idea of the secular intellectual, for whom there is 'no Archimedean perspective' outside contemporary political realities (p. 37). He argues that secular intellectuals have 'archival, expressive, elaborative, and moral responsibilities' to provide alternative readings and interpretations (p. 386). Sometimes Said seems to suggest that a historicist and comparatist reading of literary works can provide the necessary challenge to the dominant system. Yet, as he says himself, to see contrapuntal reading as an act of opposition to 'coercive domination' or a way in which to 'transform the present' is idealistic (p. 386). It is an idealism to which he clings, nonetheless.

All this puts him in a somewhat awkward position, as can be seen in the comparison of Fanon and Foucault towards the end of *Culture and Imperialism*. Said observes that Fanon represents both 'native and Western' interests, while Foucault 'seems actually to represent an irresistible colonizing movement that paradoxically fortifies the prestige of both the lonely individual scholar and the system that contains him' (p. 336). Said sees himself as aligned with Fanon rather than Foucault, yet while Said could hardly be said to ignore the neo-imperial context of *his own* theoretical position in *Culture and Imperialism*, the second part of the comment does apply, ironically enough, to Said himself, to a certain extent. His voice is both that of the 'lonely individual scholar' (or, as he would call it, the 'secular or oppositional intellectual') and that of someone positioned in a prestigious part of the Western academy. The oppositional stance of the secular intellectual cannot be dissociated from the question of positionality, especially in the postcolonial world. Said's influence on the field of postcolonial studies and these questions of complicity and positionality will be the focus of the final chapter.

4

Said and Postcolonial Studies

Introduction

Any appreciation of Said's achievement needs to include consideration of the role of his works, especially *Orientalism*, in influencing developments in the fields of postcolonial studies.[1] In postcolonial theory, Said's work has been continued, opened out, modified and challenged by the work of other scholars, notably Homi Bhabha and Gayatri Spivak. Moreover, *Orientalism* gave new impetus to the two forms of colonial discourse analysis in particular: the study of the literature of empire and the theorization of travel writing. This final chapter will offer a sketch of some of Said's most important contributions to developments in these areas of postcolonial studies. It will also argue that Said's insistence on the need for theoretical writing to have an effect on the real world distinguishes his writing from much of the work in the field.

Said and the field of postcolonial studies

The term 'postcolonial studies' is now generally accepted as the name of a field of interdisciplinary studies which encompasses a wide variety of types of analysis. What links them is a concern with the imperial past, with the different varieties of colonialism within the imperial framework, and with the links between the imperial past and the postcolonial present. Postcolonial studies can be said to include two main kinds of work: what Moore-Gilbert calls post-

colonial criticism, including the study of 'Commonwealth literature', and postcolonial theory. These are often approached through
various theoretical perspectives including feminist theory, deconstruction, psychoanalysis and minority discourse and cultural
studies. The field as a whole assumes a continuity between the colonial and postcolonial periods, and is concerned with all aspects of
the relationship between the imperial or postcolonial centre or
metropolis and the colonial or postcolonial periphery.

Given the enormous variety of work in the field, it is not surprising that there is a certain amount of dissatisfaction with the term
'postcolonial'. However, there is also general acceptance, for the
moment, that there is no realistic alternative. Anne McClintock, Ella
Shohat, Vijay Mishra and Bob Hodge, and Patrick Williams and
Laura Chrisman all criticize the term 'postcolonial', and all
continue to use it. There are three reasons for their dissatisfaction.
First, it suggests, wrongly, that the era of Western domination
and exploitation of non-Western countries is over, whereas, as
Williams and Chrisman say, although colonialism may have been
dismantled, the global imperialism of Western capital continues.[2]
Second, the term occludes two important distinctions. If 'postcolonial' is taken to refer to all countries that experienced imperial
domination and colonization, the difference between the histories
and situations of the colonies that were occupied by settlers and
those that were not is obscured. Settler colonies such as Australia,
New Zealand, Canada and South Africa are not at all comparable
to non-settler colonies in terms of their populations, their relations
to the imperial centre or the way in which they gained independence. They also differ among themselves. The second significant
type of difference obscured by the term is that among the non-settler
colonies themselves, whose histories, trajectories of development
and struggles for independence took widely varying forms.[3] Interestingly, in *The Empire Writes Back*, Bill Ashcroft, Gareth Griffiths
and Helen Tiffin include settler and non-settler colonies as well as
the writers of colour in the USA in their definition of the postcolonial field. They point out the significance of the variations of colonialism and postcolonialism in these various contexts, although
much of their discussion emphasizes the similarities rather than the
differences.

Most writers dealing with the field of postcolonial studies feel
that they have to situate postcolonialism in relation to postmodernism. One of the criticisms that Mishra and Hodge make of the

editors of *The Empire Writes Back* is that they end up by collapsing postcolonialism into postmodernism.[4] Similar criticisms have been made of Bhabha, as will be seen below. Postcolonialism, postmodernism and the relationship between the two have all been widely debated. The controversy is far too extensive to be adequately discussed here, although two opposing positions should be noted. Ashcroft, Griffiths and Tiffin argue that the challenge to the Western metropolitan centre on the part of the ex-colonial peripheries predated the postmodern questioning of the unified Western subject and centre, and should be seen as one source of postmodern thought.[5] However, this view is not widely shared. Conversely, Kwame Anthony Appiah argues that postcolonialism and postmodernism need to be sharply distinguished from each other. He sees postmodernism as a primarily Western phenomenon linked to the transcendence of various forms of modernism and associated with the global dominance of capitalism. On the contrary, he sees postcolonialism as being in search of 'an ethical universal' and 'a *transnational* rather than a *national* solidarity' (emphasis in the original), both of which challenge the global money economy he and others associate with postmodernism.[6]

Said's greatest influence has been on the area which is now known as postcolonial theory or postcolonial discourse studies. The centrality of his work, and especially of *Orientalism*, is widely acknowledged,[7] although there is some debate as to why his work has been so productive. Said's key contributions in *Orientalism* include the use of Foucault's idea of a discourse in linking the domains of culture and politics, the elaboration of the idea of the 'textual attitude' and the distinction between latent and manifest Orientalism. Moreover, even the aspects of *Orientalism* which were (and are) the subject of intense critical scrutiny can be seen in retrospect to have been productive in that they generated work which filled in the gaps and challenged various aspects of the theoretical framework of the book. Thus Said's varying and conflicting definitions of Orientalism, his lack of emphasis on elements of heterogeneity and change, the contradictions between Western humanism and Foucault's and Gramsci's ideas, and the neglect of gender, have all contributed greatly to the development of both postcolonial theory and colonial discourse analysis.

Why exactly this has been so is the subject of some disagreement. Bart Moore-Gilbert observes that both Foucault's and Gramsci's theories, which are so important for Said, are 'deeply Eurocentric'.

He argues that Foucault's hypothesis about the change in the structures and operation of power in society around 1760 is inapplicable
to the colonial world, where power continued often to operate as
and in spectacle. Foucault's argument is that in the course of the
eighteenth century, the shift from autocratic to more democratic
regimes meant that power was exercised in less obvious, though no
less repressive, ways. In the colonial situation, however, autocracy
and public punishment still held sway. Moore-Gilbert also notes
that Gramsci's concept of hegemony does not really apply to the
colonial situation.[8] However, Williams and Chrisman suggest that
it was precisely Said's 'bringing together . . . of two apparently very
different areas: post-structuralism in the shape of Foucault, and
Western Marxism, in the shape of Gramsci',[9] that made *Orientalism*
so useful and so productive. Studies of the postcolonial field often
routinely include chapters on Said, and often focus specifically on
Orientalism.[10]

But it is not only *Orientalism* which has provided the impetus for
new work. Concepts such as 'worldliness', 'secular criticism'
and 'travelling theory' have also been highly influential. Said's
engagement with elements of post-structuralist theory is extended
and changed beyond recognition in the work of Bhabha and Spivak.
Ideas like 'the voyage in', 'imaginative geography', overlapping
and intertwined histories and experiences, and the rejection of a
'politics of blame' in *Culture and Imperialism* have also left their
mark. Said's use of Fanon and of resistance to imperialism have
been very important. His analyses of literary and political representation, the opposition between the metropolitan centre and the
colonial periphery, the figure of the exile or migrant and the position of writers in relation to their audiences and constituencies have
all helped to define the field of postcolonial studies as a whole.

Thus writers as diverse as Benita Parry, Chandra Mohanty and
Rosalind O'Hanlon,[11] to name only these, take Said as a key reference and starting point for their discussions of various aspects of
the postcolonial situation, even when they criticize certain features
of his work. Similarly, despite his many disagreements with Said,
Aijaz Ahmad identifies him and Fredric Jameson as the two most
important cultural critics writing in English.[12] Other theorists of the
postcolonial situation such as Bhabha and Spivak and writers
dealing with the issue of minority discourse also draw much of their
inspiration from Said's work. Since the mid-1980s there has been a
series of conferences on such topics as 'Europe and Its Others' and
'Cultural Readings of Imperialism', to name only two, whose titles

and contents bear testimony to Said's continuing and productive role in the development of the field.[13] What follows will focus on three significant areas: first, on Said, Bhabha and Spivak in relation to postcolonial theory,[14] especially as regards issues of representation and positionality; second, the study of the literature of empire; third, the theorization of the field of travel writing. The second and third of these can both be seen as types of colonial discourse analysis.

Postcolonial theorists: Edward Said, Homi Bhabha and Gayatri Spivak

Postcolonial theory is an area that has developed largely as a result of Said's work. Along with Said, Homi Bhabha and Gayatri Spivak form what Robert Young has called the 'Holy Trinity' of postcolonial theorists.[15] All three agree that theory should not exist separately from action, but the way in which these two realms intersect in their work is very different. While all three use elements of post-structuralist theory, Said has grown more and more dissatisfied with theory in general and certain elements of post-structuralism in particular than either Bhabha or Spivak. His approach is characterized by an emphasis on historicism and empiricism that often contrasts strongly with Bhabha's and Spivak's reliance on psychoanalysis, deconstruction and so on.

The uses of theory

In Said's writings on criticism and theory there is a fundamental paradox: they are the work of a man who has declared that he is generally not interested in theory 'as a subject in and of itself'.[16] Despite this, several of Said's early essays deal with the theories of Foucault and others,[17] and *Orientalism* and *Culture and Imperialism* offer general and theorized accounts of the phenomena they analyse. As I have already argued, in later works Said expresses his disapproval of the apolitical nature of theoretical models like deconstruction and Foucault's discourse theory. He also contests the recent theoretical orthodoxy of postmodernism by challenging Lyotard's view that the era of grand narratives of emancipation and enlightenment is at an end. The problem with Lyotard is that, Said says, 'He *separates* Western postmodernism from the non-European world, and from the consequences of European modernism – and modernization – in the colonized world' (emphasis in the original).[18] For many people in the non-Western world, Said contends, the grand narratives are still very relevant since the freedoms they represent have not yet been achieved.

Said demands that theory operate in civil society, and not merely in the academy. Said criticizes the narrow professionalism of the literary critic and recommends *'amateurism'* (*RI*, p. 61, and see pp. 55–61) and a strategy of *'interference'* (O, p. 24, emphasis in the original). Interference means, first, the use of the 'visual faculty', and second, the opening up of 'the culture to experiences of the Other which have remained "outside" (and have been repressed or framed in a context of confrontational hostility) the norms manufactured by "insiders"' (O, p. 25). Both of these characterize Said's presentation of the Palestinians in *After the Last Sky*, and the second has been the focus of much of his work since *Orientalism*. The object of such interventions is to avoid the lamentable 'depoliticization' of intellectual life (O, p. 20) that he sees as characterizing much of Western academia. This is what Said himself has tried to do in many of the articles that he publishes regularly both in the Western press and elsewhere.[19] In sum, for Said theory should be linked to practice; if not, he is sceptical of its value.

Neither Bhabha nor Spivak shares Said's scepticism about theory. Both agree with Said that theory and practice should reinforce each other, but there is no equivalent in their work or their lives to Said's commitment to the Palestinian cause. Some of Bhabha's essays analyse aspects of the British political scene, and Spivak sometimes includes economic and political factors in her analyses of the postcolonial situation. Generally, however, their writings operate on an abstract theoretical level and their ideas are expressed in language which is far less accessible than Said's.

As the title of 'The commitment to theory' indicates, Bhabha attributes a positive role to theory. He is aware that theory is often seen as the 'elite language of the socially and culturally privileged'. As such it is associated both with 'the vagaries of the depoliticized Eurocentric critic' and the political and economic inequalities represented by the opposition between the West and the rest of the world (*LC*, pp. 19, 20). However, he rejects the idea that theory necessarily supports or is compromised by Western privilege, arguing that a distinction should be made between 'the institutional history of critical theory and its conceptual potential for change and innovation' (p. 31). Asking 'what the function of a committed theoretical perspective might be' in the context of 'the cultural and historical hybridity of the postcolonial world' (p. 21), he argues that it would be necessarily anti-binary, 'a negotiation (rather than a negation) of oppositional and antagonistic elements'. This would involve a rethinking of the political and the discursive or theoretical (pp. 22, 23). For Bhabha, theory's 'radical contribution' is 'This emphasis on the representation of the political, on the construction of discourse', a point he illustrates with an analysis of the position of working-class women in the British miners' strike of 1984–5 (pp. 27–8).

Bhabha's rejection of the binary opposition between the theoretical and the political domains means that he sees no distance or difference between theoretical and political action (p. 30). He uses Fanon's idea of revolutionary cultural and political change as a 'fluctuating movement' to argue for 'the necessity of theory'. He also proposes a 'Third Space of enunciation' which shows systems of meaning to be ambivalent, and which replaces cultural, historical and national homogeneity with the heterogeneity and hybridity of the postcolonial world (p. 37).

Spivak takes a position on theory that locates her in between Said and Bhabha. She is aware of the potential elitism of the use of post-structuralist theory, especially by the postcolonial intellectual. Nonetheless, she defends deconstruction since it 'problematizes the positionality of the subject of investigation'. It will not allow this subject to speak as if she were detached from the issues she is analysing (*PCC*, p. 121). As Spivak says at the end of 'The Rani of Sirmur', 'A careful deconstructive method, displacing rather than only reversing oppositions . . . by taking the investigator's own complicity into account . . . does not wish to officiate at the grounding of societies, but rather to be the gadfly who alone may hope to take the distance accorded to a "critical" thought' (RS, p. 147). This resembles Said's view that the postcolonial intellectual should offer a critical but involved perspective on social and political issues, although Spivak considers the radical potential of deconstruction as an analytic tool to be far greater than Said does.

Finally, Bhabha and Spivak part company from Said in relation to the style of their work. Bhabha's rebarbative and arcane style is notorious. Robert Young has argued that Bhabha writes as he does in order to prevent the facile recuperation of his ideas by the academic establishment.[20] If this is indeed Bhabha's aim, then he has not achieved it, since his work has great influence precisely within that establishment. It can be argued that Bhabha's style of writing limits the transmission of his ideas to a very restricted academic audience, and thus detracts from their communicative and subversive potential. Occasionally Bhabha seems aware of this. He wonders if his speculations about the subversive potential of Barthes's notion of discourse outside the sentence are simply a 'daydream' (*LC*, p. 183),[21] or takes an ironic view of his 'mad talk about group-psychosis and flying chapatis', and his 'taste for in-between states and moments of hybridity' (p. 208). However, such moments are brief and infrequent, and have not led him to change his way of articulating his ideas.

Spivak is sometimes concerned with clarity, despite her mockery of the 'clarity-fetishists' (*OTM*, p. 121). After being visiting professor at Jawaharlal Nehru University in New Delhi in 1978, she claims that people found her 'more lucid'; in 1989 she claims that she 'would like to be able to write more sober prose' (*PCC*, pp. 94, 160). To do this would entail 'un-learning our privilege as our loss' in order 'to learn to speak in such a way that the masses will not regard as bullshit'. She goes on to explain that by 'the masses' she means those Indian women belonging to the category of 'unorganized peasant labour', that is, the women she has written about as 'subaltern' (pp. 9, 56). Although she often writes in a way that is incomprehensible, and not only to the masses, Spivak's concern with the lives of real as well as fictional subaltern women testifies to her awareness that activism should never be purely textual. While Young sees the idea of unlearning privilege as 'remarkably utopian', it is at least the sign of a commitment to change in the world outside academia.[22]

Compared to the dense and abstract styles of much of Bhabha's and Spivak's work, Said's is generally much more limpid. The elegance and relative simplicity of his writing have surely contributed a great deal to the widespread influence of his ideas, and can be seen as a necessary corollary to his determination to make the work of the intellectual effective in the world. What follows will compare some salient areas of Bhabha's and Spivak's work with Said's, before examining the issue of positionality.

Said, Bhabha and difference

Bhabha's importance in the field of postcolonial studies may be attributed to three factors: his insistence on the heterogeneity of colonial and postcolonial experience, his concept of hybridity in colonial and postcolonial societies, and his concept of mimicry. All three – heterogeneity, hybridity and mimicry – can be seen as continuing the work Said began in *Orientalism*, but they do so in unexpected ways. Bhabha takes up points which in *Orientalism* are relatively marginal or, as he says, 'underdeveloped' (*LC*, p. 73), and changes them almost completely. He acknowledges Said's 'pioneering theory' and argues that it can be 'extended to engage with the alterity and ambivalence of Orientalist discourse' (p. 71). The key word here is 'ambivalence'.[23] Bhabha's work depends on a series of varying articulations of the idea that colonial power and colonial discourse are not monolithic or unified. Instead, they are split because of a fundamental ambivalence in the colonizer's relation to the colonized and thus in the language or discourse in which this relationship is expressed.

Generally, Bhabha is much more sympathetic than Said to certain aspects of postmodernist and post-structuralist theory, although he also feels that postmodernism is 'profoundly parochial' if it limits itself to 'a celebration of the fragmentation of the "grand narratives" of postenlightenment rationalism' (*LC*, p. 4). He claims that he tries 'to rename the postmodern from the position of the postcolonial' (p. 175), but to some critics he seems to do the opposite.[24] Bhabha's analyses of the colonial and postcolonial situations are often focused on speculations about the individual or collective psyche of the colonizer or the colonized, or both together in what he calls 'the colonial subject', rather than on material political and social phenomena. Unlike Said, Bhabha emphasizes the contradictions and conflicts in colonial power and discourse and argues that they ultimately lead to the subversion of colonial or neo-colonial authority.

Bhabha first engages with Said's ideas in 'Difference, discrimination, and the discourse of colonialism' (1982),[25] where he argues that Said's vision of colonial power as monolithic and unified conflicts with the heterogeneity implied by Foucault's idea of discourse. He then uses Said's idea of a 'new median category' (*LC*, p. 73) created by Orientalism as a springboard for his own theorizations of the nature of colonial authority and discourse, colonialist stereotypes and the psychology of the colonial subject. Bhabha picks out those moments in *Orientalism* where Orientalist discourse is described in terms of conflict or ambivalence. He argues that, for Said, Orientalism is 'a static system of "synchronic essentialism"' threatened by 'diachronic forms of history and narrative, signs of instability'. It is both official policy and a set of fan-

tasies, images and so on. Finally, it is both 'an unconscious positivity' (latent Orientalism) and a set of 'stated knowledges and views
about the Orient which [Said] calls *manifest* Orientalism'. As Bhabha
notes, in Said's work these oppositions are collapsed into the 'polit-
ical-ideological *intention* which, in his words, enables Europe to
advance securely and *unmetaphorically* upon the Orient' (*LC*, p. 71,
emphasis in the original).

For Bhabha, however, it is the oppositions and ambivalences that
are important. He derives one of his most important ideas, that of
the 'in-between', from an 'underdeveloped passage' in *Orientalism*
where Said describes the Orient as '[vacillating] between the West's
contempt for what is familiar and its shivers of delight in – or fear
of – novelty'. Said calls this the 'new median category', which
allows one 'to see new things, things seen for the first time, as
versions of a previously known thing'. Bhabha asks, 'What is this
other scene of colonial discourse played out around the "median
category"?' (*LC*, pp. 71–3). To answer this question, he introduces
his adaptation of the Freudian concept of fetishism into the reading
of the stereotype in colonial discourse. In other essays he develops
similar ideas through a set of key concepts such as hybridity,
ambivalence, mimicry, 'the in-between' and the 'third space'. All of
these concepts articulate ideas of split selves and discourses in
the relationship between the colonizer and the colonized, as well
as between dominant and subaltern classes in the postcolonial
period.

It is this emphasis on difference that constitutes both Bhabha's
main contribution to postcolonial studies and his divergence from
Said. Bhabha's emphasis on the median category, articulated as 'the
in-between', 'not quite/not white', the 'third space' and so on,
allows him to focus more extensively and effectively than Said does
on resistance to colonialism and imperialism. It also leads to his
greater attention to the voices of those who resist, whether they are
those of nineteenth-century Indian colonial subjects or contemporary non-Western writers and artists.[26]

Bhabha's tendency to develop notions of conflict and contradiction which are underplayed in Said's analysis of colonial discourse
can be seen in several of his essays. For example, in 'Of mimicry
and man' (1985) he refers to 'that conflictual economy of colonial
discourse which Edward Said describes' in his opposition between
a view of colonial domination as unchanging and a perspective of
historical development which emphasizes time and change (*LC*,
pp. 85–6). Of course, *Orientalism* does not stress this conflictual

economy, but rather the unifying features of colonial discourses over time. It is Bhabha who stresses the idea of conflict and contradiction, not Said.

Other direct references to Said's work, in 'Signs taken for wonders', 'DissemiNation' and 'The postcolonial and the postmodern', show Bhabha developing some of Said's ideas so as to stress difference and ambivalence. For example, in 'Signs taken for wonders' (1985) Bhabha invokes Said in relation to the 'tradition of English "cultural" authority' embodied in the book as a talisman of European cultural and imperial power (*LC*, p. 105). He says that 'The discovery of the English book establishes both a measure of mimesis and a mode of civil authority and order' in Conrad and Naipaul, among others. However, Bhabha's analysis of the reading of the Bible by Indian converts to Christianity in the nineteenth century sees it as '[inscribing] a much more ambivalent text of authority', creating the possibility of subversion of the cultural authority embodied in the text through the strategy of mimicry (p. 107). Similarly, Said's ideas of worldliness, secular interpretation and travelling theory are evoked as the beginning points for Bhabha's exploration of 'the ambivalence of the nation as a narrative strategy' in the essay 'DissemiNation' in *The Location of Culture* (p. 140), which then leaves Said's ideas far behind.

Finally, 'The postcolonial and the postmodern' (1992) takes Said's work in documenting Third World intellectuals' challenge to metropolitan authority as a starting point for the elaboration of Bhabha's own ideas on the splits in the discourses of the colonial and postcolonial periods. Bhabha begins by referring to Said's concept of 'the voyage in' (although he does not quote the phrase) by non-Western writers in both the colonial and postcolonial periods as an example of the 'process of cultural translation, and transvaluation' he sees as typical of the postcolonial world (*LC*, p. 174). While in *Culture and Imperialism* Said focuses both on the textual and the historico-political contexts of the works by C. L. R. James, Antonius, Guha and Alatas that he is discussing, Bhabha, typically, develops the cultural dimension almost exclusively.[27]

Hybridity, mimicry and subversion

Ambivalence, most notably in the forms of hybridity and mimicry, is Bhabha's most important means of theorizing the heterogeneity of colonial and postcolonial experience, especially in relation to resistance to the hegemonic discourses of the West. In 'Sly civility' (1985) Bhabha argues that colonial discourse in the case he is discussing is 'not simply the violence of one powerful nation writing out the history of another', but 'a mode of contradictory utterance that ambivalently reinscribes, across differential power relations, both colonizer and colonized' (*LC*, pp. 95–6). Bhabha's view of colonial discourse as contradictory and conflict-ridden runs counter to Said's presentation of it as an essentially unified and dominant system which effectively silences those it rules. This is seen in his concept of hybridity, which is much more developed and complex than Said's.

Whereas Said in *Culture and Imperialism* had used hybridity to mean the overlapping of colonizing and colonized cultures in all domains, and the characteristics of literary works produced in this situation, Bhabha develops the concept with much more emphasis on the resistance to and the subversion of colonial power. He explains in 'Signs taken for wonders' that 'Hybridity is a problematic of colonial representation and individuation that reverses the effects of the colonialist disavowal, so that other "denied" knowledges enter upon the dominant discourse and estrange the basis of its authority – its rules of recognition' (*LC*, p. 114). Colonial discourse becomes hybrid when the language of the colonized intersects with that of the colonizer, and when two systems of culture and representation conflict through different meanings attributed to the same words. This leads to subversion, potentially at least, since what begins as part of the dominant discourse turns into an inappropriate and therefore challenging reply (p. 112).

It is this attention to the processes of resistance and subversion that distinguishes Bhabha's approach from Said's. The third chapter of *Culture and Imperialism* is entitled 'Resistance and opposition', and it talks about the literature of resistance and formulates the model of contrapuntal reading as a strategy for doing justice to this literature and showing the imperial complicity of Western-authored works. But Said does not show how resistance to colonial discourse actually operates as Bhabha does in the case of the potential Indian converts to Christianity and so on. This is ironic, since Bhabha describes mimicry – the strategy through which subversion occurs – in terms of Said's opposition in *Orientalism* between 'the synchronic panoptical vision of domination – the demand for identity, stasis – and the counter-pressure of the diachrony of history – change, difference' (*LC*, p. 86). Bhabha sees mimicry as both a means of facilitating the operation of imperial power, when used by the colonizer, and resisting it, when used by the colonized.[28]

Yet, if Bhabha's transformations of some of Said's ideas have the advantage of illuminating the processes of discursive resistance and subversion, they are also problematic in terms of agency, intention and history. As Moore-Gilbert says, it is never clear whether the colonial subject is conscious of the ambivalence and mimicry of his (*sic*) discourse. If mimicry is not conscious on the part of the colonized, then it cannot be intentionally subversive. Moreover, the ambivalence in the discourse of the colonizer does not make that discourse any less effective as a tool of imperial repression.[29]

Bhabha's neglect of history, or of the material social, political, economic and military conditions of which discourse is a part, and which are themselves part of discourse, has been frequently criticized.[30] It may be largely attributed to his reliance on the psychoanalytic theories of Freud and Lacan, and to their effect on Bhabha's ahistorical, psychoanalytic reading of Fanon. As Parry says, this annexes Fanon to Bhabha's own theory and 'obscures Fanon's paradigm of the colonial condition as one of implacable enmity between native and invader, making armed opposition both a cathartic and a pragmatic necessity'.[31] Bhabha very rarely discusses *The Wretched of the Earth*. Instead, he focuses on *Black Skin, White Masks*, arguing that Fanon shifts 'the focus of cultural racism from the politics of nationalism to the politics of narcissism' (*LC*, p. 63). This means that he ignores the book's consideration of its own historical context.[32]

Said's use of Fanon, as chapter 3 has argued, has an entirely different focus. For Said, *The Wretched of the Earth* is the significant text, and the historical and cultural dimensions of the struggle for national liberation and consciousness are the central issues. Moreover, Said's activities on behalf of Palestinian rights show that he is directly concerned with contemporary political realities. Bhabha, on the contrary, restricts himself to the realm of postcolonial and cultural theory.

Said, Spivak and colonial discourse analysis

The divergence between Said and Spivak is perhaps even greater than that between Said and Bhabha, especially in relation to gender. Unlike Bhabha, Spivak does not explicitly derive any of her ideas from Said's work, but she recognizes Said's pre-eminent role in postcolonial studies, calls him 'a sort of senior person in our midst' (*PCC*, p. 165), and refers to *Orientalism* as 'the source book in our discipline' (*OTM*, p. 56).

There are a number of parallels between Spivak's work and Said's. Like Said, Spivak is concerned with the 'epistemic violence' that imperialism inflicted on colonized countries, especially in relation to the issue of the representation of the colonized peoples and what she calls the 'worlding' of colonized countries (RS, pp. 128, 131, 133; TWT, pp. 262, 270). Like Said, she wishes to produce alternative accounts of the history of Europe's interaction with the countries it colonized and ruled. Both writers argue that texts should be considered in relation to sociopolitical realities. Both question the use of European high theory in critiques of colonialism, although Said draws on Foucault and Spivak on Derrida, to mention only these. Spivak praises Said's awareness of how the critic is influenced by his institutional role and position (CSS, p. 75), and both consider that the theorist (the critic for Said, the historian for Spivak) should be oppositional and should find some way of representing the underprivileged and the excluded.[33]

Two areas where Said and Spivak's contributions to postcolonial studies may be compared are the theorization of colonial discourse and the representation of women from the non-Western world. Spivak's analyses of colonial discourse are particularly concerned with the construction of the colonial subject through the epistemic violence of imperialism, but both she and Said are concerned to offer alternative histories or narratives.[34] For example, Spivak's 'Three women's texts and a critique of imperialism' (1985) demonstrates how, in a novel like *Jane Eyre*, various versions of English identity – Jane's, Rochester's, Rivers's – are established at the expense of the identity of the colonized woman, Bertha Mason. Spivak argues that by canonizing *Jane Eyre*, a work that creates the triumph of the individual English female subject at the expense of the colonized woman, Western feminist criticism itself 'reproduces the axioms of imperialism' (TWT, p. 262). In relation to *Jane Eyre* as well as *Wide Sargasso Sea* and *Frankenstein*, Spivak argues that 'to reopen the epistemic fracture of imperialism' the critic must 'turn to the archives of imperialist governance' (p. 278). That is, cultural documents must be re-examined in order to reveal the ways in which they reinforce imperial domination. As Bart Moore-Gilbert notes, Spivak's strategy here anticipates Said's in *Culture and Imperialism*,[35] where Said offers a more general narrative about the interrelation of British culture and politics from the beginning of the nineteenth century up to the present. His focus is primarily on male-authored works, but he shares with Spivak the conviction that works of art from colonizing countries must be related not only to their own history and culture, including imperialism, but also to the history and culture of the territories they colonized.

Thus both Said and Spivak attempt to provide alternative historical narratives of the imperial process, Said in *Orientalism* and *Culture and Imperialism*, Spivak in a variety of essays, some of which are collected in *A Critique of Postcolonial Reason* (1999). 'The Rani of Sirmur' (1985) and 'Can the subaltern speak?' (1988) can be seen as the first examples of Spivak's exploration of the 'archives of imperial governance' and of her theorization of the concept of the subaltern, especially of the 'female subaltern consciousness'. Spivak explains the term 'worlding' as deriving from Heidegger's essay 'The origin of the work of art', and as meaning the inscription of the Indian subject as Europe's Other, the object of imperialism (RS, pp. 133–4). She analyses three different examples of colonialist 'Othering' in order to show the 'planned epistemic violence of the imperialist project' (p. 131). This violence involves 'establishing the "native" as [the] self-consolidating Other' of Europe, through the operation of the systems of law, ideology and the human sciences (p. 130). Spivak's approach, like Said's in *Orientalism*, relies on Foucault's discourse theory, and the concept of 'epistemic violence' fulfils the same function in Spivak's work as Orientalism as a dominant discourse does in Said's. A significant difference between them, of course, is that Spivak focuses on the experience of a colonized woman, the Rani. She argues the 'planned epistemic violence' of imperialism ensures that the Rani's voice cannot be heard, since she has no space from which to speak. This is because she is entirely a product of colonial discourse and emerges 'only when she is needed in the space of imperial production' (pp. 131, 146). It is an added irony, although one that Spivak would probably consider inevitable, that the Rani barely appears in Spivak's text either, since she is relegated to the last quarter of the article.[36] Like Said, Spivak unwittingly silences and marginalizes the voices of those colonial subjects whom she wishes to bring into the sphere of representation.

However, her formulation of the concept of 'the female subaltern consciousness' is motivated by her desire to do justice to the heterogeneity of the experience of colonized peoples. While she begins from Gramsci's concept of the subaltern, she argues that any account of 'the phased development of the subaltern' based on

Gramsci's work is 'thrown out of joint' by the epistemic violence of colonialism, and she uses the work of the *Subaltern Studies* group since they have had to confront the complications of this situation. Moreover, if the *Subaltern Studies* group finds that, in Spivak's words, 'in the context of colonial production, the subaltern has no history and cannot speak', then 'the subaltern as female is even more deeply in shadow' (CSS, pp. 82–3). Hence her famous conclusion that 'The subaltern cannot speak' (p. 104). This does not mean that the various types of people who make up the dominated or subordinate classes *literally* cannot express their resistance. Rather, their resistance or any expression of resistance on their behalf cannot be separated from the categories of the dominant discourse, which also creates them as subordinate beings. Hence, they cannot express themselves autonomously, as an independent group.[37]

Significantly, both Said's attempts to speak for the dispossessed and excluded and Spivak's formulations of a theoretical model of the heterogeneous experience of colonized subjects focus more on the modes of functioning of the power and discourse of the imperial centre than on the resistance of the colonized. This is much less true when they write about contemporary non-European or non-Western writers, artists and their works, although the influence of the West can still be felt in various ways.

Said, Spivak and non-Western writers and works

Said has written quite extensively about the situation of Arab writers and their works, and also about the way in which Arab literature is regarded in the West. He has also offered several quite detailed accounts of the Egyptian actress, dancer and film star, Tahia Carioca. Spivak, for her part, has translated and written commentaries on several short stories by the Bengali writer, Mahasweta Devi, and she has also analysed the position of subaltern women in R. K. Narayan's *The Guide*.

Said's discussions of works of Arab literature can be related both to his analyses of the influence of Orientalist attitudes in Western culture and to his desire to make contemporary Arabic literature better known in the West. In two separate essays, the Foreword to Elias Khoury's *Little Mountain* (1989) and 'Embargoed literature' (1990), Said makes the point that works of Arabic literature are less well known than they might be in the West since Arabic is, as he was told by a New York publisher, a 'controversial' language. This is because of its association with Arabs and with Islam, which are often reduced to the negative stereotypes of the terrorist and/or fundamentalist (FW, pp. ix–xi; *PolD*, pp. 372–3). Said is at pains to counter this image of literary works in Arabic. As in his work as a whole, he concentrates on fiction and pays most attention to the novel, although he also writes about autobiographical and historical works, popular culture and, on one occasion, medieval Arabic linguistic theory.

In his discussions of Arab fiction, Said focuses especially on the works of the Egyptian Nobel prize-winner, Naguib Mahfouz, on those of Lebanese writers like Elias Khoury and Halim Barakat, and Palestinian writers and poets like Ghassan Kanafani, Emile Habibi and Mahmoud Darwish. Said generally approaches the Arab novel by referring both its development and specific works to Western traditions, examples and models. In the Introduction to Halim Barakat's *Days of Dust*, he begins by contrasting the established tradition and genealogy of the European and American novel with the much shorter history of the novel in the Arab world. Individual works are also explained and analysed through comparison and contrast with Western works. In the Foreword to Elias Khoury's *Little Mountain*, for example, he compares Naguib Mahfouz to Balzac and Galsworthy and Flaubert, among others (FW, pp. xvi, xviii). Similarly, 'Embargoed literature' presents Adonis as 'a symbolist and surrealist' and 'a combination of Montale, Breton, Yeats, and the early T. S. Eliot' (*PolD*, p. 375).

Against this Western, primarily European background, Said traces the historical development and current situation of the Arab novel. When he describes its development from 1948 to 1983, he puts the question of Israel and the Palestinian situation at the centre of his historical analysis, arguing that it was a central and traumatic experience for all Arab writers, not only for Palestinians (Int, pp. xiv–xix). In his discussions of Mahfouz, however, there is a slightly different emphasis. Said contrasts the relatively secure and steadily developing world of Mahfouz's novels with the radical formal instability of works by Kanafani, Habibi, Khoury and so on. Said explains the stability of Mahfouz's fictional world, at least in his earlier works, by reference to the survival of Egyptian civil society, despite the turbulence of twentieth-century Egyptian history (FW, p. xii). Conversely, the disruption and fragmentation of Palestinian and Lebanese communities produces what Said calls the formal uncertainties or 'postmodern' combination of different narrative elements to be found in Khoury's *Little Mountain*, Kanafani's *Men in the Sun* and Habibi's *The Pessoptimist* (FW, pp. xiv–xviii). In his review of *Aisha*, by the younger Egyptian writer, Ahdaf Soueif, however, Said compares the novel to other 'formless works' of modern fiction in Arabic.[38] This suggests that Egyptian civil society in the 1980s provides a less stable background for the novelist than it used to do.

Said's analyses of modern Arab fiction provide an excellent example of secular criticism in action, in that they link the discussion of texts as significant form to that of texts as worldly, that is involved in social and political issues and realities.[39] For Said the Arab novel is an 'engaged', 'embattled' and 'highly risky and problematic' form (FW, pp. x, xi, xiv), because of its apparently inevitable involvement in politics. Although Said does not always insist on the centrality of the traumas of Palestinian history for all Arab writers, he does see them as invariably politicized by the disruptions of many of their societies. However, he links this to a consideration of formal elements such as repetition in Khoury's *Little Mountain* (FW, p. xix), narrative composed of disparate scenes or the constant interference of the past in the present in Kanafani's *Men in the Sun* (Int, pp. xxi–xxv).

There are other features of Said's analyses of the Arab novel that link them to the rest of his work. He has a tendency to focus on 'dissenting and oppositional' works that challenge the *status quo*, a tendency which can be related to his interest in alternative forms of knowledge from *Orientalism* onwards (PolD, p. 375). Moreover, his suggestion that the 'reading and interpretation of contemporary literature' can be 'meliorative activities' in the sense that they can lead to more toleration of other cultures and peoples recalls a similar hope in *Culture and Imperialism* (PolD, p. 378; CI, p. 385).

In addition to Arab fiction, Said pays attention to autobiographical or documentary works that bear witness to Palestinian history and experience (ALS, pp. 75–6), a type of writing to which he has recently contributed with his memoir, *Out of Place*. He quotes Darwish's identity card and Habibi's Pessoptimist as 'Two great images' embodying the 'unresolved existence' (p. 26) of Palestinians. In this context he discusses *The Fertile Memory*, directed by Palestinian film-maker Michel Khleifi, partly out of a recognition that, in his analysis of Palestinian experiences of exile and dispossession, women have been relatively neglected (pp. 77–84). He also reviews Albert Hourani's *A History of the Arab Peoples*, which, like George Antonius's *The Arab Awakening*, is praised because it presents Arab societies and Islam non-reductively, without recourse to Orientalist clichés or stereotypes, and avoids the rhetoric of blame (*PolD*, pp. 379–83; *CI*, pp. 19, 295–300).

Most of Said's writing on Arab literature focuses on contemporary fiction. The only time that he deals with any aspect of popular culture or with a woman artist is in his three presentations of Tahia Carioca. All of these exemplify the conventional postcolonial opposition between the male Western-educated and -based researcher and the relatively uneducated female Eastern artist. They also reproduce the unequal configuration of power characteristic of much anthropological research, which has recently been criticized by feminist and radical anthropologists and others, including Said himself in 'Representing the colonized' (1989). Despite this, in his presentations of Carioca, Said shows no awareness of how the unequal power relations between colonial and postcolonial powers impinge on scholarly writing and research, including his own.

In 'The Arab right wing' Said describes Carioca's performance in *Yahya al-Wafd* (*Three Cheers for the Delegation*). He begins with his changing physical impression of her. When he saw her before, she was an 'extraordinarily graceful dancer'. Now she has 'tripled in size', looks like 'a pickle barrel' and is 'scarcely able to move except with a thousand wheezes and squeaks'. This suggests that a woman has no right to appear on stage unless she is lithe and beautiful. Then Said moves on to Carioca's collusion, as he sees it, in the play's espousal of establishment right-wing capitalist philosophy, and thus her betrayal of her previous political convictions. He says: 'Tahia Carioca had once been a member of the Egyptian Communist Party, had been imprisoned for subversive activities, and for a long time was in public disgrace as a Leftist agitator. Here she was vulgarly representing a return to the pre-Nasser past, and more or less extolling the virtues of the Sadat policy of *al-Infitah* (or "free" market profiteering).' Finally, he asserts that Carioca's real-life marriage 'to the play's author, a man at least twenty years her junior, who also played the part of her husband in the play' (*PolD*, p. 227) 'make[s] matters worse' but, '*illustrate my point even better*' (my emphasis). Said seems to be implying that Carioca's performance in the play and her marriage are unseemly betrayals of both political convictions and appropriate behaviour for a woman.

In the interview with Wicke and Sprinker, Carioca appears in the context of Said's research in Egyptian cinema. He explains that he was looking for pictures of her, and continues:

Now, the woman herself, Tahia Carioca, was recently divorced. Her last husband, who was thirty years younger than she, left her, and in the process took all her property. She lives in a little apartment by herself, and apparently he took all of her films, all her prints, as well as all her pictures. She has nothing. So I went to the central cinema archives in downtown Cairo with a film-maker friend of mine, a Lebanese woman who makes documentaries. (I, p. 224)

There is no comment at all from Said on Carioca's divorce, on her loss of all her possessions or on the fact that she is divorced, a difficult situation for a woman in an Islamic country. However, Said does not omit the detail that the dancer's 'last husband' was 'thirty years younger than she'. If this is the same man referred to in the account of the play *Yahya al-Wafd*, Said is now more precise about the age difference. Having failed to find Carioca useful as a source of photographs, Said dismisses her and continues his frustrating search in the chaotic archives. Said agrees with Jennifer Wicke that, in the organization of the archives of Egyptian cinema and, it is implied, other domains too, 'There is a kind of entropy but with no sense of loss.' Said says: 'I feel the loss because I'm coming from here [the USA] and I have a deadline and all that sort of thing, but in the economy of the city, that's not the way it works' (I, p. 225). The breathtaking over-generalization at the end of the sentence, based on one example of Said's own personal experience, embodies one of the classic Orientalist stereotypes that Said criticizes in *Orientalism*. The West is efficient, productive and thus concerned with time; the East is non-efficient, non-productive and therefore does not see time as important. The West speaks; the East is spoken about.

The same is not entirely true of Said's presentation of Carioca in 'Homage to a belly-dancer', since the article includes an account of his interview with her. Here again, though, Said's is the authoritative voice. He first presents Carioca as 'like Oum Kalthoum, the remarkable symbol of a national culture', but as a symbol that 'embodied a very specific kind of sexiness'. The account of her dancing and her film career is sympathetic, even adulatory, but, as before, the actress is described in primarily physical terms, and the play *Yahya al-Wafd* is discussed in essentially the same way. Said presents Carioca in divided terms, as someone who has been many times married, but who is now 'a venerable old woman'. He sums up her life in similarly divided and emblematic terms. He says she was 'A dutiful daughter then, a pious older Muslim now. Yet Tahia was also an emblem of all that was unadministered, uncontrolled, unco-opted in her culture: for such energies the career of *almeh*, dancer, and actress non-pareil was a perfect resolution' (pp. 6–7). The division of Carioca into dutiful and pious woman on the one hand and sex symbol on the other seems to reflect a profoundly traditional and stereotyped view of women.[40] In all three presentations, in varying degrees, Said's is the voice from the powerful Western metropolis; it is the voice of (male) scholarly authority, while the non-Western world, represented by Carioca, is primarily an object of knowledge.

Said's writings on non-Western writers, works and artists show his desire to make Arab literature better known in the West; they also show his tendency to take Western, primarily European, literary traditions and works as his basic framework of reference and to speak from a Western metropolitan location. Spivak's writings on non-Western works have a more specific focus – the female subaltern – but they also deal with the relation between the West and non-Western works, as well as with the question of authority. All these can be seen in her work on Mahasweta Devi and R. K. Narayan.

Despite her reservations about postcolonial intellectuals who turn Third World literary and non-literary texts and experiences into commodities to be consumed in the West, Spivak herself plays this kind of intermediary role in relation to Devi's work, as she recognizes (*IOW*, p. 253). Spivak's translations of them are significant in themselves, but the commentaries she has produced on them and on Narayan's *The Guide* also show the development of her concept of the female subaltern as well as the similarity between her attitude to the intellectual's role and Said's.

The Translator's Foreword (1981) to 'Drapaudi', and the Translator's Preface and the conversation with the author preceding Devi's *Imaginary Maps* (1995), all show Spivak's awareness of the possible charge of commodification of Devi's works. She is anxious to avoid both this and the cultural relativism she sees as a permanent danger in the study of non-Western works in a Western academic environment. She argues that her relation to the subaltern is one of 'Ethical singularity', which she explains as similar to the kind of equal engagement with one other person which involves responsibility and accountability on both sides. 'Ethics is the experience of the impossible', she says, insisting that this does not mean that ethics are impossible (*IM*, p. xxv). Spivak seems to be suggesting that her translations and commentaries on Devi's works should be seen as a kind of academic activism rather than commodification and as an attempt to talk to the subaltern rather than talk of her. However, she can only carry out this project through the intermediary of Devi and her work with the tribal peoples of India. As Spivak says, there is a great difference between Devi's fictional female subaltern figures, who cannot be assimilated by postcolonial hegemonic 'India', and Devi's own activism which aims to obtain civil and political rights for tribal people and outcastes in that same society (*OTM*, p. 51). There is a similar distance between both of these and Spivak's role as an oppositional critic, not least because of her remoteness from the Indian context, of which she is generally aware.

This awareness emerges, along with other aspects of Spivak's work, in her analysis of Narayan's *The Guide* in 'How to read a "culturally different" book' (1994). The essay links a discussion of Western pedagogy related to a non-Western text with a critique of Western feminist writing and a consideration of the problems of representation and self-representation of one type of female subaltern in India. These are connected through Spivak's analysis of the role of the *devadasi* or temple-dancer Rosie/Nalini in *The Guide*, and of the situation of such subaltern women in contemporary India. The pedagogical strand of the argument concerns the question of how a feminist teacher in the USA might teach Narayan's novel, while Frédérique Marglin's *Wives of the God-King* (1985) is the focus of Spivak's critique of the Western anthropological approach to the *devadasis*.

The discussion of the representation and self-representation of the female subaltern as *devadasi* shows how Spivak's use of the concept has changed. Earlier, it will be recalled, Spivak had concluded that 'The subaltern cannot speak' (CSS, p. 104). Here her position is less negative. She acknowledges the extreme difficulty of the subaltern women of the *devadasi* category from different parts of India communicating with each other, since they cannot do so in their mother tongues (HTR, p. 133). She notes that the *devadasis* are effectively written out of Marglin's book, since they do not have access to the dominant discourse of Marglin and her male Indian informants, and they cannot be satisfactorily represented in this discourse either (p. 134). Moreover, even Indian feminist activists working with the *devadasis* cannot allow the women to emerge as agents, since they do not fit into the activists' 'idiom of . . . capital logic'. Spivak concludes that the *devadasi* 'slips through both cultural relativism and capital logic' and so 'can yield "real" information as agent with the greatest difficulty'. Spivak now recognizes that the problem is not that the subaltern cannot speak, but that, because she does not use any version of the dominant discourse, she is hard to hear and understand (pp. 138, 143).

Said's and Spivak's writings on non-Western works reflect their commitment to 'writing back' to the West, despite or because of their relatively privileged positions within the West's academic and social institutions. Both agree that while the issue of representing the marginalized and underprivileged is a deeply problematic enterprise, it is nonetheless a necessary part of the intellectual's job. The issue of representation is inevitably mixed up with that of positionality, since postcolonial intellectuals like Said, Bhabha and Spivak operate at a distance from those whom they are representing. All three are aware of the potential problems posed by the institutional positioning of the critic, but for Spivak this is a much more central issue than it is for Said, while Bhabha offers no explicit discussion of it at all.

Representation: positionality and complicity

For Said, as for Spivak, the issue of representation is central to the intellectual's role. As I have argued earlier, Said sees the intellectual as a necessarily oppositional figure whose main function is 'to provide alternatives: alternative sources, alternative readings, alternative presentation of evidence'.[41] Presenting alternatives raises the issue of positionality. If the intellectual must speak truth to power, refuse to be co-opted and be critical and sceptical, this might seem to presuppose a marginal position. In a 1988 interview with Bruce Robbins, Said argues that the intellectual should not be an outsider, 'hovering on the margins'.[42] Almost ten years later, in a 1997 essay, Said gives two alternatives for the postcolonial intellectual. The first, which he rejects, is to choose 'silence, exile, cunning', and so on. The second is to accept the responsibility of representation and to try to influence public policy on behalf of those whom it too easily oppresses. While this project is 'deeply flawed and perhaps too marginalized', Said says, it must be attempted, since although 'what injustice and power inflict on the poor, the disadvantaged, and disinherited' cannot be adequately spoken of, 'there are approximations to it, not representations of it'.[43] His position is that the intellectual should not shy away from the responsibility of representing the political and human rights of others, despite the difficulty of doing so adequately.

Spivak is far more aware than either Said or Bhabha of the question of positionality. She is constantly alert to the possible complicity of the critic in the systems and institutions she is criticizing, and frequently highlights elements of her own biography and position. She relates the theoretical issues she discusses to the pedagogical context in the USA, India and Australia, and occasionally expresses her awareness of the need to write more intelligibly. She acknowledges deconstruction as a key factor in raising the question of the critic's position and in suggesting that no position can be justified absolutely. While Spivak's self-description as someone without roots or someone who belongs to two cultures without entirely fitting into either of them resembles Said's comments on his situation, Spivak also comments on the authority that her position as an eminent American academic gives her in ways that Said does not.[44]

In a 1987 interview, Spivak describes herself as 'bicultural', but she then explains that this means that she is 'not at home in either of the places' she inhabits (*PCC*, p. 83). Like Said, she views this as an advantage, since she feels that 'it's important for people not to feel rooted in one place' (p. 37, and see p. 93). She expresses scepticism about identity labels, since 'There are many subject positions which one must inhabit; one is not just one thing' (p. 60). She rejects the 'Third World woman' label in relation to herself since it fails to reflect the specificity of 'someone who was born in Calcutta in the '40s in a metropolitan professional middle-class family' (p. 114). When she offers her own 'alibi', she describes herself as 'born a Brahmin, upper-class, senior academic in the United States, highly commodified distinguished professor', adding, ironically, 'what do you want?' (p. 86). More seriously, she asserts that 'being an Indian without nationalism and being a Bengali without regionalism' is the biggest problem for her (p. 115). Like Said, Spivak rejects notions of identity based on national or regional identity.

While Spivak agrees with Said that the intellectual has a responsibility to engage with crucial issues in the world outside the educational system, she makes no utopian claims about social change. In 'Feminism and critical theory' (1986) Spivak admits that 'I think less easily of "changing the world" than in the past'. Instead, she says: 'I teach a small number of the holders of the can(n)on, male or female, feminist or masculist (*sic*), how to read their own texts, as best I can' (*IOW*, p. 92). Elsewhere she describes her attempts to teach American students that indoctrination is not confined to the Soviet Union and the Islamic world (p. 99), and to show them that saying, ' "I am only a bourgeois white male, I can't speak" ', is a sign of laziness and bad faith and is intellectually unacceptable (*PCC*, p. 62).

There are several points of similarity in Said's and Spivak's approaches to the issue of representation, with its corollaries of positionality and complicity. Both discuss quite explicitly the need for postcolonial intellectuals to represent those less fortunate than themselves. Both know that intellectuals are always influenced and may be compromised by their institutional role and position (CSS, p. 75; *RI*). Finally, both are aware that the use of sophisticated theoretical models may limit their ability to speak to a wider audience and influence opinions and events outside the world of education.

Bhabha approaches these issues rather differently. Much of his work is concerned with representation and location, especially in relation to the place of the subject in the hybrid postcolonial world. But he never explicitly discusses the problems of the postcolonial intellectual in representing – that is, speaking for as well as about – others. Nor does he consider the ambiguities of his own position. Finally, the issue of how to move from theory to practice (or politics) is subsumed in his model of postcolonial hybridity into the idea of the inevitable interrelation and interdependence of the two domains.

In 'DissemiNation' in *The Location of Culture*, Bhabha approaches the issue of representation by redefining both the nation and nationalism as heterogeneous, ambivalent narrative strategies and locations, that is, discourses and places where many different cultures intersect and conflict. He argues that a national perspective, whether elite or subaltern, can never achieve ' "representative" authority' (*LC*, p. 144) since it is always concerned with the negation of internal differences in order to achieve the desired homogeneity and uniformity. He is concerned with representation as part of discourse rather than as a political act, although he would deny that the separation is a valid one. Bhabha suggests that the heterogeneity of the nation as a space is primarily derived from its conflicting minorities and their discourses; since the nation is heterogeneous and ambivalent, so any representation of it must also reflect those qualities. Like Said and Spivak, Bhabha challenges nationalism when it is defined simply as the opposite of colonialism, which he sees as a dead end. But his discussions of the issue remain in the realm of the abstract and the theoretical, and are often related as much or more to cultural matters rather than to those of politics or economics.

On the issues of positionality and complicity, Bhabha does not foreground the problems and possible contradictions of his own location, as Said and Spivak do. At times he refers briefly to his own experiences, but the references are never developed. For example, at the beginning of 'DissemiNation', he gestures at his 'own experience of migration' in his evocation of two different types of twentieth-century migration, that of more or less voluntary bourgeois exile and that of imposed diaspora or dislocation (*LC*, p. 139). However, neither his own experience of migration nor his relation to the two types of exile is discussed in any detail. Similarly, the concluding essay in *The Location of Culture* begins by evoking some stylized examples of racist behaviour. These are followed by the statement: 'whenever and wherever I am when I hear a racist, or catch his look, I am reminded of Fanon's evocatory essay "The fact of blackness" and its unforgettable opening lines' (p. 236). Again, however, the reference to personal experience is fleeting, and it does not develop into a reflection on Bhabha's own experience of racism.

Thus Bhabha can ask, 'Where does the postcolonial subject lie?' He can answer that, in relation to this subject, 'the articulations of difference – race, history, gender – are never singular, binary, or totalizing' (Free, pp. 56, 57). But he never asks where *his* own location as a postcolonial subject is, or pays any attention to the concrete manifestations of the heterogeneity which he so frequently writes about. In a similar way, he justifies his use of post-structuralist theory because he sees it as emerging from 'postcolonial contramodernity' (*LC*, p. 175). By this he means that contemporary critical theory and its practitioners, like himself, can learn from the experience of those who have suffered 'subjugation, domination, diaspora, displacement' (Free, p. 48). The experience of these people can offer the postcolonial theorist both a learning experience and a tool of analysis so that, Bhabha argues, he can 'revise the known' and 'rename the postmodern from the position of the postcolonial' (*LC*, p. 175). Again, though, the revision and the renaming take place at the level of abstract theory rather than that of any type of specific or concrete practice.

Finally, Bhabha's position in his writing may be taken as an example of the 'in-between' state he so often evokes. His favourite strategy is to read 'against the grain' (*LC*, p. 24). This can take the form of free adaptation of various kinds or of reading catachrestically, that is, in an inappropriate way. For example, on one occasion Bhabha says that 'I have freely adapted some of Benjamin's phrases and interpolated the problem of modernity into the midst of his argument on Epic theater. I do not think that I have misrepresented his argument' (Free, pp. 60–1, n. 12).[45] Discussing his presentation of John Berger's argument, on another occasion, Bhabha admits that he has compiled a quoted passage 'from statements that are scattered throughout the text' (*LC*, p. 268, n. 59). Elsewhere, Bhabha says that his reading of Bakhtin and Guha 'will be catachrestic: reading between the lines, taking neither him at his word nor me fully at mine' (*LC*, p. 188). Such reading strategies are clearly part of Bhabha's version of 'the historical and literary project' of 'the postcolonial intellectual' (p. 173), to which he occasionally refers, but which he does not explicitly define. But they also raise the issue of responsibility, a word Bhabha rarely if ever uses, and an issue that he does not directly approach, unlike Said and Spivak.

The other area of postcolonial studies that shows the influence of Said's work, and especially of *Orientalism*, is colonial discourse analysis. The imperial connections of literary works in English have increasingly received attention, and travel writing has come to be taken seriously as a field of study, with several writers focusing on its theorization, especially in relation to the factor of gender.

Orientalism and the literature of empire

Largely thanks to Said's influence, nineteenth- and twentieth-century British fiction is increasingly interpreted in terms of its relation to imperialism. Canonical texts like E. M. Forster's *A Passage to India* have been resituated in the historical and political framework of British colonization by recent critics such as Jenny Sharpe and Zakia Pathak and her co-authors.[46] For example, Jenny Sharpe's essay 'The unspeakable limits of rape: colonial violence and counter-insurgency' reads *A Passage to India* in the light of Anglo-Indian fears and phobias in the wake of the Indian Mutiny of 1857 and the Amritsar massacre of 1919. There are also a number of studies that approach British fiction in terms of colonial discourse analysis. Some of the most important of these are Abdul JanMohamed's *Manichean Aesthetics: The Politics of Literature in Colonial Africa* (1983), Peter Hulme's *Colonial Encounters: Europe and the Native Caribbean 1492–1797* (1986) and Patrick Brantlinger's *Rule of Darkness: British Literature and Imperialism 1830–1914* (1988). Suvendrini Perera's *Reaches of Empire: The English Novel from Edgeworth to Dickens* (1991) and Jenny Sharpe's *Allegories of Empire: The Figure of*

Woman in the Colonial Text (1993) examine both canonical and non-canonical English novels from the dual perspectives of feminism and postcolonial theory. Moreover, studies like Barbara Harlow's *Resistance Literature* (1987) or Thomas Richards's *The Imperial Archive: Knowledge and the Fantasy of Empire* (1993) also extend the study of the links between politics, history and literature in ways related to Said's concerns in *Orientalism*. Some of these works, notably those by Hulme, Brantlinger and Richards, follow Said in using Foucauldian discourse theory to analyse the colonial situation.

JanMohamed's book is an attempt to contextualize the colonial encounter through a study of works by Joyce Carey, Isak Dinesen, Nadine Gordimer, Chinua Achebe, Ngugi wa Thiongo and Alex La Guma. JanMohamed discusses the influence of colonialism in the various stereotypes projected upon the colonized but derived from 'the settler's own anxieties and negative self-images', and in the mixture of dependency, antagonism and ambivalence which characterizes the relationship between settlers and colonized people(s). He traces three main themes, that is, the influence of colonial society on literary works, the negative influence of colonialist literature on African fiction and the issue of realism in African fiction. Although he obviously draws on both Fanon and Memmi, JanMohamed cites Sartre, Eagleton and Jameson as the most important influences on his own work. There is no specific reference to Said, but the book's emphasis on the importance of the 'socio-political aspects of colonialism' in the study of colonial and postcolonial literature can be linked to Said's insistence on the interrelation of the political and the literary.[47]

Unlike JanMohamed, Hulme cites Said as a 'pervasive influence' especially in relation to the clarification of his ideas 'about the discourse of colonialism'.[48] The book depends on Said's discussion of colonial discourse, although Hulme deals with Europe's relations with the Caribbean rather than the Orient. He uses a method of detailed analysis of specific texts, which include canonical literary works such as *The Tempest* and *Robinson Crusoe* as well as non-literary material. Like Said, Hulme sees the strategies and tropes of colonial discourse as characteristic of a wide variety of texts. Both also argue that there is a continuity between the imperialism of Spain and England in the Caribbean and Central America and the postcolonial role of the USA in the same area.[49] However, Hulme adopts an explicitly Marxist framework of reference and method of analysis. This means that, unlike Said, he examines the relationship between racial stereotypes, various aspects of colonial discourse from narrative structures to single words and 'some notion of "historical truth"'.[50] The quotation marks around the last two words shows Hulme's awareness of the fraught nature of the enterprise.

Patrick Brantlinger, Suvendrini Perera and Jenny Sharpe all focus primarily on nineteenth-century British literary works in relation to imperialism. Brantlinger's *Rule of Darkness* is organized chronologically. It begins with texts from the 1830s and 1840s, including works by Marryat, and then moves to works from the 1850s by Thackeray, Dickens, Bulwer-Lytton, Reade and Marcus Clarke, and the treatment of the Middle East by writers from Byron to Burton. This is followed by a Foucauldian or Saidian genealogy of the myth of the Dark Continent in the nineteenth century, a discussion of literary representations of the Indian Mutiny and an overview of occultism and imperialism in late Victorian and Edwardian writings. Finally, there is an analysis of Joseph Conrad. Brantlinger's book can be seen to be developing the study of the relation between literature and imperialism along lines similar to those explored in *Orientalism*, although he attempts to provide a view of the development of imperialism as a historical process, which Said does not. Specifically, Brantlinger examines how nineteenth-century theories of race and evolution contributed to the myth of the Dark Continent, which, he argues, was a Victorian invention. Perera's *Reaches of Empire* reads selected canonical works by Edgeworth, Austen, Gaskell, Dickens, Charlotte Brontë and Thackeray in relation to imperial ideology and gender issues. Sharpe adopts a similar approach in *Allegories of Empire*, but she concentrates on the depiction of women in nineteenth- and twentieth-century works dealing with the colonial situation in India.

Unlike most of the works discussed so far, Barbara Harlow's *Resistance Literature* extends Said's work in *Orientalism* in relation to contemporary non-European literature, dealing with autobiographical and other narratives of resistance as well as resistance poetry. In the Preface to the book, Harlow thanks Edward Said and Gayatri Spivak for their 'support and example'.[51] Her study analyses non-canonical works by non-Western writers, including a number by Palestinians. For Harlow, Said is most important for his writing on Palestine, and especially for essays like 'Permission to narrate' and 'Orientalism reconsidered'. Harlow quotes both of these, and the title of her book alludes to Said's reference to 'repressed or resistant history' in the latter, as well as to the narrat-

ives of resistance by Palestinian and other writers that she discusses.[52] Thomas Richards's *The Imperial Archive,* as its title suggests,
draws on Foucault's idea of the archive as well as Said's approach
to the connections between literature, geography and imperialism.
It takes the British Museum as the embodiment of the imperial
archive of the title, explores the significance of mapping in the imperial process and discusses *Kim, Dracula, Tono-Bungay* and *The
Riddle of the Sands* in detail.

Orientalism and the study of imperial travel writing

One development in postcolonial studies that can be largely attributed to *Orientalism* is the analysis of the hitherto generally neglected
genre of travel writing as an example of colonial discourse.[53] The
dual influences of *Orientalism* and of feminist theory have combined
to ensure that travel writing by women often takes centre stage. It
was, perhaps, Said's almost total neglect of gender in *Orientalism*
that prompted women critics to turn to the field and often, but not
always, to focus on women's writing. For example, 1986 saw the
publication of Rana Kabbani's *Imperial Fictions: Europe's Myths of
Orient.* This was followed in 1991 by Lisa Lowe's *Critical Terrains:
French and British Orientalisms,* Sara Mills's *Discourses of Difference:
An Analysis of Women's Travel Writing and Colonialism* and Dennis
Porter's *Haunted Journeys: Desire and Transgression in European Travel
Writing.* 1992 saw the appearance of both Billie Melman's *Women's
Orients: English Women and the Middle East, 1718–1918, Sexuality,
Religion and Work* and Mary Louise Pratt's *Imperial Eyes: Travel
Writing and Transculturation.* In 1993 David Spurr's *The Rhetoric of
Empire: Colonial Discourse in Journalism, Travel Writing, and Imperial
Administration* was published, soon followed by Tim Youngs's *Trav-
ellers in Africa: British Travelogues, 1850–1900.* Mills's and Melman's
books are concerned exclusively with women's travel writings.
Lowe and Pratt analyse writing by both men and women. Kabbani
and Youngs focus on works by various male authors. Spurr's book
analyses various types of colonial discourse in terms of twelve
rhetorical tropes. All of these works extend and develop Said's
analysis of Orientalism in various ways, often by changing the
terms of the theoretical discussion to include gender, in some cases
using Foucault in new ways to do so.

Rana Kabbani explains in the Preface to the 1994 edition of her
Imperial Fictions that she writes as a Muslim feminist. However, the

book does not analyse women's writing, since Kabbani sees women as 'token travellers' who were forced to articulate patriarchal values because of their colonial and imperialist context.[54] There is some attention to gender issues in the work of male writers, notably in chapters 2 and 3. Although there is only one passing reference to Said in the introduction, the book is obviously inspired by *Orientalism*, and it is organized in a very similar way. It begins with a brief overview of the representation of Islam in some literary works ranging from medieval epics and romances to eighteenth-century prose and poetry, before discussing various key nineteenth- and twentieth-century figures, from Edward William Lane to V. S. Naipaul. Kabbani's book continues and extends Said's work by offering some analysis of Orientalist painting in chapter 3 and some attention to Orientalist representations of women.

Works by Mills, Porter, Lowe, Melman and Pratt develop Said's ideas further. Sara Mills's *Discourses of Difference* (1991) analyses the intersection of gender with travel writing, colonialism and imperialism. Mills uses a Foucauldian model of discourse, noting that this model offers the advantages of separating the author from the voices of the text, theorizing the text's different narrative voices, and thus articulating the contradictory position occupied by women's travel texts in relation to colonial power structures and discourses. The first part offers a theoretical discussion of these issues, while the second uses a Foucauldian approach to the production and reception of women's travel texts, before offering detailed case studies of works by Alexandra David-Néel, Mary Kingsley and Nina Mazuchelli. Mills engages explicitly with the theoretical discourse on Orientalism, of which she takes Said as the most important exemplar. She argues that the analysis of women's writing would entail a thorough revision of the theoretical framework of Orientalism. This is so because there is a need for a model capable of including the contradictions and conflicts between the dominant colonial discourse and women's discourses, which she sees as often being 'counter-hegemonic'.[55]

In *Haunted Journeys* Dennis Porter develops some of the ideas that he first explored in his critique of Said's view of Orientalist discourse in '*Orientalism* and its problems' (1983), notably his challenge to Said's monolithic view of Orientalist discourse. He finds Foucauldian discourse theory of the type used by Said in *Orientalism* insufficiently discriminating, since it does not take into account the individual idiosyncrasies or the subversive potential of the language of particular works. He focuses on avowedly non-fictional

works by British and French male authors, drawn from a variety
of domains, from the eighteenth century to the postcolonial
period, and offers detailed analysis of his chosen texts. These range
from Boswell's account of the Grand Tour to works by Barthes
and Naipaul. He explains that his book is historical, but not a
history, and argues that Foucault, Freud and the theories of textuality to which he refers need to be historicized. Said is a key reference point throughout the study. Both he and Porter stress the
individual and the idiosyncratic, both regard the traveller's attitude
to what he sees as a mixture of practicality and fantasy, both see
considerable continuity in the characteristic features of the discourse of travel writing, and both note the hegemonic power of the
Western centre.[56]

Like Mills, both Lisa Lowe and Billie Melman see women's travel
texts as having a contradictory relationship to the dominant discourses of colonialism.[57] Like Porter, both focus on the variety and
heterogeneity of Orientalist writing. Liza Lowe's *Critical Terrains:
French and British Orientalisms* (1991) explicitly acknowledges Said's
'gracious encouragement' of her project.[58] Like Mills, Lowe both
follows and modifies Said's approach, and challenges his monolithic or homogeneous definition of Orientalism. Melman, similarly,
engages with Said's theoretical framework in *Orientalism*, both
acknowledging her debt to him and taking him and others to task
for their neglect of the factors of gender and class.

Although *Critical Terrains* follows Said in basing its theoretical
perspectives on Foucault and Gramsci, Lowe is both more explicit
in her self-positioning in relation to her sources and more consistent in her use of them than Said is. She brings together a modified
version of Foucault's concept of discourse and the concepts of hegemony and subalternity derived from Gramsci to demonstrate that
Orientalism can best be theorized and its texts analysed through the
concept of a set of unstable 'critical terrains'. These are characterized by the potentially contradictory discourses that encode various
social, cultural and textual practices, and that either endorse or
undermine hegemony in various ways.[59] The idea of instability is
a key one for Lowe since it allows for differences in Orientalist
discourse between national traditions and individual writers and
within the work of individual writers, such as Flaubert. Lowe
demonstrates several different types of this instability in a variety
of texts drawn from the fields of fiction, travel, criticism, theory and
philosophy which embody some of the discourses of British and
French Orientalism from the eighteenth to the twentieth century.

In analysing works by Lady Mary Wortley Montagu, Montesquieu, Flaubert, Kristeva and Barthes, among others, Lowe rejects the idea of describing difference in terms of binary opposition because she sees it as 'based on a logic inscribed by discourses of domination' and thus a perpetuation of that logic.[60]

Like Lowe's *Critical Terrains*, Billie Melman's *Women's Orients: English Women and the Middle East 1718–1918* (1992) is a substantial contribution to the field. Melman both acknowledges her debt to Said and challenges his and other scholars' neglect of the factors of class and gender.[61] Like Lowe, Melman emphasizes the factor of gender and the heterogeneity of the Orientalist tradition and challenges a conceptualization based on binary oppositions. She argues that 'an alternative view of the Orient' emerged in works by women in the eighteenth and nineteenth centuries.[62] These works she divides into three categories: 'Harem Literature', 'Evangelical Ethnography' and 'feminine travelogues'. All three are based on the encounter between the woman writer's own culture and that in which she is travelling, which Melman sees as offering an 'analogy between the polygamous Orient and the travelling women's own monogamous society'. This analogy sometimes 'led to self-criticism rather than cultural smugness and sometimes resulted in an identification with the other that cut across the barriers of religion, culture and ethnicity', since women were both inside and outside the dominant structures and discourses of colonialism.[63]

Mary Louise Pratt's *Imperial Eyes*, like the works by Mills, Lowe and Melman, demonstrates its author's awareness of the need for an elaboration of Said's theoretical apparatus. She also calls for a broadening of perspective to include the voices of non-Europeans and non-Westerners. Unlike *Orientalism*, *Imperial Eyes* includes sections on travel literature on the Americas as well as on Africa, but Pratt's starting point of 1750 corresponds more or less to Said's location of the beginning of modern Orientalism in the late eighteenth century (*O*, p. 120).[64] Pratt introduces some new terminology and some elements of a new typology of Orientalizing travel writings. She introduces the terms, 'contact zone', 'anti-conquest', and 'autoethnography' or 'autoethnographic expression'. By the first she means 'the space of colonial encounters', while 'anti-conquest' refers to 'the strategies of representation whereby European bourgeois subjects seek to secure their innocence in the same moment as they assert European hegemony'. Finally, 'autoethnography' or 'autoethnographic expression' are 'instances in which colonized subjects undertake to represent themselves in ways that *engage with* the colonizer's own terms' (emphasis in the original). She also introduces the trope of 'the monarch of all I survey' for the hegemonic voice of the imperialist explorer.[65] Pratt offers a much more precise and detailed analysis of some of the textual strategies of imperialist travel writings than *Orientalism* does. She considers the relationship between travel writing and other discourses, as well as the differences between various sub-genres of travel writing, with their varying complicity in the imperialist process. She tries to lessen the implicit identification with the metropolitan centre that is often found in both travel writing and analyses of it, through the concept of 'transculturation', that is, the way 'subordinated or marginal groups select and invent from materials transmitted to them by a dominant or metropolitan culture'.[66] Finally, in one chapter on travel writing about South America, she raises the issue of gender and discusses works by women travellers. Although Pratt does not mention Said, her analyses of travel writing would be unthinkable without the ground-breaking work of *Orientalism*.[67]

Similarly, David Spurr's *The Rhetoric of Empire* builds on Said's work in relation to colonial discourse analysis. Like Said, Spurr relies on a model of discourse that is essentially Foucauldian, he relates rhetorical tropes to the practice of colonial authority, and he conceives of colonial discourse as operating both during and after the period of imperial possession of territories. He distinguishes twelve rhetorical features of colonial discourse: surveillance, appropriation, aestheticization, classification, debasement, negation, affirmation, idealization, insubstantialization, naturalization and resistance. As he notes, the list is not exhaustive, nor are the categories always strictly separated from each other. Although he deals with journalism, travel writing and imperial administration, most of his examples are taken from literary journalism.

Tim Youngs's *Travellers in Africa* focuses on the accounts of British travellers' journeys to Africa between 1850 and 1900. Young begins by summarizing the aspects of Said's *Orientalism* that he follows. These are the emphasis on the importance of representations and images and of their cultural and political contexts and, more specifically, Said's concepts of 'strategic location' and 'strategic formation' in relation to travel writing as a genre.[68] Youngs does not discuss individual writers separately. Rather, his book is organized around a miscellany of issues: the 1867 military expedition to Abyssinia, the analysis of food and eating habits and of the range of objects and commodities mentioned in travel narratives,

Stanley's expedition to relieve Emin Pasha and Conrad's *Heart of Darkness* as a travel narrative.

Orientalism has also influenced other works relating both to imperialism and to gender issues that are more difficult to categorize. For example, Jane Miller's *Seductions: Studies in Reading and Culture* (1990) contains a critique of *Orientalism* from a feminist perspective in the chapter which examines women in relation to imperialism, colonialism, slavery and racism. The book as a whole includes discussions of women's place in Raymond Williams's work and in Volosinov's and Bakhtin's theories of language and literature, as well as autobiographical and biographical studies. Reina Lewis's *Gendering Orientalism: Race, Femininity and Representation* (1996) begins with a discussion of Said's *Orientalism* and then uses a feminist version of Said's approach to discuss the work of Henriette Brown as 'a woman Orientalist artist'. The book also includes a chapter on George Eliot's 'Orientalization of Jews in *Daniel Deronda*'.[69] Finally, Meyda Yeğenoğlu's *Colonial Fantasies: Towards a Feminist Reading of Orientalism* (1998) engages with Said's theoretical model in some detail in its Introduction, notably in relation to the ideas of representation, binary oppositions and sexuality. Later in the book Yeğenoğlu uses Said's opposition between latent and manifest Orientalism to argue that to see Orientalism as unified in various ways does not mean to see it as monolithic. Moreover, she maintains that the contradictions and splits in Orientalist texts are precisely one means through which Orientalist hegemony is maintained.[70] She also engages with the work of Homi Bhabha, Benita Parry, and Robert Young, among others. Her book develops a feminist reading of various Orientalist issues and tropes such as the veil (in relation to both Western fantasy and liberation struggles in formerly colonized countries), the presence of European women in the harem and the connections between Orientalism, Western feminism and the Enlightenment.

Conclusion

Said's position in the field of postcolonial studies is central. *Orientalism* is a work whose theoretical and methodological inconsistencies have proved far less important in the long run than its broad vision and its engagement with historical and political issues. In postcolonial theory, Homi Bhabha and Gayatri Spivak have developed the theoretical outlines of the field, and their approaches both complement and challenge Said's work. In colonial discourse analysis, a wide variety of critics have continued and extended Said's analyses in *Orientalism, Culture and Imperialism* and elsewhere. But Said has also influenced debate in the wider public arena, notably through his commitment to the Palestinian cause and his insistence on the intellectual's responsibility in the area of human and political rights. The significance of Said's role outside the academic context will be the focus of the conclusion.

Conclusion

Throughout his career, Said has questioned the assumptions underlying particular disciplines, discourses, or cultural or critical practices, and rejected notions of purity – whether of race, religion or critical system – as dangerous and destructive. He has also attacked totalizing systems as uninformative and oppressive and espoused the alternatives of secularism and geographical, social and cultural interconnectedness. Born in East Jerusalem in British Mandate Palestine, educated in Jerusalem and Cairo, and then at Princeton and Harvard, and in the late 1990s University Professor at Columbia, Said is part of a complex set of conflicting yet interdependent languages, religions, cultures and traditions. He has constantly sought to position himself in relation to this complex background. He has assumed what he sees as the responsibilities of both his birth as a Christian Palestinian and his current status and role as an eminent American academic and intellectual, with all the potential contradictions these various parts of his identity and background imply.

Inside and outside the academy, Said's work is both pre-eminent and controversial. In academic terms, *Orientalism* continues to provoke debate, and Said is the most significant but also the most contested figure in the domain of postcolonial theory.[1] From December 1998 to December 1999, he was also the President of the MLA (the Modern Language Association of America), a highly visible position in American academia with international significance. In the public sphere, largely because of his espousal of the Palestinian cause, he is an equally important and equally contested figure. He has made several significant contributions to public debates: first, he has defended Palestinian rights; second, he has drawn attention to the continuing role of the imperialist heritage in Western culture and politics; third, he has challenged the intellectual conformism of the Western metropolis and helped to change it.

Said's defence of Palestinian rights makes him an exemplar of the committed intellectual in the late twentieth century. He has helped to change the way the situation in the Middle East is perceived and represented in the intellectual community and in the media in the USA.[2] Moreover, Said has not restricted his defence of the power-less, the oppressed and the dispossessed to the Palestinians, but has defended the notion of universal human rights, free of the idea's usual exclusive association with European thought.

Said is also one of those who have forced the West to recognize the link between its own metropolitan culture and the non-Western world, and to face up to the historical facts and the continuing implications of its imperialist past.[3] The consequences of this real-ization are to be seen in the development of the field of postcolo-nial theory in the academy, but they also extend far beyond the sphere of literary or cultural studies. Said's work has been a major factor which has forced the West to recognize the place of the non-Western world in its creation and its image of itself and, perhaps, to begin to do justice to it, however belatedly. Here again, a paradox appears, for many of the literary and musical works Said analyses belong to the Western canon, and most of his writing is done in English. Yet, given Said's personal history, and given the history of the twentieth century, it could hardly be otherwise. If Said is to be heard on the world stage, then he must write in English, and if he is to influence work in the academy, he must focus on works that command a wide audience.

It is Said's insistence on the continuing influence of the imperial heritage that has enabled him to challenge and change the intellec-tual conformism of the West. The enterprise is a difficult one, and Said's own position in relation to the issue of intellectual authority has frequently been criticized for succumbing to the temptation of power as an authoritative intellectual when he represents the underprivileged. That is, in attacking the authority of the estab-lishment, Said himself might be said to claim an inverted version of that authority as an oppositional intellectual, even as he contests the whole notion of authority. Said is aware, at least intermittently, of the problems associated with the issue of representation, but he has chosen to make use of his persuasive powers as a public intellectual and to shoulder the responsibility nonetheless.

The question then arises, and it has been most extensively discussed perhaps by Bart Moore-Gilbert, how far does the position of the postcolonial intellectual, ensconced in the Western academy, prevent him or her from being truly radical?[4] In other words, is the postcolonial intellectual who has made what Said himself has called the 'voyage in' to the Western metropolis necessarily completely co-opted by its values? Bruce Robbins argues that the success of intellectuals like Said and others in establishing themselves in Western metropolitan culture can both challenge its authority and change it.[5] If the 'voyage in' could be seen as inevitable, given the current imbalance of economic, political, social and discursive power, then the only place from which Said and others like him can launch their attacks on Western hegemony and *be heard* is in the West itself. Where else can they speak from, if not the centre, and in the language of the centre?

Said speaks from near the centre but with a constant awareness of his responsibilities to those on the periphery. It is a strategic choice of position, allowing him the possibilities of both intervention and distance. It sometimes leads to theoretical inconsistencies of an ironic or frustrating kind, but it also enables him to speak out and defend the rights and values in which he believes.

Notes

Introduction

1 Said has also written quite extensively about music, a topic that will not be discussed in this work.
2 Said, *Covering Islam*, p. xlix.
3 Said, 'Afterword to the 1995 printing', *Orientalism*, p. 338.
4 Osborne, 'Orientalism and after', p. 79.
5 In *Edward Said: The Paradox of Identity*, Bill Ashcroft and Pal Ahluwalia view Said in similar terms, arguing that Said's construction of his identity and his writing on Palestinian politics and literary and cultural theory are inextricably intertwined. They see his concept of worldliness as the key to his work as a whole, and take the paradoxes of his position to be typical of the hybridity and contradictions of the postcolonial situation (pp. 3, 12, 30).
6 In 'Identity, authority, and freedom', p. 11, Said says: 'I belong to more than one world. I am a Palestinian Arab, and I am also an American.'
7 'Palestine, then and now', pp. 47, 50. The presentation of Said's life here is based on the following articles and books by Said: *Out of Place*; *After the Last Sky*, pp. 88, 91, 116–19, 169–72; 'Edward Said: an exile's exile'; 'Palestine, then and now'; 'Return to Palestine-Israel' in *The Politics of Dispossession*; 'Lost between war and peace'; and 'Between worlds'.
8 Salusinszky, 'Edward Said', p. 128; see also 'Edward Said: an exile's exile', p. 30.
9 'Palestine, then and now', pp. 48, 50–1.
10 The controversy that erupted in September 1999 about Said's early life can be seen largely as a politically motivated attempt to discredit Said, and, through him, the Palestinian cause. Said's memoir, *Out of Place*, published in 1999, makes it clear that Said spent most of his childhood in Cairo, with extended visits to Palestine on several occasions. However, it is equally clear that he was born in Jerusalem, and did attend St George's school there before the family left for Cairo in 1947. Despite the assertions of Justus Reid

Weiner, Said has never claimed that he was a refugee; indeed, he explicitly rejected the word in talking to Imre Salusinszky. See Salusinszky, 'Edward Said', p. 127, and Jaggi, 'Out of the shadows', p. 6.

11 Osborne, 'Orientalism and after: Edward Said', pp. 66, 67. See also Said, 'Interview: Edward W. Said', *Diacritics*, p. 35; 'Between worlds', p. 5; *Out of Place*, p. 293. See also Ashcroft and Ahluwalia, *Edward Said*, p. 2.

12 'Palestine, then and now', p. 50.

13 Ibid., p. 55.

14 'Lost between war and peace', p. 14.

15 For more extensive discussion of Said's views on the intellectual as expressed in his *Representations of the Intellectual*, see Ashcroft and Ahluwalia, *Edward Said*, pp. 131–46.

16 The analysis of Jane Austen's *Mansfield Park* in *Culture and Imperialism* is one exception. Said has also written about the Egyptian novelist Ahdaf Souief in 'Edward Said writes about a new literature of the Arab world', and 'Review of Ahdaf Souief's *In the Eye of the Sun*'. In addition, there is his review of Joan Didion's *Miami* in 'Miami twice', and his discussion of Tahia Carioca, the Egyptian actress and dancer. See ch. 4, pp. 126–31 for an analysis of Said's views of Soueif, Carioca and other Arab writers and artists.

17 Osborne, 'Orientalism and after', p. 68.

18 Said, *After the Last Sky*, p. 77.

19 Said, 'Between worlds', p. 3. For comments on Said's fascination with Conrad, see Ashcroft and Ahluwalia, *Edward Said*, pp. 14–16, 39–40, 106–7.

20 Salusinszky, 'Edward Said', p. 134.

21 See Brennan, 'Places of mind, occupied lands', p. 75, and Ashcroft and Ahluwalia, *Edward Said*, p. 95.

22 For a detailed analysis of Said's elaboration of the concept of worldliness in *The World, the Text, and the Critic*, see Ashcroft and Ahluwalia, *Edward Said*, pp. 31–56.

23 For example, see his critique of Hartman's formalistic approach to fiction as opposed to poetry in 'What is beyond formalism?', pp. 939–40, 945.

24 The essay appears in the later volume unchanged, except for a rewritten introductory section. Said distinguishes, here and elsewhere, between Derrida's ideas and the use made of them by his followers.

25 Said, Afterword to the 1995 printing, *Orientalism*, p. 329.

26 Foucault, 'Truth and power', in *Power/Knowledge*, p. 131; see also pp. 112–13.

Chapter 1 *Orientalism*

1 Salusinszky, 'Edward Said', p. 137.

2 For example, Linda Hutcheon in *A Poetics of Postmodernism* sees Said as bringing theory out of the academy and into the world, pp. xi, 16, 24, 61, 66.

3 Ahmad sees *Orientalism* as very much part of a *Zeitgeist* in this respect and refers to S. H. Alatas's *The Myth of the Lazy Native* (1977) and Brian Turner's *Marx and the End of Orientalism* (1978) as two contemporary works of the same type. See *In Theory*, pp. 173, 334.

4 Some Orientalists did not greet *Orientalism* with the same enthusiasm. Bernard Lewis and other Orientalists regarded Said's work as both mis-

guided and unjust as a study of their field. See Lewis, 'The question of Orientalism'. See Mani and Frankenberg, 'The challenge of Orientalism', p. 175, for comments on the book's reception by Orientalists. Arab reviewers were also sometimes very critical of Said; see Sivan, 'Edward Said and his Arab reviewers', and Little, 'Three Arab critiques of Orientalism'.

5 See Ahmad, *In Theory*, pp. 52–62 for an essentially similar account of the same period in English departments of American universities.

6 Edward W. Said, 'Afterword to the 1995 printing', *Orientalism*, p. 329.

7 Ahmad takes issue with Said's description of the Third World; see *In Theory*, pp. 291–2.

8 See Williams, *Keywords*, p. 159, and Ashcroft, Griffiths and Tiffin, *Key Concepts in Post-Colonial Studies*, pp. 122–3.

9 Moore-Gilbert, *Postcolonial Theory*, pp. 46–7.

10 In later works too, Said makes a clear distinction between different types of Western and non-Western literary works and how they should be approached. See *Culture and Imperialism*, pp. 373, 383–4, and 'Figures, configurations, transfigurations', pp. 7, 13–14.

11 See MacKenzie, *Orientalism*, p. 11, for his observation that Said's 'historicism . . . is in itself essentially ahistorical'. He makes the same point about *Culture and Imperialism*, pp. 34, 37.

12 Foucault, 'History of systems of thought', p. 199.

13 Ibid., p. 200.

14 Childs and Williams, *An Introduction to Post-Colonial Theory*, p. 101.

15 Moore-Gilbert, *Postcolonial Theory*, p. 42, and Young, *White Mythologies*, p. 130, also make this comparison.

16 The articles in question are: 'Michel Foucault as an intellectual imagination' (1972), 'An ethics of language' (1974), the final chapter of *Beginnings*, 'The problem of textuality' (1978), later reprinted in *The World, the Text, and the Critic* as 'Criticism between culture and system', 'Traveling theory' (1982), reprinted in the same volume, 'Michel Foucault 1927–1984' (1984), and 'Foucault and the imagination of power' (1986).

17 In 'Michel Foucault as an intellectual imagination', pp. 5–7, 10, 12, 15, Said apparently accepts Foucault's dismissal of the importance of the individual subject, author and work, as he does in *Beginnings*, pp. 308, 313. In *Orientalism* this is no longer so.

18 Foucault, 'Truth and power', in *Michel Foucault: Power/Knowledge*, ed. Colin Gordon, p. 131.

19 Foucault, *Histoire de la sexualité. I: La Volonté de savoir*, p. 122.

20 Said, 'An ethics of language', p. 37.

21 Said, 'From silence to sound and back again', pp. 17, 18. See also Ashcroft and Ahluwalia, *Edward Said*, pp. 72–3.

22 Bhatnagar, 'Uses and limits of Foucault', p. 12.

23 Fanon, *The Wretched of the Earth*, p. 77.

24 Said, 'Foucault and the imagination of power', p. 152.

25 Said's lack of attention to resistance has been criticized by Moore-Gilbert, *Kipling and* Orientalism, pp. 8, 198, and *Postcolonial Theory*, pp. 48–53; Pathak et al., 'The prisonhouse of Orientalism', pp. 209–10; Ahmad, *In Theory*, p. 174; Parry, 'Overlapping territories and intertwined histories', pp. 24–7; O'Hanlon, 'Recovering the subject'.

26 Hourani, 'The road to Morocco', pp. 29–30; Kopf, 'Hermeneutics versus history'; Moore-Gilbert, *Postcolonial Theory*, pp. 45–56; Young, *White Mythologies*, pp. 127–9; Mani and Frankenberg, 'The challenge of Orientalism', pp. 175–7, 184, 191; Porter, '*Orientalism* and its problems', pp. 181–90; Clifford, 'On *Orientalism*', pp. 261–2, 271; Ahmad, *In Theory*, pp. 183–4.

27 Childs and Williams, *An Introduction to Post-Colonial Theory*, p. 115.

28 *White Mythologies*, pp. 139, 140. Similarly, Moore-Gilbert argues in *Postcolonial Theory* that Said himself shows a 'conflictual and uneven' recognition that 'colonial discourse is in fact fractured in its operations, aims and affective economy', p. 44.

29 Ahmad, *In Theory*, p. 164.

30 Said, 'The problem of textuality', pp. 710–11.

31 Said, 'Foucault and the imagination of power', p. 154. Although Said does not discuss resistance in *Orientalism*, he does so in *Culture and Imperialism*. See above, ch. 3, pp. 81, 86–8, 91–2.

32 Porter, '*Orientalism* and its problems', pp. 180–1, 192.

33 This raises the issue of positionality, which is somewhat contentious, both in *Orientalism* and elsewhere. See the final section of this chapter and chapter 4, pp. 133–5. Prasad suggests that Said misreads Gramsci; see 'The "other" worldliness of postcolonial discourse', p. 82.

34 This contradiction has engaged the attention of Clifford, 'On *Orientalism*', pp. 259, 261–74; Ahmad, *In Theory*, pp. 162–70; Cain, *The Crisis in Criticism*, pp. 209–15; Bové, *Intellectuals in Power*, pp. 26–33, 276–8; Young, *White Mythologies*, pp. 119–40; Moore-Gilbert, *Postcolonial Theory*, pp. 42–3, among others.

35 Williams, *Keywords*, p. 58, and see p. 150.

36 Clifford, 'On *Orientalism*', p. 261.

37 See Williams, *Keywords*, p. 89, in relation to Herder, for example.

38 Wicke and Sprinker, 'Interview with Edward Said', p. 230.

39 Ashcroft, Griffiths and Tiffin, *Key Concepts in Post-Colonial Studies*, p. 235.

40 Appiah, 'Is the post- in postmodernism the post- in postcolonial?', p. 353.

41 Lorde, 'The master's tools will never dismantle the master's house'.

42 Eliot, 'Tradition and the individual talent', p. 41.

43 Bové examines the first of Said's descriptions of the Orientalist at some length. He notes Said's debt to Eliot and to I. A. Richards and argues that the analysis demonstrates the strength of Said's approach in applying the tools of humanist criticism to domains other than literature. However, he also argues that even adversarial criticism such as Said's perpetuates the humanist emphasis on conventional authority in the form of the figure of the leading intellectual. See *Intellectuals in Power*, pp. 29–31, 216, 276–9.

44 Clifford, 'On *Orientalism*', p. 263.

45 Williams, 'Appendix: media, margins, and modernity', p. 197.

46 Ahmad, *In Theory*, p. 197. Ironically, Ahmad himself pays hardly more attention to gender than Said does.

47 See Pratt's comments on *Culture and Imperialism* in her contribution to the essay 'Edward Said's *Culture and Imperialism*', pp. 7–8. Perhaps the most ambitious attempt to date to include both gender and sexuality in a theorization of Orientalism is Meyda Yeğenoğlu's *Colonial Fantasies*, which seeks

to combine Said's approach with elements of a deconstructive reading practice.

48 Fanon, *The Wretched of the Earth*, pp. 106 and 148–205 *passim*.
49 Mills, *Discourses of Difference*, pp. 156–8. For an example of this, see Kingsley, *Travels in West Africa*, pp. 86–7.
50 Melman, *Women's Orients*, pp. 77–98; Lowe, *Critical Terrains*, pp. 40–52.
51 See Paxton, 'Complicity and resistance in the writings of Flora Annie Steele and Annie Besant'. For French-Sheldon, see Boisseau, 'They called me *bebe bwana*'.
52 See Kingsley's *Travels in West Africa*, pp. 40–1, 82; see also Birkett, *Mary Kingsley*, pp. 111–24, for a discussion of Kingsley's opposition to the British government's policy on the hut tax, and pp. 125–50, for her criticism of British colonial policy in West Africa more generally. For both, see also Birkett, *Spinsters Abroad*, pp. 232–4.
53 See Stark, *Letters III*, for comments on the need for British imperialists to differentiate themselves from the image of other 'European profiteers' in the Arab world and to 'unify our Arabian policy', pp. 30, 93. For Gertrude Bell, see Lady Bell, ed., *The Letters of Gertrude Bell*, for Bell's criticism of the British policy of 'muddling through' and her assertion of the need for a coherent policy in relation to the Arab world, p. 306. Bell also talks about the need to adjust British imperial policy to Arab ambitions, and, after the 'relapse into barbarism' of World War I, she wonders how Europe can 'claim to teach others' how to manage their affairs, p. 404. Other examples of women travellers and writers who adopted imperialist and masculinist views more or less uncritically are Mary Hall and Mary Eliza Bakewell Gaunt; see Romero, ed., *Women's Voices on Africa*, pp. 70–90 for Hall and pp. 91–104 for Gaunt.
54 Carr, 'Woman/Indian', p. 46.
55 Ibid., p. 49; for a list of these qualities, see p. 50.
56 See Ahmad, *In Theory*, p. 171, for comments on what Ahmad calls Said's strategic deployment of 'words like "we" and "us"'.
57 See Kabbani, *Imperial Fictions*; Lowe, *Critical Terrains*; Melman, *Women's Orients*; Mills, *Discourses of Difference*; and Pratt, *Imperial Eyes*; and see above, ch. 4, pp. 140–4, for a further discussion of these works.
58 See Spivak, 'The Rani of Sirmur', p. 128, and Mohanty, 'Under western eyes'.
59 Said, 'Interview', *Diacritics*, p. 47. In 'Orientalism reconsidered', he calls himself 'an Oriental responding to Orientalism's asseverations', p. 18.
60 Clifford, 'On *Orientalism*', p. 266, and see Bové, *Intellectuals in Power*, pp. 27–33.
61 Pathak et al., 'The prisonhouse of Orientalism', pp. 216, 195, 203.
62 In 'Orientalism reconsidered', Said answers criticism of his failure to discuss German Orientalism and the ahistoricity and inconsistency of the book; he also comments on Bernard Lewis's and Daniel Pipes's discussions of the book, pp. 14, 18–20. As in his response to Lewis's belated review of *Orientalism* in *New York Review of Books* in 'Orientalism: an exchange', exchanges between Said and Orientalists such as Lewis and Pipes sometimes become acrimonious. Said's 'Afterword' to the 1995 edition of *Orientalism* again takes up the argument with Lewis, as well as commenting more briefly on Hourani's review of the book.

63 Ahmad, *In Theory*, pp. 175–6.
64 Bové, *Intellectuals in Power*, pp. 26–33, 212–37.

Chapter 2 Imperialism in the Middle East: Palestine, Israel and the USA

1 See Marrouchi, 'The critic as dis/placed intelligence', for a discussion of the significance of the essay form for Said.
2 See also Robbins, 'American intellectuals and Middle East politics', p. 41.
3 For one example, see Said's film for BBC 2, 'In search of Palestine' (17 May 1998).
4 See above, ch. 3, pp. 86–7 and 92–3, for an analysis of Said's discussion of nationalism in relation to Fanon.
5 As Radhakrishnan argues, for example, in his contribution to 'Edward Said's *Culture and Imperialism*', p. 18.
6 Salusinszky, 'Edward Said', p. 143.
7 For discussion of Said and the Palestinian counter-narrative, see Ashcroft and Ahluwalia, *Edward Said*, p. 115.
8 Krupnick, 'Edward Said: discourse and Palestinian rage', pp. 21–3, emphasis in the original.
9 Shohat, 'Antinomies of exile', pp. 131–2.
10 In 'Broadcasts', in *Blaming the Victims*, Christopher Hitchens makes a similar argument about the supposed broadcasts by Arab leaders instructing Palestinians to leave their homes. See also Chomsky, 'Middle East terrorism and the American ideological system', *Blaming the Victims*, pp. 134–5.
11 See also Said, 'Who is worse?', p. 19.
12 Chomsky's 'Middle East terrorism and the American ideological system' supports Said's view of Israeli action in Lebanon in the 1970s and 1980s.
13 See also Sayigh, *Too Many Enemies*, pp. 117–22, 130.
14 This point is made in many essays and interviews, notably in the 'Orientalism revisited' interview with Barsamian in *The Pen and the Sword* and in the Introduction and 'The prospects for peace in the Middle East' in *The Politics of Dispossession*. See Ashcroft and Ahluwalia's discussion in *Edward Said*, pp. 116–19.
15 See Dunsky, 'Ending a one-sided view of violence', for criticism of this falsely idealizing view of Israel in the American media and public discourse.
16 He distinguishes between the European media and their American counterparts; see, for example, *Covering Islam*, pp. 123–30.
17 The point is also made by Chomsky, in 'Middle East terrorism and the American ideological system', *Blaming the Victims*, pp. 105–6.
18 For Said's criticism of negative popular stereotypes of Arabs see also *Orientalism*, pp. 284–8.
19 Rushdie, *Imaginary Homelands*, pp. 129–47.
20 Khalidi, 'Edward W. Said and the American public sphere', p. 168.
21 Osborne, 'Orientalism and after', p. 82.
22 The Introduction had appeared in the *London Review of Books* in 1993 as 'The morning after'.
23 Said, 'Between worlds', p. 7; see also Ashcroft and Ahluwalia, *Edward Said*, p. 127.

24 Hentzi and McClintock, 'An Interview with Edward W. Said', p. 7. See also Said, *The Politics of Dispossession*, p. xxiv, and Osborne, 'Orientalism and after', p. 67.

25 Khalidi, 'Edward W. Said and the American public sphere', p. 171.

26 See Bhatia, 'Arafat drops pretence at democracy', 'Tenth Palestinian dies in cell' and 'Fear cloaks brutality of Arafat's police'; Borger, 'Ashrawi quits over crookery in Arafat ranks' and 'Palestinian "taxmen" exact price of freedom'.

27 Said, 'He won't gag me'.

28 Said, 'Lost between war and peace', p. 14.

29 Marquand, 'Conversations with outstanding Americans', p. 12.

30 Said, 'Lost between war and peace', p. 12.

31 Said, 'He won't gag me'.

32 Khalidi, 'Edward W. Said and the American public sphere', p. 167. For the articles, see Hirst, 'Shameless in Gaza'; Hockstader, 'In Gaza, peace has brought only poverty' and 'Nightlife rocks where violence ruled'.

33 Said, 'Palestinian prospects now' (1979), p. 4. See also 'The burdens of interpretation and the question of Palestine' (1986), p. 34; '*Intifada* and independence' (1989), pp. 9, 12; 'A real state means real work' (1998). For an explicit statement of Said's agreement with the two-state solution in 1984, see *The Politics of Dispossession*, p. 266.

34 Said, '*Intifada* and independence', p. 9.

35 Said, 'A real state means real work'. See also 'The one-state solution' (1999).

36 Buttigieg and Bové, 'An interview with Edward W. Said', *boundary 2* (1993), p. 14; see also Ashcroft and Ahluwalia, *Edward Said*, p. 127.

37 Ahmad, *In Theory*, p. 171.

38 JanMohamed, 'Worldliness-without-world, homelessness-as-home', p. 97.

39 Mitchell, 'The panic of the visual', pp. 15, 17–18.

40 Bowman, 'Tales of the lost land', pp. 41–4. Bowman also discusses two other versions of a Palestinian narrative, by Fawaz Turki and Raja Shehadeh, which provide interesting alternatives to Said's.

41 Other examples of the same type of differentiation and distantiation are to be found in *The Politics of Dispossession*, pp. 283, 284.

42 For some of Said's comments on nationalism, see *Representations of the Intellectual*, pp. 19–33, his discussion of Fanon in *Culture and Imperialism* and chapter 3, pp. 86–7 and 92–3 above.

43 Salusinszky, 'Edward Said', p. 129.

44 Rushdie, *Imaginary Homelands*, p. 168; see also Marquand, 'Conversations with outstanding Americans: Edward Said', p. 10.

45 Salusinszky, 'Edward Said', p. 133.

46 Osborne, 'Orientalism and after', p. 76.

47 Griffin, 'Ideology and misrepresentation', pp. 624–5; Said, 'Response' to Robert J. Griffin and Daniel and Jonathon Boyarin, pp. 645–6. For another example of Said's apparently unconscious exploitation of the authority of his position at the centre of academic life, see chapter 3, pp. 101–2 above.

48 Said and Donato, 'An exchange on deconstruction and history', pp. 70–1.

49 'Birzeit students meet Edward Said': http://www.birzeit.edu/ourvoice/society/nov/said1198.html.

Chapter 3 After *Orientalism: Culture and Imperialism*

1 See Buttigieg and Bové, 'An interview with Edward Said', *boundary 2* (1993), pp. 1, 2, 4, 5. For the comments about settler colonialism, see Said, 'Response', in 'Edward Said's *Culture and Imperialism*', p. 21.

2 Pratt in 'Edward Said's *Culture and Imperialism*', p. 8; Arac, ibid., p. 11.

3 The title could be translated as *The Marvels of Works in Biography and History*. My thanks to Lahcen Haddad and Abderrahman El-Moudden for the translation.

4 This is a key phrase for Said. In *Beginnings* he identifies the source of the idea as Jakob Burckhardt, but without giving any more precise reference, p. 330.

5 Moore-Gilbert, 'Which way post-colonial theory?', p. 566; Childs and Williams, *An Introduction to Post-Colonial Theory*, p. 103; MacKenzie, *Orientalism*, pp. 34–5.

6 See MacKenzie, *Orientalism*, pp. xvi, 35, 155: MacKenzie argues that Said misunderstands *Aida*.

7 For other comments on gender issues in *Culture and Imperialism*, see Afzal-Khan's review of the work, and Pratt in 'Edward Said's *Culture and Imperialism*', pp. 7–8.

8 Moore-Gilbert, 'Which way post-colonial theory?' pp. 557, 563.

9 Pratt in 'Edward Said's *Culture and Imperialism*', p. 7.

10 See the previous chapter.

11 See Buttigieg and Bové, 'An interview with Edward Said', *boundary 2*, (1993), p. 8.

12 Other references to Eliot in *Culture and Imperialism* are to his poetry, pp. 339 and 401–2, but they are far less important than the essay.

13 Jewsiewicki and Mudimbe, 'For Said', p. 37.

14 Gates, 'Critical Fanonism', p. 459.

15 Fanon, *The Wretched of the Earth*, pp. 311, 313, 315.

16 See Radhakrishnan's contribution to 'Edward Said's *Culture and Imperialism*', p. 16.

17 Williams is not consistent in locating structures of feeling: he vacillates between ascribing them to one particular generation or class or historical period. See *Marxism and Literature*, p. 134; *Politics and Letters*, pp. 157–8. See also *The Long Revolution*, pp. 41–71.

18 *Marxism and Literature*, pp. 132–4.

19 *Politics and Letters*, pp. 157–66, especially pp. 161–2.

20 See Ashcroft and Ahluwalia, *Edward Said*, pp. 90–1, for a similar point.

21 See ibid., pp. 9–16, for a slightly different approach to this contradiction in Said's work.

22 Pratt in 'Edward Said's *Culture and Imperialism*', pp. 6, 3.

23 Said, 'The politics of knowledge', p. 18.

24 Ibid., pp. 18, 19, emphasis in the original.

25 Ibid., p. 19.

26 Brantlinger, 'Victorians and Africans', p. 217, and see pp. 185–222 *passim*.

27 See Ahmad, *In Theory*, pp. 216–17. Ahmad is discussing 'Figures, configurations, transfigurations', the article published in 1990 on which Said bases

this part of *Culture and Imperialism*. There is no difference in the views expressed in the article and in the book.

28 Pratt in 'Edward Said's *Culture and Imperialism*', p. 3.
29 Wilson, 'Edward Said on contrapuntal reading', pp. 265, 267–73.
30 For Said's other discussions of the term in music, see *Musical Elaborations*, 'In the chair' and 'Bach's genius, Schumann's eccentricity, Chopin's ruthlessness, Rosen's gift'. See also Ashcroft and Ahluwalia, *Edward Said*, pp. 93–4.
31 Jewsiewicki and Mudimbe, 'For Said', p. 49.
32 Wicke and Sprinker, 'Interview with Edward Said', p. 230. See also Ashcroft and Ahluwalia, *Edward Said*, pp. 25–6, 127 for a discussion of Said's version of universalism.

Chapter 4 Said and Postcolonial Studies

1 Said's work has also influenced the fields of geography, anthropology, art history and so on, but the analysis of his influence in these areas is beyond the scope of this study.
2 Williams and Chrisman, *Colonial Discourse and Post-Colonial Theory*, p. 1.
3 McClintock, 'The angel of progress', and Shohat, 'Notes on the "postcolonial"', pp. 99–104.
4 Mishra and Hodge, 'What is post(-)colonialism?', pp. 281–4.
5 Ashcroft, Griffiths and Tiffin, *The Empire Writes Back*, pp. 12, 156, 164.
6 Appiah, 'Is the post- in postmodernism the post- in postcolonialism?' p. 353. The most influential account of the links between postmodernism and global capitalism is Fredric Jameson's *Postmodernism, or, The Cultural Logic of Late Capitalism* (1991).
7 Some examples are: Ahmad, *In Theory*, p. 14; Behdad, *Belated Travellers*, pp. 9–10; Breckenridge and van der Veer, *Orientalism and the Postcolonial Predicament*, pp. 3, 4–5; Ghandi, *Postcolonial Theory*, pp. 64–6; Holmlund, 'Displacing limits of difference', pp. 3–5; McClintock, *Imperial Leather*, p. 14; MacKenzie, *Orientalism*, pp. 4, 10; Marrouchi, 'Counternarratives, recoveries, refusals', p. 215; Parry, 'Problems in current theories of colonial discourse', p. 27; Sarkar, 'Orientalism revisited'; Williams and Chrisman, *Colonial Discourse and Post-Colonial Theory*, p. 5.
8 Moore-Gilbert, *Postcolonial Theory*, pp. 158–61.
9 Williams and Chrisman, *Colonial Discourse and Post-Colonial Theory*, p. 6.
10 For example: Moore-Gilbert, *Postcolonial Theory*; Young, *White Mythologies*; Ghandi, *Postcolonial Theory*; Childs and Williams, *An Introduction to Post-Colonial Theory*.
11 Parry, 'Overlapping territories and intertwined histories'; Mohanty, 'Under western eyes'; O'Hanlon, 'Recovering the subject'.
12 Ahmad, *In Theory*, p. 159.
13 See Barker et al., eds, *Europe and Its Others* and Ansell-Pearson et al., eds, *Cultural Readings of Imperialism*.
14 There are a growing number of works on contemporary literary theory or on postcolonial theory which devote a chapter to Said. Examples of the former are: Gorak, *The Making of the Modern Canon*; Spikes, *Understanding Contemporary American Literary Theory*; Steele, *Critical Confrontations*; Varadharajan, *Exotic Parodies*; and McGowan, *Postmodernism and Its Critics*. Two

examples of the latter are the works by Ghandi and Childs and Williams mentioned in n. 10 above. There is also much work being done in minority discourse studies and the study of women in colonialism. For an example of the first, see JanMohamed and Lloyd, eds, *The Nature and Context of Minority Discourse*; for a list of some of the texts on women in colonialism, see Moore-Gilbert, *Postcolonial Theory*, pp. 213–14.

15 Young, *Colonial Desire*, p. 163. Ashcroft and Ahluwalia also point out the significance of Homi Bhabha and Gayatri Spivak, and the difference between their approaches and Said's; see their *Edward Said*, pp. 22, 32.

16 Osborne, 'Orientalism and after', p. 73.

17 For early discussions of Foucault and other theorists, in addition to *Beginnings* and *The World, the Text, and the Critic*, see 'Notes on the characterization of a literary text' (1970), 'Linguistics and the archeology of mind' (1971), 'Molestation and authority in narrative fiction' (1971), 'Michel Foucault as an intellectual imagination' (1972), 'An ethics of language' (1974) and 'Conrad and Nietzsche' (1976). See also Ashcroft and Ahluwalia, *Edward Said*, pp. 4, 22, 23, 32.

18 Said, 'Representing the colonized', p. 222 and see p. 224. See also Ashcroft and Ahluwalia, *Edward Said*, pp. 19–20.

19 Said writes for the *Guardian*, the *Observer* and the *London Review of Books* in Britain and *The Nation*, *Harper's* and the *New York Review of Books*, among others, in the USA, as well as for *Al-Hayat* and other newspapers in the Arab world.

20 See Young, *White Mythologies*, pp. 146, 156. Moore-Gilbert makes the same suggestion in relation to both Bhabha and Spivak, and ultimately accepts that Bhabha's style is problematic because obscure; see *Postcolonial Theory*, pp. 166–8.

21 See Moore-Gilbert, *Postcolonial Theory*, p. 140, for a comment on this passage.

22 Young, *White Mythologies*, p. 170.

23 Young, *Colonial Desire*, p. 161.

24 Moore-Gilbert, *Postcolonial Theory*, p. 128.

25 The essay was first presented as a paper in 1982, published in a slightly revised form in 1992, and is included in *The Location of Culture* (1994).

26 For example, see Bhabha's comments on the resistance to the Indian catechist Anund Messeh in the essay 'Signs taken for wonders' (*LC*, pp. 102–6, 116–22) and on Renée Green, Toni Morrison and Nadine Gordimer in the Introduction to the book.

27 He does so by using Roland Barthes's idea of the language 'outside the sentence' before returning to Guha's analysis of Indian peasant insurgency and then to Bakhtin and Arendt. As Moore-Gilbert notes, Bhabha neither indicates that he mixes details of his own with those of Barthes, nor that Barthes's perspective can be seen as traditionally Orientalist in some ways; see *Postcolonial Theory*, pp. 115, 128.

28 For an excellent discussion of the different ways Bhabha uses the term 'mimicry', see Childs and Williams, *An Introduction to Post-Colonial Theory*, pp. 129–34.

29 Moore-Gilbert, *Postcolonial Theory*, pp. 131–5.

30 See ibid., p. 143; JanMohamed, 'The economy of Manichean allegory', p. 79; Loomba, 'Overworlding the "Third World"', p. 309; Marrouchi, 'Counternarratives, recoveries, refusals', p. 220; Parry, 'Problems in current

theories of colonial discourse', p. 43, and 'Signs of our times', pp. 11–12, 16, 18; Young, *White Mythologies*, pp. 144, 146.

31 Parry, 'Problems in current theories of colonial discourse', pp. 31–2.

32 Moore-Gilbert, *Postcolonial Theory*, pp. 116, 138, 143. Bhabha also misreads Fanon's *Black Skin, White Masks* badly, transforming the little boy who looks at the Negro into a little girl, as Christine Holmlund points out. See Holmlund, 'Displacing limits of difference', pp. 8, 19, n. 50. For other criticism of Bhabha's neglect of gender, class and caste, see Loomba, 'Overworlding the "Third World"', p. 316.

33 For a lengthier and somewhat different account of the stylistic, thematic and methodological differences between Said and Spivak, see Moore-Gilbert, *Postcolonial Theory*, pp. 74–83.

34 Some of Spivak's essays on this topic are mainly concerned with the critique of Western feminism and its neglect or marginalization of non-Western women and thus bear little relation to Said's work. For example, see 'Feminism and critical theory' (1986), 'French feminism in an international frame' (1981), both in *In Other Worlds*, and 'French feminism reconsidered' in *Outside in the Teaching Machine* (1993).

35 Moore-Gilbert, *Postcolonial Theory*, p. 94.

36 In 'Problems in current theories of colonial discourse', pp. 34–5, Parry criticizes Spivak for effacing the colonized subaltern woman's voice in her own writing, and for effacing native resistance to British rule more generally.

37 See Ashcroft, Griffiths and Tiffin, *Key Concepts in Post-Colonial Studies*, pp. 218–19.

38 See 'Edward Said writes about a new literature of the Arab world'.

39 Said makes the link between significant form and worldliness in his essay 'The World, the Text, and the Critic' (1975) in relation to medieval Arabic linguistics (*WTC*, p. 39).

40 Said's reaction to Carioca may also be related to his statement in *Out of Place* that, when he was an adolescent, 'to me dance was a spectacular kind of sexual experience only to be had vicariously and surreptitiously' (p. 98). As an adolescent Said once saw Carioca dance.

41 See also *Representations of the Intellectual* and 'Figures, configurations, transfigurations' for further elaboration of the intellectual's responsibilities.

42 Robbins, 'American intellectuals and Middle East politics', p. 45.

43 Said, 'From silence to sound and back again', p. 21.

44 See Young, *White Mythologies*, pp. 161–2, 169–72, for discussion of Spivak's attention to positionality in her work.

45 Bhabha, 'Freedom's basis in the indeterminate', pp. 60–1, n. 12. Moore-Gilbert notes that Bhabha 'often bends his sources – at times radically – to his own needs and perspectives'; see *Postcolonial Theory*, p. 115.

46 Sharpe, 'The unspeakable limits of rape'; Zakia Pathak et al., 'The prison-house of Orientalism'. See also Sharpe, *Allegories of Empire*, and Moore-Gilbert, *Writing India 1757–1990*, for discussions of the representation of India in British literature.

47 JanMohamed, *Manichean Aesthetics*, p. 3.

48 Hulme, *Colonial Encounters*, p. xv, and see also p. 267, n. 2.

49 Ibid., p. 6.

50 Ibid., p. 50.

51 Harlow, *Resistance Literature*, p. xx.

52 Ibid., p. 28.
53 As Ashcroft and Ahluwalia observe, the importance of *Orientalism* in this regard has not often been acknowledged; see *Edward Said*, p. 26.
54 Kabbani, *Imperial Fictions*, p. 7.
55 Mills, *Discourses of Difference*, pp. 22–3; see also p. 58.
56 Porter, *Haunted Journeys*, pp. 3–21.
57 MacKenzie, *Orientalism*, offers a discussion of Lowe, Melman, Porter and Pratt, pp. 21–5.
58 Lowe, *Critical Terrains*, p. xi.
59 Ibid., pp. 10–11.
60 Ibid., p. 24.
61 Melman, *Women's Orients*, p. xxii.
62 Ibid., p. 7.
63 Ibid., p. 8.
64 Pratt, *Imperial Eyes*, p. 4.
65 Ibid., pp. 6, 7, 201–13.
66 Ibid., p. 6.
67 Pratt does not mention Said, but in *Culture and Imperialism* Said refers to Pratt's book as 'remarkable', p. 423, n. 49.
68 Youngs, *Travellers in Africa*, pp. 1–3.
69 Lewis, *Gendering Orientalism*, pp. 85, 191.
70 Yeğenoğlu, *Colonial Fantasies*, pp. 70–2.

Conclusion

1 Childs and Williams, *An Introduction to Post-Colonial Theory*, p. 115.
2 On Said as a committed intellectual, see McGowan, *Postmodernism and Its Critics*, p. 146. For a comment on Said's effect on the media in the USA, see Bové, 'Introduction', *boundary 2*, 25, 2 (Summer 1998), p. 7.
3 Parry, 'Narrating imperialism', p. 229.
4 Moore-Gilbert, *Postcolonial Theory*, chs 1 and 5 *passim*.
5 Robbins, 'Secularism, elitism, progress, and other transgressions', p. 34.

Bibliography

Only works referred to in this study are included here. Works by Said are ordered chronologically in their sections, books according to the date of their first publication and articles and interviews according to the date of their first publication or the date of the collected volume in which they appear if they were not previously published. Interviews are listed under works by other authors. In the interests of showing the development of Said's thought, details of the first publication of individual essays are given in the chronological sequence; however, for ease of reference page numbers in the text relate to the collected volume in which they were published.

Works by Said

Books

Joseph Conrad and the Fiction of Autobiography (Cambridge, Mass.: Harvard University Press, 1966).
Beginnings: Intention and Method (New York: Columbia University Press, 1985 [1975]).
Orientalism (London: Penguin, 1995 [1978]).
The Question of Palestine (London: Vintage, 1992 [1979]).
Covering Islam: How the Media and the Experts Determine How We See the Rest of the World, revised edition (New York: Vintage Books, 1997 [1981]).
The World, the Text, and the Critic (London: Vintage, 1991 [1983]).
After the Last Sky: Palestinian Lives, photographs by Jean Mohr (London: Vintage, 1993 [1986]).
Musical Elaborations (London: Vintage, 1992 [1991]).
Culture and Imperialism (London: Vintage, 1994 [1993]).
Representations of the Intellectual: The 1993 Reith Lectures (London: Vintage, 1994).
The Pen and the Sword: Conversations with David Barsamian (Edinburgh: Ark Press, 1994).
Peace and Its Discontents: Gaza-Jericho 1993–1995 (London: Vintage, 1995).

The Politics of Dispossession: The Struggle for Palestinian Self-Determination 1969–1994 (London: Vintage, 1995 [1994]).

Out of Place: A Memoir (New York: Alfred A. Knopf, 1999).

——and Christopher Hitchens, eds, *Blaming the Victims: Spurious Scholarship and the Palestinian Question* (London and New York: Verso, 1988).

Other Works

'Notes on the characterization of a literary text', *Modern Language Notes*, 85 (1970), pp. 765–90.

'The Arab portrayed', in *The Arab–Israeli Confrontation of June 1967: An Arab Perspective*, ed. Ibrahim Abu-Lughod (Evanston: Northwestern University Press, 1970), pp. 1–9.

'A Palestinian perspective', in *The Arab World from Nationalism to Revolution*, ed. Abdeen Jabara and Janice Terry (Wilmette, Illinois: The Medina University Press International, 1971), pp. 192–200.

'Linguistics and the archeology of mind', *International Philosophical Quarterly*, 11, 1 (March 1971), pp. 104–34.

'Molestation and authority in narrative fiction', in *Aspects of Narrative: Selected Papers from the English Institute*, ed. J. Hillis Miller (New York: Columbia University Press, 1971), pp. 47–68.

'The Palestinians one year since Amman', *Le Monde diplomatique* (October 1971). Reprinted in *The Politics of Dispossession*.

'What is beyond formalism?', *Modern Language Notes*, 86 (1971), pp. 933–45.

'Michel Foucault as an intellectual imagination', *boundary 2*, 1 (Fall 1972), pp. 1–36.

'U.S. policy and the conflict of powers in the Middle East', *Journal of Palestine Studies*, 2, 3 (Spring 1973). Reprinted in *The Politics of Dispossession*.

'Shattered myths', in *Middle East Crucible: Studies on the Arab–Israeli War of October 1973*, ed. Naseen H. Aruri (Wilmette, Illinois: The Medina University Press International, 1975), pp. 408–47.

'An ethics of language', *Diacritics*, 4, 2 (Summer 1974), pp. 28–37.

'Conrad: the presentation of narrative', *Novel*, 7, 2 (Winter 1974), pp. 116–32.

'Conrad and Nietzsche', in *Joseph Conrad: A Commemoration* (London: Macmillan, 1976), pp. 65–76.

'The Arab right wing', published in *Information Paper no. 21* (September 1978), by the AAUG. Reprinted in *The Politics of Dispossession*.

'The problem of textuality: two exemplary positions', *Critical Inquiry*, 4 (Summer 1978), pp. 673–714.

'Reflections on American "Left" literary criticism', *boundary 2*, 8, 1 (Fall 1979). Reprinted in *The World, the Text, and the Critic*.

'Opponents, audiences, constituencies, and community', *Critical Inquiry*, 9 (September 1982), pp. 1–26.

'Traveling theory', *Raritan*, 1, 3 (Winter 1982). Reprinted in *The World, the Text and the Critic*.

'Edward Said writes about a new literature of the Arab world', review of Ahdaf Souief's *Aisha, London Review of Books*, 5, 12 (7–20 July 1983), p. 8.

Introduction to *Days of Dust* by Halim Barakat, trans. Trevor Le Gassick (Washington, DC: Three Continents Press, 1983), pp. ix–xxxiv.

'Michel Foucault, 1927–1984', *Raritan*, 4, 2 (1984), pp. 1–11.

'The mind of winter: reflections on life in exile', *Harper's Magazine* (September 1984), pp. 49–55.

' "Our" Lebanon', *The Nation* (1 February 1984). Reprinted in *The Politics of Dispossession*.

'Permission to narrate', *London Review of Books* (16–29 February 1984). Reprinted in *The Politics of Dispossession*.

'Reflections on exile', *Granta*, 13 (Winter 1984), pp. 159–72.

'An ideology of difference', *Critical Inquiry*, 12 (Autumn 1985), pp. 38–58.

'Orientalism reconsidered', in *Europe and Its Others. Volume I*, ed. Francis Barker et al. (Colchester: University of Essex, 1985), pp. 14–27.

'Foucault and the imagination of power', in *Foucault: A Critical Reader*, ed. David Couzens Hoy (London: Blackwell, 1986), pp. 149–55.

'Intellectuals in the post-colonial world', *Salmagundi*, 70–71 (Spring–Summer 1986), pp. 44–64.

'The burdens of interpretation and the question of Palestine', *Journal of Palestine Studies*, 16, 1 (Autumn 1986), pp. 29–37.

'Miami twice', *London Review of Books* (10 December 1987), pp. 3, 5–6.

'Edward Said: the voice of a Palestinian in exile', *Third Text*, 3–4 (Spring/Summer 1988), pp. 39–50.

'Identity, negation and violence', *New Left Review*, 171 (September/October 1988). Reprinted in *The Politics of Dispossession*.

Foreword to *Little Mountain* by Elias Khoury, trans. Maia Tabet (Minneapolis: University of Minnesota Press, 1989), pp. ix–xxi.

'Intifada and independence', in *Intifada: The Palestinian Uprising Against Israeli Occupation*, ed. Zachary Lockman and Joel Beinin (London: I. B. Tauris, 1990 [1989]), pp. 5–22.

'Representing the colonized: anthropology's interlocutors', *Critical Inquiry*, 15 (Winter 1989), 205–25.

Response to Robert J. Griffin and Daniel and Jonathon Boyarin, *Critical Inquiry*, 15 (Spring 1989), pp. 634–46.

'Sanctum of the strong', *The Nation* (10 July 1989). Reprinted in *The Politics of Dispossession*.

'Behind Saddam Hussein's moves', *Christian Science Monitor* (13 August 1990). Reprinted in *The Politics of Dispossession*.

'Embargoed literature', *The Nation* (17 September 1990). Reprinted in *The Politics of Dispossession*.

'Figures, configurations, transfigurations', *Race and Class*, 32, 1 (1990), pp. 1–16.

'Homage to a belly-dancer', *London Review of Books*, 12, 17 (13 September 1990), pp. 6–7.

'On Nelson Mandela, and others', *Al-Majalla* (13 March 1990). Reprinted in *The Politics of Dispossession*.

'Third World intellectuals and metropolitan culture', *Raritan*, 9, 3 (Winter 1990), pp. 27–50.

'A tragic convergence', *New York Times* (11 January 1991). Reprinted in *The Politics of Dispossession*.

'The politics of knowledge', *Raritan*, 10, 2 (Summer 1991), pp. 17–31.

'Ignorant armies clash by night', *The Nation* (11 February 1991). Reprinted in *The Politics of Dispossession*.

'The Arab–American war: the politics of information', *London Review of Books* (7 March 1991). Reprinted in *The Politics of Dispossession*.

'The prospects for peace in the Middle East', published as *Peace in the Middle East*, The Open Magazine Pamphlet Series (November 1991). Reprinted in *The Politics of Dispossession*.

'Palestine, then and now: an exile's journey through Israel and the Occupied Territories', *Harper's Magazine*, 285, 1711 (December 1992), pp. 47–55.

'Return to Palestine-Israel', *Observer* (25 October, 1, 8 November 1992). Reprinted in *The Politics of Dispossession*.

Review of Ahdaf Souief's *In the Eye of the Sun*, *Times Literary Supplement* (19 June 1992), p. 19.

'The morning after', *London Review of Books*, 15, 20 (21 October 1993), pp. 3, 5.

'The Other Arab Muslims', *New York Times Magazine* (26 November 1993). Reprinted in *The Politics of Dispossession*.

'Who is in charge of the past and the future?' *Al-Hayat* (12 November 1993). Reprinted in *Peace and Its Discontents*.

'Identity, authority, and freedom: the potentate and the traveller', *boundary 2*, 21, 3 (Fall 1994), pp. 1–18.

'Who is worse?', *London Review of Books*, 16, 20 (20 October 1994), p. 19.

Afterword to the 1995 printing, in *Orientalism* (London: Penguin, 1995), pp. 329–54.

'Bach's genius, Schumann's eccentricity, Chopin's ruthlessness, Rosen's gift', *London Review of Books*, 17, 18 (21 September 1995), pp. 10–11.

'He won't gag me', *Guardian* (23 August 1996), p. 13.

'Lost between war and peace', *London Review of Books*, 18, 17 (5 September 1996), pp. 10–14.

'Palestinians vent fury of the dispossessed', *Guardian Weekly*, 155, 14 (6 October 1996), p. 12.

'From silence to sound and back again: music, literature, and history', *Raritan*, 17, 2 (Fall 1997), pp. 1–21.

'In the chair', *London Review of Books*, 19, 14 (17 July 1997), pp. 3, 5–6.

Introduction to the Vintage edition, in *Covering Islam: How the Media and the Experts Determine How We See the Rest of the World*, revised edition (New York: Vintage, 1997) pp. xi–xlviii.

'A real state means real work', *Al-Ahram Weekly*, 397 (1–7 October 1998). 1998/397/op1.htm.http://www.ahram.org.eg/weekly/

'Between worlds', *London Review of Books*, 20, 9 (7 May 1998), pp. 3, 5–7.

'Birzeit students meet Edward Said', http://www.birzeit.edu/ourvoice/society/nov/said1198.html.

'Israel-Palestine: a third way', *Le Monde diplomatique*, 531 (6 September 1998), pp. 6–7.

'The one-state solution', *New York Times Magazine* (10 January 1999), pp. 36–9.

——and Eugenio Donato, 'An exchange on deconstruction and history', *boundary 2*, 8, 1 (Fall 1979), pp. 65–74.

——and Bernard Lewis, 'Orientalism: an exchange', *New York Review of Books*, 29, 13 (12 August 1982), pp. 44–8.

[and others], 'Edward Said's *Culture and Imperialism:* a symposium', *Social Text*, 40 (Fall 1994), pp. 1–24.

Works by Other Authors

Afzal-Khan, Fawzia, Review of *Culture and Imperialism*, *World Literature Today*, 68 (Winter 1994), pp. 229–30.

Ahmad, Aijaz, *In Theory: Classes, Nations, Literatures* (London and New York: Verso, 1994 [1992]).

Alloula, Malek, *The Colonial Harem*, trans. Myrna Godzich and Wlad Godzich (Minneapolis: University of Minnesota Press, 1986 [1981]).

Ansell-Pearson, Keith, Benita Parry and Judith Squires, eds, *Cultural Readings of Imperialism: Edward Said and the Gravity of History* (New York: St Martin's Press, 1997).

Appiah, Kwame Anthony, 'Is the post- in postmodernism the post- in post-colonial?', *Critical Inquiry*, 17 (Winter 1991), pp. 336–57.

'Arafat "bans Said's books"', *Guardian* (22 August 1996), p. 14.

Ashcroft, Bill, Gareth Griffiths and Helen Tiffin, *The Empire Writes Back: Theory and Practice in Post-Colonial Literatures* (London and New York: Routledge, 1993 [1989]).

——, *Key Concepts in Post-Colonial Studies* (London and New York: Routledge, 1998).

Ashcroft, Bill and Pal Ahluwalia, eds, *Edward Said: The Paradox of Identity*, London and New York: Routledge, 1999.

Barker, Francis, Peter Hulme, Margaret Iversen and Diana Loxley, eds, *Europe and Its Others*, 2 vols (Colchester: University of Essex, 1985).

——, eds, *Literature, Politics and Theory: Papers from the Essex Conference 1976–84* (London and New York: Methuen, 1986).

Barker, Francis, Peter Hulme and Margaret Iversen, eds, *Colonial Discourse/Post-colonial Theory* (Manchester and New York: Manchester University Press, 1994).

Beauvoir, Simone de, *Le deuxième sexe* (Paris: Gallimard, 1976 [1949]).

Bennett, Tony, 'Critical illusions' in *Outside Literature* (London and New York: Routledge, 1990), pp. 193–220.

Behdad, Ali, *Belated Travellers: Orientalism in the Age of Colonial Dissolution* (Cork: Cork University Press, 1994).

Bell, Lady, ed., *The Letters of Gertrude Bell* (Harmondsworth: Penguin, 1987 [1927]).

Bhabha, Homi, 'Signs taken for wonders: questions of ambivalence and authority under a tree outside Delhi, May 1817', in *Race, Writing and Difference: Special Issue of the Journal*, ed. Henry Louis Gates, *Critical Inquiry* (1985), pp. 163–84. Reprinted in *The Location of Culture*.

——, 'Sly civility', *October* (Winter 1985). Reprinted in *The Location of Culture*.

——, 'Of mimicry and man: the ambivalence of colonial discourse', *October: Anthology* (Boston: MIT Press, 1987). Reprinted in *The Location of Culture*.

——, 'The commitment to theory', in *Questions of Third Cinema*, ed. J. Pines and P. Willemen (London: The British Film Institute, 1989), pp. 111–32. Reprinted in *The Location of Culture*.

——, 'Postcolonial criticism, in *Redrawing the Boundaries: The Transformation of English and American Literary Studies*, ed. Giles Gunn and Stephen Greenblatt (New York: Modern Languages Association, 1992), pp. 437–65. Reprinted in *The Location of Culture* as 'The postcolonial and the postmodern'.

——, *The Location of Culture* (New York and London: Routledge, 1997 [1994]).

——' Freedom's basis in the indeterminate', in *The Identity in Question*, ed. John Rajchman (New York and London: Routledge, 1995), pp. 47–61.

Bhatia, Shyam, 'Arafat drops pretence at democracy', *Guardian Weekly*, 155, 16 (11 August 1996), p. 5.

——, 'Tenth Palestinian dies in cell', *Guardian Weekly*, 155, 24 (15 December 1996), p. 2.

——, 'Fear cloaks brutality of Arafat's police', *Guardian Weekly*, 156, 6 (9 February 1997), p. 7.

Bhatnagar, Rashmi, 'Uses and limits of Foucault: a study of the theme of origins in Edward Said's *Orientalism*', *Social Scientist/Trivandum*, 158 (July 1986), pp. 3–22.

Birkett, Dea, *Spinsters Abroad: Victorian Lady Explorers* (Oxford: Blackwell, 1989).

——, *Mary Kingsley: Imperial Adventuress* (London: Macmillan, 1992).

Boisseau. T. J., ' "They called me *bebe bwana*": a critical cultural study of an imperial feminist', *Signs*, 21, 1 (Autumn 1995), pp. 116–46.

Borger, Julian, 'Ashrawi quits over crookery in Arafat ranks', *Guardian* (7 August 1998), p. 11.

——, 'Palestinian "taxmen" exact price of freedom', *Guardian* (21 August 1998), p. 12.

Bové, Paul, 'Intellectuals at war: Michel Foucault and the analytics of power', *SubStance*, 37–8 (1983), pp. 36–55.

——, *Intellectuals in Power: A Genealogy of Critical Humanism* (New York: Columbia University Press, 1986).

——, 'Introduction', *boundary 2*, 25, 2 (Summer 1998), pp. 1–9.

Bowman, Glenn, 'Tales of the lost land: Palestinian identity and the formation of nationalist consciousness', *New Formations*, 5 (Summer 1988), pp. 31–52.

Boyarin, Daniel and Jonathon Boyarin, 'Toward a dialogue with Edward Said', *Critical Inquiry*, 15 (Spring 1989), pp. 626–33.

Brantlinger, Patrick, 'Victorians and Africans: the genealogy of the myth of the Dark Continent', in *'Race', Writing, and Difference*, ed. Henry Louis Gates, Jr. (Chicago and London: University of Chicago Press, 1986 [1985]), pp. 185–222.

——, *Rule of Darkness: British Literature and Imperialism 1830–1914* (Ithaca and London: Cornell University Press, 1990 [1988]).

Breckenridge, Carol A. and Peter van der Veer, *Orientalism and the Postcolonial Predicament: Perspectives on South Asia* (Philadelphia: University of Pennsylvania Press, 1993).

Brennan, Tim, 'Places of mind, occupied lands: Edward Said and philology', in *Edward Said: A Critical Reader*, ed. Michael Sprinker (Oxford and Cambridge, Mass.: Blackwell, 1993 [1992]), pp. 74–95.

[Bruzonsky, Mark], 'Palestinian prospects now: Edward W. Said speaks with Mark Bruzonsky', *Worldview*, 22, 5 (May 1979), pp. 4–10.

[Buttigieg, Joseph A. and Paul A. Bové], 'An interview with Edward W. Said', *boundary 2*, 20, 1 (Spring 1993), pp. 1–25.

Cain, William E., 'Reviewing the state of criticism, III: Edward Said. *Orientalism*', in *The Crisis in Criticism: Theory, Literature, and Reform in English Studies* (Baltimore and London: Johns Hopkins University Press, 1984), pp. 209–15.

Carr, Helen, 'Woman/Indian: "the American" and his Others', in *Europe and Its Others*, vol. 2, ed. Francis Barker et al. (Colchester: University of Essex, 1985), pp. 46–60.

Chaudhuri, Nupur and Margaret Strobel, eds, *Western Women and Imperialism: Complicity and Resistance* (Bloomington and Indianapolis: Indiana University Press, 1992).

Childs, Peter and R. J. Patrick Williams, *An Introduction to Post-Colonial Theory* (New York and London: Prentice Hall/Harvester Wheatsheaf, 1997).

Chomsky, Noam, 'Middle East terrorism and the American ideological system', in *Blaming the Victims: Spurious Scholarship and the Palestinian Question*, ed. Edward Said and Christopher Hitchens (London and New York: Verso, 1988), pp. 97–147.

Clifford, James, 'On *Orientalism*', in *The Predicament of Culture: Twentieth-Century Ethnography, Literature, and Art* (Cambridge, Mass. and London: Harvard University Press, 1988), pp. 225–76.

Dunsky, Marda, 'Ending a one-sided view of violence', *Guardian Weekly*, 156, 5 (2 February 1997), p. 17.

Eliot, T. S., 'Tradition and the individual talent', *The Sacred Wood: Essays on Poetry and Criticism* (London: Faber and Faber, 1997 [1920]), pp. 39–49.

Enloe, Cynthia, *Bananas, Beaches and Bases: Making Feminist Sense of International Politics* (Berkeley and Los Angeles: University of California Press, 1990 [1989]).

Fanon, Frantz, *Black Skin, White Masks*, trans. Charles Lam Markmann (London: Pluto Press, 1986 [1952]).

——, *The Wretched of the Earth*, trans. Constance Farrington (New York: Grove Press, 1968 [1961]).

Foucault, Michel, *Histoire de la sexualité. Volume I: La Volonté de savoir* (Paris: Gallimard, 1976).

——, 'History of systems of thought', in *Language, Counter-Memory, Practice: Selected Essays and Interviews*, ed. Donald F. Bouchard (Ithaca, N.Y.: Cornell University Press, 1993 [1977]), pp. 199–204.

——, *Power/Knowledge: Selected Interviews and Other Writings 1972–1977*, ed. Colin Gordon, trans. C. Gordon et al. (New York and London: Harvester Wheatsheaf, 1980).

Gates, Henry Louis, Jr., ed., *'Race', Writing, and Difference* (Chicago and London: University of Chicago Press, 1986 [1985]).

——, 'Critical Fanonism', *Critical Inquiry*, 17 (Spring 1991), pp. 457–70.

Ghandi, Leela, *Postcolonial Theory: A Critical Introduction* (New York: Columbia University Press, 1998).

Gorak, Jan, *The Making of the Modern Canon: Genesis and Crisis of a Literary Idea* (London and Atlantic Highlands, NJ: Athlone Press, 1991).

Gramsci, Antonio, 'The intellectuals', in *Selections from the Prison Notebooks* (London: Lawrence and Wishart, 1996 [1971]), pp. 5–23.

Griffin, Robert J., 'Ideology and misrepresentation: a response to Edward Said', *Critical Inquiry*, 15 (Spring 1989), pp. 611–25.

Harlow, Barbara, *Resistance Literature* (New York and London: Methuen, 1987).

[Hentzi, Gary and Anne McClintock], 'An interview with Edward W. Said', *Critical Texts*, 3, 2 (Winter 1986), pp. 6–13

Hirst, David, 'Shameless in Gaza', *Guardian*, G2 (21 April 1997), pp. 8–9.

Hitchens, Christopher, 'Broadcasts', in *Blaming the Victims: Spurious Scholarship and the Palestinian Question*, ed. Edward Said and Christopher Hitchens (London and New York: Verso, 1988), pp. 73–83.

Hockstader, Lee, 'In Gaza, peace has brought only poverty', *Guardian Weekly*, 159, 13 (27 September 1998), p. 15.

——, 'Nightlife rocks where violence ruled', *Guardian Weekly*, 160, 13 (28 March 1999), p. 19.

Hourani, Albert, 'The road to Morocco', review of *Orientalism* by Edward Said, *New York Review of Books* (8 March 1979), pp. 27–30.

Holmlund, Christine Anne, 'Displacing limits of difference: gender, race, and colonialism in Edward Said and Homi Bhabha's theoretical models and Marguerite Duras's experimental films', *Quarterly Review of Film and Video*, 13, 1–3 (1991), pp. 1–22.

Hulme, Peter, *Colonial Encounters: Europe and the Native Caribbean, 1492–1797* (New York and London: Methuen, 1986).

Hutcheon, Linda, *A Poetics of Postmodernism: History, Theory, Fiction* (New York and London: Routledge, 1990 [1988]).

Jaggi, Maya, 'Out of the Shadows', *Guardian* (11 September 1999), pp. 6–7.

Jameson, Fredric, *The Prison-House of Language* (Princeton, N.J.: Princeton University Press, 1972).

——, *Postmodernism, or, The Cultural Logic of Late Capitalism* (Durham, N.C.: Duke University Press, 1991).

JanMohamed, Abdul. R., *Manichean Aesthetics: The Politics of Literature in Colonial Africa* (Amherst: University of Massachusetts Press, 1988 [1983]).

——, 'The economy of Manichean allegory: the function of racial difference in colonialist literature', in *'Race,' Writing, and Difference*, ed. Henry Louis Gates, Jr. (Chicago and London: University of Chicago Press, 1986 [1985]), pp. 78–106.

——, 'Worldliness-without-world, homelessness-as-home: toward a definition of the specular border intellectual', in *Edward Said: A Critical Reader*, ed. Michael Sprinker (Oxford and Cambridge, Mass.: Blackwell, 1993 [1992]), pp. 96–120.

——and David Lloyd, eds, *The Nature and Context of Minority Discourse* (New York and Oxford: Oxford University Press, 1990).

Jewsiewicki, Bogumil and V. Y. Mudimbe, 'For Said: why even the critic of imperialism labors under Western skies', *Transition*, 63 (1996), pp. 34–50.

Kabbani, Rana, *Imperial Fictions: Europe's Myths of Orient* (London: Pandora, 1988 [1986]).

Kermode, Frank, *The Sense of an Ending: Studies in the Theory of Fiction* (London and New York: Oxford University Press, 1967).

Khalidi, Rashid I., 'Edward W. Said and the American public sphere: speaking truth to power', *boundary 2*, 25, 2 (Summer 1998), pp. 161–77.

Kingsley, Mary, *Travels in West Africa* (London: Everyman, 1993 [1897]).

Kopf, David, 'Hermeneutics versus history', *Journal of Asian Studies*, 39, 3 (May 1980), pp. 495–506.

Krupnick, Mark, 'Edward Said: discourse and Palestinian rage', *Tikkun*, 4, 6 (November–December 1989), pp. 21–4.

Lewis, Bernard, 'The question of Orientalism', *New York Review of Books* (24 June 1982), pp. 49–56.

——and Edward Said, 'Orientalism: an exchange', *New York Review of Books*, 29, 13 (12 August 1982), pp. 44–8.

Lewis, Reina, *Gendering Orientalism: Race, Femininity and Representation* (London and New York: Routledge, 1996).

Little, Donald P., 'Three Arab critiques of Orientalism', *The Muslim World*, 69, 2 (April 1979), pp. 110–31.

Lodge, David, *The Modes of Modern Writing: Metaphor, Metonymy, and the Typology of Modern Literature* (London: Edward Arnold, 1977).

——, *Working with Structuralism* (London: Routledge and Kegan Paul, 1981).

Loomba, Ania, 'Overworlding the "Third World"', in *Colonial Discourse and Post-Colonial Theory: A Reader*, ed. Patrick Williams and Laura Chrisman (New York and London: Harvester Wheatsheaf, 1994 [1993]), pp. 305–23.

Lorde, Audre, 'The master's tools will never dismantle the master's house', *This Bridge Called My Back: Writings by Radical Women of Color*, ed. Cherrie Moraga and Gloria Anzaldua (New York: Kitchen Table: The Women of Color Press, 1983 [1981]), pp. 98–101.

Lowe, Lisa, *Critical Terrains: French and British Orientalisms* (Ithaca, N.Y. and London: Cornell University Press, 1994 [1991]).

McClintock, Anne, 'The angel of progress: pitfalls of the term "post-colonialism"', *Social Text*, 31–2 (1992), pp. 84–98.

——, *Imperial Leather: Race, Gender and Sexuality in the Colonial Context* (New York and London: Routledge, 1995).

McGowan, John, *Postmodernism and Its Critics* (Ithaca, N.Y. and London: Cornell University Press, 1991).

MacKenzie, John M., *Orientalism: History, Theory and the Arts* (Manchester and New York: Manchester University Press, 1995).

Mani, Lata and Ruth Frankenberg, 'The challenge of Orientalism', *Economy and Society*, 14, 2 (May 1985), pp. 174–92.

[Marquand, Robert], 'Conversations with outstanding Americans: Edward Said', *Christian Science Monitor* (27 May 1997), pp. 10–11.

Marrouchi, Mustapha Ben T., 'The critic as dis/placed intelligence: the case of Edward Said', *Diacritics*, 21, 1 (Spring 1991), pp. 63–74.

——, 'Counternarratives, recoveries, refusals', *boundary 2*, 25, 2 (Summer 1998), pp. 205–57.

Melman, Billie, *Women's Orients: English Women and the Middle East, 1718–1918, Sexuality, Religion and Work*, second edition (London: Macmillan, 1995 [1992]).

Miller, Jane, *Seductions: Studies in Reading and Culture* (London: Virago, 1990).

Mills, Sara, *Discourses of Difference: An Analysis of Women's Travel Writing and Colonialism* (New York and London: Routledge, 1993 [1991]).

Mishra, Vijay and Bob Hodge, 'What is post(-)colonialism?', in *Colonial Discourse and Post-Colonial Theory: A Reader*, ed. Patrick Williams and Laura Chrisman (New York and London: Harvester Wheatsheaf, 1994 [1993]), pp. 276–90.

[Mitchell, W. J. T.], 'The panic of the visual: a conversation with Edward W. Said', *boundary 2*, 25, 2 (Summer 1998), pp. 11–33.

Mohanty, Chandra Talpade, 'Under western eyes: feminist scholarship and colonial discourses', in *Colonial Discourse and Post-Colonial Theory: A Reader*, ed. Patrick Williams and Laura Chrisman (New York and London: Harvester Wheatsheaf, 1994 [1993]), pp. 196–220.

Montagu, Lady Mary Wortley, *The Selected Letters of Lady Mary Wortley Montagu*, ed. Robert Halsband (London: Longman, 1970).

Moore-Gilbert, Bart, *Kipling and Orientalism* (London and Sydney: Croom Helm, 1986).

——, 'Which way post-colonial theory? current problems and future prospects', *History of European Ideas*, 18, 4 (1994), pp. 553–70.

——, *Writing India 1757–1990: The Literature of British India* (Manchester and New York: Manchester University Press, 1996).

——, *Postcolonial Theory: Contexts, Practices, Politics* (New York and London: Verso, 1997).

Netanyahu, Benjamin, *A Place Among the Nations: Israel and the World* (London and New York: Bantam, 1993).

O'Hanlon, Rosalind, 'Recovering the subject: *Subaltern Studies* and histories of resistance in colonial South Asia', *Modern Asian Studies*, 22, 1 (1988), pp. 189–224.

[Osborne, Peter], 'Orientalism and after: Edward Said', in *A Critical Sense: Interviews with Intellectuals* (London and New York: Routledge, 1996), pp. 65–86.

Parry, Benita, 'Problems in current theories of colonial discourse', *Oxford Literary Review*, 9, 1–2 (1987), pp. 27–58.

——, 'Overlapping territories and intertwined histories: Edward Said's postcolonial cosmopolitanism', in *Edward Said: A Critical Reader*, ed. Michael Sprinker (Oxford and Cambridge, Mass.: Blackwell, 1993 [1992], pp. 19–47.

——, 'Signs of our times: discussion of Homi Bhabha's *The Location of Culture*', *Third Text* (Winter 1994), pp. 5–24.

——, 'Narrating imperialism: Nostromo's dystopia', in *Cultural Readings of Imperialism: Edward Said and the Gravity of History*, ed. Keith Ansell-Pearson et al. (New York: St. Martin's Press, 1997), pp. 227–46.

Pathak, Zakia, Saswati Sengupta and Sharmila Purkayastha, 'The prisonhouse of Orientalism', *Textual Practice*, 5, 1 (Spring 1991), pp. 195–218.

Paxton, Nancy L., 'Complicity and resistance in the writings of Flora Annie Steel and Annie Besant', in *Western Women and Imperialism: Complicity and Resistance*, ed. Nupur Chaudhuri and Margaret Strobel (Bloomington and Indianapolis: Indiana University Press, 1992), pp. 158–76.

Perera, Suvendrini, *Reaches of Empire: The English Novel from Edgeworth to Dickens* (New York: Columbia University Press, 1991).

Porter, Dennis, *Haunted Journeys: Desire and Transgression in European Travel Writing* (Princeton, N.J.: Princeton University Press, 1991).

——, 'Orientalism and its problems' (1983), in *Colonial Discourse and Post-Colonial Theory: A Reader*, ed. Patrick Williams and Laura Chrisman (New York and London: Harvester Wheatsheaf, 1994 [1993]), pp. 150–61.

Prasad, Madhava, 'The "other" worldliness of postcolonial discourse: a critique', *Critical Quarterly*, 34, 3 (Autumn 1992), pp. 74–89.

Pratt, Mary Louise, *Imperial Eyes: Travel Writing and Transculturation* (London and New York: Routledge, 1992).

——, in [Said, Edward and others] 'Edward Said's *Culture and Imperialism*: a symposium', *Social Text*, 40 (Fall 1994), pp. 2–10.

Radhakrishnan, R., in [Said, Edward and others] 'Edward Said's *Culture and Imperialism*: a symposium', *Social Text*, 40 (Fall 1994), pp. 15–20.

Richards, Thomas, *The Imperial Archive: Knowledge and the Fantasy of Empire* (New York and London: Verso, 1993).

[Robbins, Bruce], 'American intellectuals and Middle East politics: an interview with Edward W. Said', *Social Text*, 19–20 (Fall 1988), pp. 37–53.

——, 'Comparative cosmopolitanism', *Social Text*, 31–32 (1992), pp. 169–86.

——, 'Secularism, elitism, progress, and other transgressions: on Edward Said's "voyage in"', *Social Text*, 40 (Fall 1994), pp. 25–37.

Romero, Patricia W., ed., *Women's Voices on Africa: A Century of Travel Writings* (Princeton, N.J. and New York: Markus Wiener Publishing, 1992).

Rushdie, Salman, *Imaginary Homelands: Essays and Criticism 1981–1991* (London: Granta Books, 1991).

[Said, Edward], 'Interview: Edward W. Said', *Diacritics*, 6, 3 (1976), pp. 30–47.

[Salusinszky, Imre], 'Edward Said', in *Criticism in Society* (New York and London: Methuen, 1987), pp. 122–48.

Sarkar, Sumit, 'Orientalism revisited: Saidian frameworks in the writing of modern Indian history', *Oxford Literary Review*, 16, 1–2 (1994), pp. 205–24.

Sayigh, Rosemary, *Too Many Enemies: The Palestinian Experience in Lebanon* (London and New Jersey: Zed Books, 1994).

Sharpe, Jenny, *Allegories of Empire: The Figure of Woman in the Colonial Text* (Minneapolis and London: University of Minnesota Press, 1993).

——, 'The unspeakable limits of rape: colonial violence and counterinsurgency', in *Colonial Discourse and Post-Colonial Theory: A Reader*, ed. Patrick Williams and Laura Chrisman (New York and London: Harvester Wheatsheaf, 1994 [1993]), pp. 221–43.

Shohat, Ella, 'Antinomies of exile: Said at the frontiers of national narrations', in *Edward Said: A Critical Reader*, ed. Michael Sprinker (Oxford and Cambridge, Mass.: Blackwell, 1993 [1992]), pp. 121–43.

——, 'Notes on the "post-colonial"', *Social Text*, 31–2 (1992), pp. 99–113.

Sivan, Emmanuel, 'Edward Said and his Arab reviewers', in *Interpretations of Islam, Past and Present* (Princeton, N.J.: The Darwin Press, 1985), pp. 133–54.

Spelman, Elizabeth V., *Inessential Woman: Problems of Exclusion in Feminist Thought* (Boston: Beacon Press, 1988).

Spikes, Michael P., *Understanding Contemporary American Literary Theory* (Columbia, S.C.: University of South Carolina Press, 1997).

Spivak, Gayatri Chakravorty, 'The Rani of Sirmur', in *Europe and Its Others*, vol. 1, ed. Francis Barker et al. (Colchester: University of Essex, 1985 [1984]), pp. 128–51.

——, 'Feminism and critical theory', in *For Alma Mater: Theory and Practice in Feminist Scholarship*, ed. Paula A. Treichler, Cheris Kramarae and Beth Stafford (Urbana: University of Illinois Press, 1985), pp. 119–42. Reprinted in *In Other Worlds*.

——, 'Three women's texts and a critique of imperialism', in *'Race,' Writing, and Difference*, ed. Henry Louis Gates, Jr. (Chicago and London: University of Chicago Press, 1986 [1985]), pp. 262–80.

——, *In Other Worlds: Essays in Cultural Politics* (New York and London: Routledge, 1988 [1987]).

——, *The Post-Colonial Critic: Interviews, Strategies, Dialogue* (New York and London: Routledge, 1990).

——, *Outside in the Teaching Machine* (London and New York: Routledge, 1993).

——, 'How to read a "culturally different" book', in *Colonial Discourse/Postcolonial Theory*, ed. Francis Barker et al. (Manchester and New York: Manchester University Press, 1994), pp. 126–50.

——, *Imaginary Maps: Three Stories by Mahasweta Devi* (New York and London: Routledge, 1995).

——, *A Critique of Postcolonial Reason: Toward A History of The Vanishing Present* (Cambridge, Mass. and London: Harvard University Press, 1999).

Sprinker, Michael, ed., *Edward Said: A Critical Reader* (Oxford and Cambridge, Mass.: Blackwell, 1993 [1992]).

——, 'The national question: Said, Ahmad, Jameson', *Public Culture*, 6 (1993), pp. 3–29.

Spurr, David, *The Rhetoric of Empire: Colonial Discourse in Journalism, Travel Writing, and Imperial Administration* (Durham, N.C. and London: Duke University Press, 1993).

Stark, Freya, *Letters. Volume III: The Growth of Danger, 1935–1939*, ed. Lucy Moorehead (London: Compton Russell, 1976).

Steele, Meili, *Critical Confrontations: Literary Theories in Dialogue* (Columbia, S.C.: University of South Carolina Press, 1997).

[Stevenson, Matthew], 'Edward Said: an exile's exile', *Progressive*, 51, 2 (February 1987), pp. 30–4.

Suleri, Sara, *The Rhetoric of British India* (Chicago and London: University of Chicago Press, 1992).

Varadharajan, Asha, *Exotic Parodies: Subjectivity in Adorno, Said, and Spivak* (Minneapolis and London: University of Minnesota Press, 1995).

[Wicke, Jennifer and Michael Sprinker], 'Interview with Edward Said', in *Edward Said: A Critical Reader*, ed. Michael Sprinker (Oxford and Cambridge, Mass.: Blackwell, 1993 [1992]), pp. 221–64.

Williams, Patrick and Laura Chrisman, eds, *Colonial Discourse and Post-Colonial Theory: A Reader* (New York and London: Harvester Wheatsheaf, 1994 [1993]).

Williams, Raymond, *The Long Revolution* (New York: Columbia University Press, 1961).

——, *Keywords: A Vocabulary of Culture and Society* (London: HarperCollins, 1988 [1976]).

——, *Marxism and Literature* (Oxford and New York: Oxford University Press, 1977).

——, *Politics and Letters: Interviews with New Left Review* (London: New Left Books, 1979).

——, 'Appendix: media, margins, and modernity (Raymond Williams and Edward Said)', in Raymond Williams, *The Politics of Modernism: Against the New Conformists* (London and New York: Verso, 1994 [1989]), pp. 177–97.

Wilson, George M., 'Edward Said on contrapuntal reading', *Philosophy and Literature*, 18 (1994), pp. 265–73.

Yeğenoğlu, Meyda, *Colonial Fantasies: Towards a Feminist Reading of Orientalism* (Cambridge: Cambridge University Press, 1998).

Young, Robert, *White Mythologies: Writing History and the West* (New York and London: Routledge, 1996 [1990]).

——, *Colonial Desire: Hybridity in Theory, Culture and Race* (London and New York: Routledge, 1995).

Youngs, Tim, *Travellers in Africa: British Travelogues, 1850–1900* (Manchester and New York: Manchester University Press, 1994).

Index